Drugs and Football

By Brett Luster

PublishAmerica
Baltimore

© 2009 by Brett Luster.
All rights reserved. No part of this book may be reproduced, stored in a retrieval system or transmitted in any form or by any means without the prior written permission of the publishers, except by a reviewer who may quote brief passages in a review to be printed in a newspaper, magazine or journal.

First printing

PublishAmerica has allowed this work to remain exactly as the author intended, verbatim, without editorial input.

ISBN: 1-60813-260-9
PUBLISHED BY PUBLISHAMERICA, LLLP
www.publishamerica.com
Baltimore

Printed in the United States of America

Drugs
and Football

Buh-Bye

I wondered, "Where is my father?"
Over and over I inwardly asked myself this question.
His name was Bobbye.
Bobbye.
Buh-Bye.
See ya'.

I wanted a father. I needed a father, but there was no father to be had. I wanted a father so bad. I wanted to be accepted by him. I wished to be loved by him. I wanted a father to show me how to with women, and so on. I'm telling you, I wanted to be a son, so he could show me how to be a father.

Many men were there for me when I needed a father. I needed someone to show me special care. I needed special support. My friends' fathers taught me which ways to go, what routes to follow. I learned from their examples how to be a father. They taught me, so I would know how to be a father.

Everybody's childhood is rough on some level. Every child is small. Every child is vulnerable. So everyone can relate. Everyone can see where this is going.

I grew up half black and half white in a small, white, rural town.

Everybody has felt isolated as a youth. My case was special though, because I was the only person with so much African-American ancestry in a town of 4800 people for most of my first years on this planet. But I found as I got older, that being black in a town where people look different can be an asset. Meaning, people like uniqueness. I was shy and afraid to begin with, however. I had no father to show me the way to go. But this was a challenge; a challenge I learned to embrace. More and more men stepped up to the plate in my life. I had the opportunity to learn from the very best of men around my neighborhood. They came out of the woodwork. They stepped up at the trailer court, at grandma's, in sports. Another tricky aspect was mom sent us to Catholic schools, during the time we lived in a trailer park. This was strange—reconcilable, but strange nonetheless. We grew up around people. Our people made all the difference.

While writing this book I will try to rely heavily on my personal experiences with fathers of friends or older, edifying male influences in my life. Because I believe men like these are the ones who make a major difference in the lives of so many youths today, those who shape futures, and impart knowledge. These people share wisdom and insight. They give what they have, what has been stirring inside. These men play a vital role in our lives, especially in the formative years. People who are widely recognized on the world scene make a difference as well. However, people in your personal life, who go to the grind day in and day out, these people are so particularly special, because they do it all—because it is supposed to get done—because they care about you. Dads give such a profound contribution to the lives of all around them. They enrich the lives of all who come near. They thought of me and considered me before they decided to go out to a bar, or what kind of influence or impression that would leave. They searched their respective behaviors and reasoned what manner of implications this would have on their children or on me.

Here and there I will give reference to people who I never knew, many of them deceased. But these men made a lasting impression on me also, if not in person. Sure, I will never know these men, however, they have clarified what so much of our existence means, and have done it with such eloquence and courage. I can learn from them, even now, because their words speak to me through the decades.

Role Model

Shirley was like a mother to me while I was away from my mother. She babysat my brother Jharmel and me in East St. Louis, the most chocolate city you could imagine in the United States. She was very motherly. She possessed all the motherly qualities people look for: patience, gentleness and unconditional love. I recall Shirley as a perfect woman, without blemish, probably because for the earliest years I can remember she was a surrogate mother—and my brother and me did not go over to her house often after those two years mom let her baby sit us.

Shirley's house set on the edge of a busy highway overpass, deep into East St. Louis. Her home was humble, with a few small rooms, and a normal-size living room. Sofas were still in plastic. Pictures of her black relatives adorned the space. Everybody looked distinguished, as though the picture-taking was serious, so they had to be serious.

I would sit there on Shirley's lap, as she rested on that plastic-covered sofa. She made me feel special. Shirley caressed my head, treating me better than a lot of mothers treat their own children. I felt captivated by her love. I felt like an angel held me in her arms. She would rock back and forth, and hug me so tenderly. She held me as a tender mother should. She would hold me until my own mother returned from work.

Shirley shared the home with her parents. Shirley's brother Dwight lived under the roof as well. Dwight was the first young, strong, caring male influence in my life. His attitude was golden.

Jharmel and I scurried back to hang out with Dwight in his 9' x 7' bedroom. We would interrupt him while he was doing homework, or listening to music. But the man would always make time for us. We were a pleasant surprise, never an unwanted distraction. He always made us feel wanted.

Dwight playfully slapped us, like a wrestler. He lifted me up to the sky. Then he would toss me, and I was completely exhilarated—I was completely enthralled. This man meant a great deal to me. He was five 5' 10" and slender, confident. But I was short. I was small then, at five years of age.

He threw me upward, and wrestled me to the bed. He would throw me up again, and my little heart was filled with joy. To be with him was the greatest fortune, more valuable than any item from a treasure chest. He threw me to the sky. He tossed me on the bed. And it did not hurt. No, it felt great. It really felt great to be so wanted by a young man, who could have been with girlies or friends. He was outgoing, but he chose to throw us in the air, and toss us to the bed. We were with each other in those times, and he knew me. He knew I needed that attention. He gets my respect. Dwight will always have my deepest admiration. I wondered what he has been up to, what Dwight has been doing. He made such an impression upon me. I wanted to be like him. Hopefully he is fulfilled and overflowing with good things. Hopefully he is living out the excellent existence I knew of him as a young man.

It was at *this* age I began to develop an understanding of the boy, young adult, and man I wanted to become. Dwight gave me a very early framework of the type of person I aspired to grow into. I wanted to be caring, clean, outgoing, athletic, and someone mother would be unhesitatingly glad to call her little boy.

Dwight was such an awesome person. I've not seen him since the age of seven. I think about him often, though. I think of him—how to be a clean individual just like him—willing to take out just those precious few moments to impact the life of a child, who, hopefully will remember that interaction for at least a lifetime—and possibly forever. I've not seen Shirley since the age of seven either. My family found out about a year after we stopped going to her house Shirley had died. Nobody informed us of the funeral. Mom was upset. I was a little upset. I would have liked to have been with the family and mourned with them. Sometimes I just want to reach out and hug Shirley. Somehow, however, she is still with me. Shirley is like an angel upon my shoulder.

When writing about growing up I think about beautiful outstanding people. I just want to be a special person who can help to alleviate the sufferings of others—somehow. This could be my contribution to mankind. It was these people who made the major differences in my life. I want to be a difference maker, impacting others as they impacted me.

At the age of four I thought all the world was great. I knew the world was great. Children want so little as far as things. Only when people grow up do they crave more things. Toy trains, a big wheel, magazines, video games, cars, houses, bigger houses. Only when people were dissatisfied with the smaller things in comparison did they reach for bigger things in relation. Only when people considered themselves to be of less worth, did they seek to add riches upon the splendid treasures latent in the human heart. That way only sells a lie instead of giving all possessions to help the poor and going, and following after righteousness. This was the struggle I was up against. The terrible thing was the intangible and yet most real of all—love, joy, peace—was up against—self-centeredness, conceit, and pride.

Only through becoming less of myself could others learn from my experiences. People always have a need to be accepted. And only when people lose themselves can they find eternal life, that is, meaning in their lives. Only when people choose to live simply, so others may accept what they have given up, can people live fulfilled lives. I have heard and read about people getting bent because of the question, What is the meaning of life. The answer has always been simple.

Every time we choose to serve others we are making something great of ourselves. We are molding a masterpiece through suffering, that others may have more. Serving is low, menial, service to others. Each of us has a responsibility to serve others. I saw people all over the place who served others in their respective areas. Television played a large role in shaping my ideas of other people all over the place.

Mr. Rogers

Mr. Rogers was the sweetest, most caring individual I had ever known at kindergarten level. I knew he was a man. He was the ultimate father figure—serving his children with knowledge.

Mr. Rogers was the first person who ever taught me how powerful media, and in particular television, is. He could translate so many things to me without being overt. His actions were subtle and gentle. Mr. Rogers was not who you would normally consider a manly man. He was an even higher caliber.

He walked into the bright light, beaming onto his grey, smooth hair, parted to one side. He took his coat off, and hung it on a hanger. He was the man. I mean, he was absolutely terrific. Mr. Rogers bent down to tie his shoe on purpose. I mean, he was *tying his shoe*, to show me how to tie my shoe. Wait.

"How are *you* doing boys and girls?" he said. He was speaking right to me. I looked at him in awe and amazement. He was speaking to me. He was speaking to me.

"Oh, my, gosh," I thought. "He speaks to me through this television set. Oh, my gosh. How can he…Uhhm. He can't do that." But he just did.

Mr. Rogers took you to the land of make believe and you were there with him. He was so fluid in everything he did. Mr. Rogers was a stand-up type guy. He made you feel at home, even when you were so many miles away.

We are caught in an inescapable network of mutuality, tied in a single garment of destiny. Whatever affects one directly affects all indirectly, according to Martin Luther King. He said we are all living here in a dream right now in America. Because the goal of America is freedom. We can each be a servant of each other. Every day we have to become less that others may become more. I came up with (or borrowed) the radical idea that people should be willing to sacrifice that which is dearest to them in this world, in order that their neighbor may have.

As a boy I noticed that people all around were after things. Things were all over. You could see things. You could touch things. Some things were beautiful. Some things whisked and zipped through the sky. Those things were hard and shiny also. A magnificent display of human ingenuity, of the skills inherent in the human mind. These were not animate, though. These things could not speak to you and communicate with you as we are doing now. These things could not teach you anything in the way a friendly dialogue could. These things were just—things.

Mom was big into the arts. The arts were so wild and crazy when I grew up and a contrast to the soybean, corn, and wheat fields surrounding our fair city. I grew up in Staunton, Illinois, a rural farm town about 40 miles northeast of St. Louis.

Mom would take us to Southern Illinois University in Edwardsville, her alma mater. Mom, Jharmel and I walked into the Lovejoy library, light pouring through the incandescent ceiling, my brother and me in total amazement.

I would peer into the long, cavernous aisles of books that stretched on, and thought "So, this is what life outside of rural is like, eh?" Then, I knew if I did the right things I would be able to walk through a place like this whenever I wanted. All three of us traveled to a higher level in the library where people looked into these machines with these old news articles inside.

I wondered how you could get all those old stories in that little machine. Mom said something about fish, and, I kept wondering time after time when we went there, "What do these little machines have to do with fish?" But it was microfiche. You had to own a library card to look through a fiche.

Grandpa

I guess my early existence was similar to that of Will Hunting, in the film Good Will Hunting.

Boy comes to life.

Here it is.

He wakes up and finds himself twisted inside, and with yearnings that seem indescribable.

Boy looks up to men in his life.

He wishes to be a good man some day.

Boy looks up to that one guy in his life who makes all the difference.

He wants to be like this guy

For me, he was my mother's father, Louis Wesley Brackman.

I did not know my grandpa on my dad's side, just as I did not know my dad. I knew little of my grandma on my father's side. But Grandpa Brackman seemed like a man who was more than sufficient for two sides of the family. It felt as though he could wrap the world in his arms.

And this guy tells him things about his life. And this guy tells him things like, well, if he's a writer—to stop or not write so many ands in the beginning of your sentences so as to bore your reader with a repetitive structure. Then through the guy's determination to make this boy better, he brings out some things within himself as a youth growing up. All this while both are being consulted. Both seek to find themselves anew.

Grandpa was still standing after living through the Great Depression,

DRUGS AND FOOTBALL

a world war, the loss of two twins—a daughter and son—who died shortly after their birth. He inspired awe in me each time he let me sit on his lap, every time he let me fish with him at the Sportsman's as if I was one of the guys.

Grandpa was strong. He knew that each person is deserving of respect, the dignity of man that is owed to them. Grandpa validated me. He listened.

Grandpa was somebody who listened to me no matter what was going on in life. And that was important. An imposing figure, he usually wore sharp, grey sideburns on high cheek bones that complimented the sheen in his hair. Grandpa was utterly impressive. His body was massive for somebody his weight and height, as days tending to the family farm since the age of 15 showed in his rugged physique. He was a man of stature. He was a physical presence, standing 6', belly sticking out and in some instances, appearing as pregnant. He ate his fair share, and, when in the kitchen for a spell, walked from snack to snack, sampling the variety grandmother had chosen so adeptly. He often rocked forward when standing, and up on his toes, as to maximize the economy of his height.

Grandpa never lifted weights. He worked on the farm regularly, however, which was just as good, if not better. He bucked bails. He reared horses.

Grandpa was my hero.

Grandpa taught me the importance of work. Straight up—grandpa showed me how it was done. He got up in the early morning, went out and kicked tires on his 1985 Ford F-150. Grandpa had a routine. And he would go about it in the best way possible. He was so consistent. You knew what to expect. I knew the sun would rise. I knew grandpa would rise with it. I knew government required taxes. Grandpa would save money by eating at home with steadfastness. Grandpa let out our dog Josh for potty in the morning. And I knew grandpa would wear his boxers going to the bathroom at night.

I could confide in him with anything. I didn't tell him personal things regularly. But I could have. He'd a been all ears, because he had a big heart. You could tell it about the man. Grandpa was not some big shot movie star, but he was a person who we looked up to. He was a real American hero.

He provided for my grandmother through the Great Depression. He cared for her through colon cancer. His work at Olin provided him with little recognition.

He deserved accolades, though he rarely received them.

Grandpa had his fair share of good times. Mom said he stood in the doorway back in the day after he got home from work. He held a beer in one hand as he leaned into a wall.

"Bfffphm…" his body said through flatulence.

His children left the room straightaway.

Funny moments like these gave my grandpa the most pleasure, I think. Times with his family were the most precious treasure.

My grandpa cared about me like he would never let me go and I meant the world to him. Grandpa always looked forward to seeing his entire family. Grandpa just wanted to provide for us as best he could.

Grandpa spoke carefully, and with jovial ease, gesturing with large, calloused, liver-spotted hands. He regularly wore Osh Kosh suspenders with a cap to cover his head that was three-fourths bald.

Grandpa taught me many things in this life. He taught me once, after I took a shower, about hygiene. I think grandma put him up to this. Grandpa went into our small bathroom, and showed me how to dry off with a towel. Straight up—I think it is the most personal thing grandpa ever showed me. He said to take the towel at one side, and then another and, pull the towel across the back.

He would hum, "MM Hmm," and clear his teeth "Tsth," in only the right circumstances. Grandpa was king of his domain.

We sailed off in the small fishing boat with one oar at the Staunton Sportsman's Club. We set out on a pond usually inhabited by fish, turtles, snakes, and on some days grown men—for fishing derbies. But one day, one day we set off just a little off the shore, and grandpa set bait for me. He and I fished together, and we lived like kings that day. Though we did not catch anything, grandpa threw his line that way, "Thewp!" into the water the bait went.

"Freee—plop." Mine went too. We fished, and he listened. I listened, and he listened some more. Grandpa was not heavy on words, and knew well the art of keeping silent. Our communication was through fishing line and bobbers, tugs on poles, and the oar's glide. But my affection grew for him as he enjoyed dwelling with me in a sea of words unspoken.

And this is the best, if mysterious, service men give to young men in their charge—to live with them, letting them know if they *do* need to talk about something—anything—the elder will be there for the younger.

People do not have to go it alone. Mom said to me, Whatever does not kill you makes you stronger. I'm glad I'm here today, even though it seemed like some things were so big, giant like monsters pillaging through the forest in search of flesh. However, faith pulls me through. "Yea, though I walk through the valley of the shadow of death, I will fear no evil, for thou art with me," the psalmist says. When men are there for other men an outwardly unsearchable bond develops. I wake up every day thankful for such enduring relationships with males in my life.

We in the whole family sat together at the dinner table and grandpa just had this silent, steady quality about himself. His farming hands passed the beans, rugged and assured. Grandma and grandpa had Uncle Louis, mom, Christy, Amy, Jharmel and me to look after. We children sat in awe of the grown-ups in our lives around the shiny oval kitchen table with cheesy printing on top. Adults instilled the necessity of togetherness firmly into our little selves. A feeling of safety permeated the room when grandpa took a seat. We all wanted to be like him.

Grandpa was strong, like a fence post built of the most solid oak. When a wind would come to test the oak, there my grandmother would be, like another post put on the side, just for extra insurance, sturdy and unwavering.

Grandpa was not easy on the children. He challenged them to do more with their lives than he did. His dad died when he was in the middle of high school so grandpa had to take care of the farm and his younger brother Cecil.

I can remember pretty far back in my life, back way back, with some memories to the age of three, and some to the age of four. At five, I can think of quite a few.

Dorchester, Illinois was a tiny, tiny town of 50 residents, in the bosom of central Illinois. My grandma would take me to a Lutheran church on Sundays. Behind the church flowing fields of wheat were effervescent beneath the scarlet sky. Teachers served us children cookies and Kool-Aid teaching us basic lessons in a way that gave us a feel they were loving others as themselves.

Back at home angst riled up inside me. I sat there, a short one, at preschool age. A pencil, some paper, and curiosity filled with faith. I began to scribble. Squiggly lines filled the page. How do I make a sea, I thought. There are lines, waving up and down, there I have it. A sun with rays shining was beaming down from the corner. Grandpa makes me proud. I want to be like grandpa—like when he protects us—mom, grandma, the whole country—from bad people. I drew a short man with a round head, bending, bowed legs, and a gun with a round ball coming out of the end. A little guy was trailing the man on the ship's deck, as the man was running toward a ship across the way. The boy in the picture ran toward the bad people in the ship. Little man fired round bullets from the obnoxious gun, with a curved trumpet style end of the barrel. The man hung back and told the lad, "Get 'em son." I just wanted to make my grandpa proud of me. I figured there were some people who were bad inherently, when they carried guns and were trying to beat up Americans.

Grandpa made me feel good about being someone. He made me feel good about working to build up a country that was doing something for the right reasons.

We are the same who accepted the most wretched. Comedian Jerry Seinfeld even quipped we were accepting, but do we really need to call out for the worst anybody's got?

Give us your poor, tired and huddled masses. That ain't no joke. People in America used to be poor. We used to huddle into masses when assembling for soup lines during the Depression of the 1930s. But somehow, all of us, Germans, Poles, Jews, Slavs, Italians—we all got through together. We made it through because we believe in the nation that would give birth to those peoples' children, and grand children and great grandchildren…

DRUGS AND FOOTBALL

My mother

My mother, what a dream
What a dream you hold, mother
Land of me
Land of free
You nurture,
You nature
Let your nature be
Be your nature this promise,
Land of the free
Land of the free
You and me
You shelter
Give me feed
You let me be
The sights I see
Tranquil blossoms
Your swaying reeds
Let me be
Just you and me

Hold me in your arms
Mother of free
This promise
Of freedom
Will ever ring

I call your name
O' mother of me
You promise me
You let me see
The promise, free

Say the word
And let it be
The promise free
Starts with me

He made me glad our country made it through together. He made me glad to live in this country. However, he brought home some prejudice with him from the Pacific Ocean.

Grandpa fought against the Japanese in World War II. I used to think some people were inherently bad and all of that group of people were out to kill the good people. I am convinced today, however, everyone is evil in natural desires, but always striving toward doing good in their spirit.

My brother Jharmel wants to do good in his life. He has been an inspiration to me, even from the very outset of our lives. When I was a pipsqueak, about three feet tall, Mrs. Buffington brought me into the kindergarten room at St. Michael's and was motioning for me to sit down. Jharmel hesitatingly went away from me, upstairs to the big kid's classes in the third grade. He slowly moved, looking back slightly with his eyes, not wanting to leave me for, what would be the first occasion we were separated in a school setting. I glanced at him and as the teacher led him away, I began sobbing uncontrollably. Mrs. Buffington had to explain to me in the well-kempt basement at St. Michael's grade school, Jharmel was just going away for the day. "You can see him after school," she assured me. I was emotionally a wreck in there. But I learned to let go of him. I learned to let go, because I can always have someone in my heart the best way I remember them.

The way they appear, and who they are, are what goes on inside of me. Where people are right now. How people are right now internally is the very most important part of them. And in my heart, so long as I have the person from the best way they used to be, to the very best of what they are capable of, which is one and the same, then there is no contradiction. It would be selfish to expect someone to be the best of what they can be without being most critical of myself. I can and *must* change. But for right now, I must imagine someone as the very best of their potential.

Somehow, however, it seemed as though Jharmel was trying to get me at times. We fought and fought, and I probably understand him better now through our occasional discord.

St. Michael's had some profound mystery about it, and so did the Catholic Church in general. We attended church weekdays. Our eight grade school classes walked up the large steps, then entered the tall doors. We had this feeling we were being taken care of. We filed in as orderly as possible past the foyer, past the wooden and glass doors, into the vast sanctuary, minds wandering all about with childish curiosity.

Even today the immensity of Catholic cathedrals makes me stand in awe. Everything about them is intricate. I looked up into the expanse reaching for 40 feet upwards in amazement. I sensed this utter peace, this—nothing will happen to you. You will be okay. You are home.

We walked and were parallel with the ornate wooden pews, exhibiting a small cross symbol at the end. Pews on each side of the church stretched down 15 feet. I looked up as we continued walking closer. I was in full view of the wide open variety of color pouring through the large stained glass windows on my right and left. We continued walking past all the pews—there were so many of them. And I looked up to the right.

There hung the stations of the cross—12 pictures depicting the most significant moments of crucifixion day. You could see the terrible suffering Christ endured, to do what He had to come to do for humanity. Viewing those images on a weekly basis gave me an early framework of the meaning of sacrifice.

It was displayed for us day after day in vivid, graphic art. Soldiers whipping the man. Christ falling. Simon carrying the cross. The ladies wiping the blood from his brow. The whole scene was hardcore, horrific. And yet I could not keep my eyes away.

Mystery was, He did not have to go to the cross. He chose to abide by what He said. What He said got Him in trouble. He stood for something greater than Himself, and would not deny His Father's words. He knew where He came from. He knew where He was going.

We shuffled in to the left side. I scanned the whole scene, seeing a statue on each side of the altar, one of Mary, another of Joseph. I then looked up, deep past the tan carpet steps leading up to the sacristy. Up above there, suspended on the cross was Christ, in a twisted agony for all the world to see. He was 85 percent naked.

All that covered him was a loincloth and a penetrating crown of thorns. This was His end, our beginning. It was so fresh in me. I saw someone who gave exactly His all. I was in a deep, reverential admiration.

The musty incense wafted gently past our pubescent nostrils. It was intoxicating, this aroma that smelled thousands of years old. It was an ancient scent, and captivated the onlooker to this broken view.

Pain is interesting because of what it brings us through. Not that pain should be sought after or desired, but pain teaches us lessons. First, pain lets us know we are alive.

I rode a bike that was way too big for me at five years of age. My brother, my mom and I were over at Jose Manzano's apartment in Collinsville. Now Jose had been my mother's friend for quite some time, and he owned a bicycle much larger than is fit for a five year-old boy. My 4' frame, and the large, gangly cycle, did not mix. As I made my way down the street, still wobbling, trying to gain balance, I saw a figure jump out in front. My brother was trying to be a funny guy, but he completely caught me off-guard.

The next moment and the minutes that followed will be etched in my memory for the rest of my days. Trembling started to increase and I feh…fe…fell to the ground, banging! My little knee to the gravel-covered ground. I lay on the ground, tossing back and forth crying like there was no tomorrow. My mother came running from Jose's first floor apartment and Jharmel stood on the side like a spectator at a dune buggy rally who had just gotten sideswiped by one of the vehicles.

I wailed and cried, cried and wailed all the way into the front room, 30 yards from where I landed with the bike, just sitting there as my mother did her best to comfort me as only she could with her words of conciliation. I bled continuously from the wound and the sight of the blood probably exacerbated the sobbing. After a while, mother's gentle words were a balm to my bent, hurt feelings.

"How could Jharmel, the flesh of my blood, do such a thing?" was my first thought. He was a role model. The one whose shirt I tugged on for safety. He knew me. He knew me better than me. "My first word in this life was 'Awmel'," I thought. "How could he do such a terrible thing to his brother?"

Then reasoning set in...he was just joking around. He knew what pulled my strings. We were both rotten. We each laughed at inappropriate things, watched inappropriate television. At other times I had cried unnecessarily. So yeah, this act of chicanery was a forgivable, if not pain-free, act.

Though I put my body in harm's way many times after this, I rode bicycles larger than me only with great caution. The wreck when I was a youngster makes me think about getting out and doing. "What if I never tried to ride a bike in the first place?" I thought, or "What if I never registered for college?" I could have traded that day's mishap for a game of kickball in some barren lot. But taking chances, allowing yourself to become vulnerable is a big, essential part of life.

I just remember as a small boy being joyous and balled up, across the lap of my grandmother's brown comfort chair in the living room. Walls were covered with pictures of Aunt Lois, grandpa, grandma, Amy, Jharmel and the rest of the family. Cartoons would play on the television Smurfs outfitted in white Hershey's Kiss hats on their blue noggins. My joy was boundless because this great family was there. Mother, in her voice, itself childlike, would ask me, "Shortest of days, do you want a sandwich?" My reply: "Yes mom. Put mayonnaise on it please and cut it in half."

She would walk past the imposing, rather random bookcase on her left and out of the room. Mom walked east into the kitchen, a 10' x 10' room with high white ceiling with water stains on it, washer and dryer sat in the left corner, with a stove to the right corner. Cabinets with goodies were catty-corner to the entrance up, out of the reach of children.

Mother walked sprightly in her hefty frame, boosted by the drama of her personality. A spring air rested outside as a bare breeze blew, sun shining down and into the living space, reflecting off white patches in the wall not covered by deer parts, or family photos. This was family. With such a sure infrastructure I wanted to branch out. My mission from that moment was to meet people and change the world.

But there was something I was missing. I had to fill some void inside.

Suburbs and the Trailer Park

Afro-Americans were few and far between in and around Staunton. I had no black friends. A large number of black folks, however, lived on the eastern side of the Mississippi River from St. Louis.

We got 50 percent closer to there when mom moved us from the safety of grandma and grandpa's home in Staunton to Edwardsville. Mom taught Spanish at Lincoln High School in East St. Louis.

I would see at St. Mary's school the parents and children trying to look, and thereby to feel, beautiful. They were after things of this world, of what is sought after based upon appearance.

First impulse, I wanted to be like that. I wanted all that. I wanted architecture. I wanted art. I wanted to be cultured, though living in Edwardsville Estates, a trailer park, on the edge of the city. And this was not just any city, mind you. This was the most affluent, progressive city in the St. Louis Metro-East.

People all over Edwardsville were clamoring and trying to look beautiful. People smiled in Edwardsville. They smiled a lot, trying to keep a smile. But when we force smiles on our faces and try to make it all right by ourselves, then is when we have messed up. A scripture in the Christian faith goes,

"Blessed are those who persevere through trials, because after they have stood the test they will receive the crown of life God has promised to those who love Him."

No matter how much I tried—no matter how much I wanted to be accepted, certain people already accepted me for who I was. These people I called friends.

Genuine friends cared about being with you. Friends were not encumbered by the distractions of a wishful life—a wishful life in regard to those who wished for that which they did not already possess. John Ruskin wrote in a book, Unto This Last, That which a man cannot buy with cash, he should not own. This revelation was being woven into me over and over, marinating into the fibers of my being. I sought things less and less as childhood matured into adolescence. I strove to bring out what was already inside, hidden as a treasure, the treasure of my fragmented, human heart.

At St. Mary's grade school, I was surrounded by white children during first and second grade. Often my clothes would smell of urine from my nervousness and anxiety in bed during nighttime. But I could cope with that, as I tried to act like I was the only one who could smell the odor. Anyway, me being the only mixed child in the bunch, I felt a sort of isolation, like I was out of place in uniform, dressed to look the same, but irretrievably, aesthetically, different. 'Twas always hard to live, but everybody's got struggles. At an early age I walked into the bathroom of our trailer.

I stood there, looking at myself in the mirror in disbelief, in frustration. "How was this? How could I have all this going for me, a family that loved me, a fascination for girls at school, and all the friends a child could ask for, and be a different color than them all?" I looked strange, I reasoned, scratching at my caramel skin, wondering if maybe it would come off so I could be white, like the rest of the children. As I sobbed there in the mirror, wondering who else in the world was like me, I felt alone, isolated, outlandish. I wanted to be like everyone. I wanted to be accepted. Who would accept me for who I was? However, a soothing, inner voice came, and God spoke still, uttering, "Be different, I made you for a purpose, and you are mine." I cried, as tears came so easily. He made me unique. I *faintly* understood this then. The voice was more of a balm of affirmation, a fix when I needed to know the world needed me. Some poor choices, however, slowed me down to that final analysis.

Mike Mitchell was a rugged, ruddy young man, two grades older than I was and definitely a role model for my behavior. His face was of a soft countenance, but his body, strong and tough, even if a little chubby. He was half a foot taller than me, with dusty brown, blond hair down to his shoulders. Mike played the Nintendo game Contra with commendable dexterity, and the only one who was better was his mother, who would play for hours on end. Even if for sheer age, I'd looked up to the boy, trying to be a man.

Mike Mitchell was a leader. He lead me into the dirt trails that bordered a field behind my trailer. An older man's house lie on the other side of the dust path. We were leery, if not afraid, of the man and his house. Yikes!

We walked a quarter mile through a brief series of twists and turns. We saw a rusty microwave, refrigerator and grocery cart from many years before.

We were in nature also. Trees lined backs of some folks' lawns to our left. This was middle of the summer in unadulterated, dingy nature. Even the dirt was hot. Mike and I got to speaking about bb guns. We saw some on the ground. I asked him if you could re-use bb's.

"Of course not," Mike said.

He knew I was naïve, however. Just breathing that warm, stale air was enough to fill my lungs and penetrate my being with expectation. I could anticipate a better life than would normally be expected from such surroundings.

But the whole experience was great. The people who lived there were living, breathing hard-working folks. The whole environment made me appreciate all types of people. Something about that whole scenario was a wonderful blessing. In the people I saw something redemptive.

They were just trying to make it.

All the while I was growing up in the trailer court, people taught me many thousands of things. I absorbed some, others I discarded.

Misstep

Mike and I were in Edwardsville Estates, a trailer park on the fringes of Edwardsville, an affluent suburb of St. Louis. We sat across the street from my trailer behind the single-wide of an eccentric, purple-haired woman.

He was so confident, so sure, and almost everything he was, I wanted to be, until there came an episode that would test my mettle as never before.

Mike pulled out some chewing tobacco. I was only seven years old and felt the pangs of temptation banging at my very core. Mike asked if I wanted some and I hesitated at first, but then I gave in, and, upon consent alone, felt a sudden, unclean rush. The tobacco made me feel light-headed, yet the physical effects were incomparable to the emotional anguish that soared through my members. This experience gave me red eyes and a guilty conscience. I was with Mike only shortly, then went home—and prayed. I thought I was going to hell, not knowing how God would ever forgive me for tarnishing his gift, His temple, which is my body. Trembling, I was thinking and praying. It was not until my sophomore year in high school, however, that I comprehended the fact that what a person does to himself affects others also.

People say sometimes, "I regret…" or, "If I could do that differently…" Well, when you live your life, you are living it. People make mistakes. I wouldn't go back and change anything about my life. You learn from what you did, because those who do not learn from the past are doomed to repeat it. So it's useless to look back with regret.

Over and over, I think about my life, and how the rough ways were made smooth, like a once erratic chorus line playing out into a beautiful symphony. Even though potholes and dirt crevices caused me to stumble, the journey was that much more palatable. Because we are human beings, striving for ourselves, to please people in high positions, and to please the Creator.

I can only live with the hope of doing *everything* to the best of my ability.

"Jars of Clay" sang a song describing the power of children and their dreams. Song goes, "And they say that I can move the mountains, and send them crashing to the sea. And they say that I can walk on water if I would follow and believe. With faith like a child."

Martin Luther King Jr. said he couldn't be all he could be until the least of his brothers were all they could be. That means if a man walks into an alley to shoot up heroin, that needle not only destroys his veins, self-esteem and compromises his future, but endangers the lives of people around him. They have put forth effort to rear the man, no matter what level of their commitment. Whatever is done to the self directly, even if not seen by others, affects others indirectly.

When an investor goes to a bank, puts in $10,000 in a savings account, before long, he *will* gain interest. When men sow into the lives of children, no matter how small the amount, they will receive, and usually indirectly, a return in interest. Because the investment the man makes is of the most valuable treasure. Time equals love, joy, and ultimately, peace in the heart of a small person; people are our greatest resources.

My Grandpa, Louis Wesley Brackman was my hero. He was born a farmer and reared in Staunton, Illinois in the midst of the Great Depression. Grandpa made an affect on my life, not through showy outward display, but grandpa was there. He directly affected my outcome.

Whenever I had a choice to go with grandpa or grandma, the vast majority of times I chose grandpa. I did not prefer him, but we were guys. We had things to discuss. His devotion to family persuaded me in my relationships, on the football team, in jobs. His impact continues even today.

DRUGS AND FOOTBALL

It was not what my grandfather embodied while he was here on earth only, but the impression he left in me and the rest of his family after he was gone. He sowed a strong, vibrant seed of "time", and his seed continues to reap a harvest in us and the people we visit.

I never saw him cry, never saw him show that type of emotion. But he was caring, in his own way. He represented a fading sun in the distance, a cowboy, who knew where the road went.

Sports Giants

My mom worked in East St. Louis, a contrast to the rustic farm upbringing she lived for the first 22 years of her life. She never looked back though, along the litter-strewn alleys of the city, among lots choked by their decadent grace of waist-high weeds. Momma knew why she was there and it made her tougher.

Working there and staying in the trailer court made her more of a person than she would have been had she shrugged off the challenge of East St. Louis and settled for work at Edwardsville, or some other well-to-do suburban municipality.

My experience with East St. Louis is that the town, just by going there, makes you aware of your own blackness. An Asian hairdresser from Wichita could move to East St. Louis and feel black. The city just gave a person that special burden.

And no other place did I feel manlier at the age of eight than in the presence of Mr. Bailey, the Lincoln High School principal. Early in grade school I regularly visited Lincoln with mom and hung out with Bailey.

He was a very active man, experienced in, and proponent of, wrestling. He had a slender, more-than-six foot frame, wide shoulders, grey, thick hair, and a mustache that gave him a special, serious appeal. He was always funny around me. Bailey would often take me into the halls just in front of the broad entrance doors of the school. Bailey had a rough and tussle demeanor about him, an attitude that made people recognize he didn't take nothin' from nobody.

He threw me around like a lion preparing a cub for the jungle's war, tossing me to and fro. Bailey was a masculine guy, but with the sensitivity it took to lead a group of educators in an economically pressed city. Bailey called me boy quite a lot through his silvery mustache, as he explained how we needed to get together so he could teach wrestling and boxing. I had to be tough, for Bailey was a man's man. He didn't take nothin' from nobody, and that was final.

As I wandered near the three-foot-across door of my mother's Spanish classroom adjacent to the basketball court, I, at three feet tall, would watch Leviathan teenagers pass by, with afros, curls, weaves and high sneakers—all decked out, for the days of adolescence were in full swing. I wanted to be just like them. I wanted to be big and black and strong, just like those guys. They taught me, too. A guy explained to me how to shoot a basketball.

"Grip the ball with your hands on the outside so you have more control," he said. Such a hold helped you to influence the shot's accuracy much better I learned later.

Being so close to the gym gave me some interesting insight into the life of East St. Louis' finest young men. In pursuit of their educational advancement, African-American folks found their way into the sun-drenched courts of Lincoln's storied basketball court. In the years since, many talents have shone there. LaPhonso Ellis, fifth pick in the 1993 NBA draft; Darius Miles, who went into the pros after his senior year; and Cuonzo Martin, Big Ten standout for Purdue University, all played at Lincoln. And on that court was my education into the mind of the Negro.

In East St. Louis Lincoln High School, black male and female's brains may as well have been basketballs in between classes and into the next period. Oh how easily were the bright youth of Lincoln swayed into those wide doors and onto the shined, waxy courts of orange and black. I had the pleasure of getting rebounds for one chap who put on a show for me and the rest of the people in attendance.

He was a studious, gentle lad, who looked as if he was willing to pass off the attention to others. The boy had to have been at least a sophomore, with a chiseled face, a wiry frame and a smooth rotation. His short black hair compressed onto his head like a hindered accordion.

One—there's the first, from the three-point line no less. Two—good shot, way to go, give him some respect and get the ball back to him. Three—he's on a roll, hitting the shots with grace...what focus and fluidity of motion. Dropping three three-pointers in a row was something of beauty and grace. This young lad, of barely dating age was showing me how to physically be a man with his finesse and unflappable rotation. Four—now he had me in complete awe. Was I worthy of such an effortless-looking display? This dark black brother appeared unflustered, almost machine-like in his constancy, unflinching, and at a stroke like somebody with more years, more experience—. But what he was doing in his nonchalance was playing the game as a child, how it should always be played.

Five—his total baskets in succession was unheard of from a high school player just shooting the breeze. He was on his way to basketball becoming a basketball legend. Keeping his streak alive, and with tiger-like precision, he focused onward without a passing, fleeting look. Six—I was in utter amazement, dumbfounded, with mouth agape. This is who I wanted to be like. The smooth motion in his shot made him the more attractive as a role model, and by this point, I wished he were my father. On his seventh attempt, he missed; side glances and glares beaming in on him were hot, like a noon day heat on a sweltering adobe hut. That could have been it. He had to miss some time. But he was great. He taught me the importance of being suave, when it comes to high school.

Privilege and the Trailer Court

I attended St. Mary's School in Edwardsville then, in first and second grade. Nikki Keller came to St. Mary's with her tanned white skin, straight black hair like a Native American, and chubby, round face. Nikki told the class on one occasion of how her family was driving on a vacation, and a boulder fell upon their Porsche. Nobody was hurt. I could not relate, though I naturally felt sympathy for her. Her family owned Keller Construction, still a chief business in the booming city of Edwardsville. A rusty, orange, dirty semi trailer with K E L L E R printed across in separate lettering, each symbol the size of a man sat on the left-hand side, half a mile from a much-used city park. Workers would drive Keller trucks across town. You would see them parked outside restaurants, new businesses. Her name was all over the city.

There was always this dichotomy, a contrast between my school life at a parochial school, where we received an excellent education, and parents of friends were wealthy, and our trailer park—where children ran around the court with one another with little parental supervision, dirty, and looking like ragamuffins.

Edwardsville Estates trailer park was a large oval of a court with trailers on each side of the road. The court raced around like a short NASCAR track, a mile long. The people had ability...they had something going for them. Those folks were alive. No matter what their condition. It gave me great warmth in spirit to be in the presence of all these people.

I played with some other little ones in the yard of an abandoned trailer, three lots down. I was on the porch. I stepped on a rusty nail.

"Awwwwgh!" I said. I immediately began crying. It went through my shoe, and pierced my flesh and it was nasty.

Few times in my life have I cried so hard. My foot was bleeding. I was in need of medical attention. But momma came to the rescue.

There I was screaming and in pain, and somehow momma knew where I was. Maybe somebody told her. Maybe she heard my wailing. Any way, she showed up and carried my seven-year old body away from my pain. After I was in mother's arms everything was alright. The feeling was still there, but soothed.

I felt like a little girl in front of my friends as mom carried me away in her arms. However, she was my heroine that day. Mom rescued me from distress.

Living in Edwardsville Estates was a completely different world than St. Mary's grade school. The trailer court was low-income, with blow up pools in yards many paces from the trailers. Some people kept dogs in large metal cages, looking onto the overtly large speed bumps set in place to promote cautious driving. Children were just like me, snot-nosed, dirty, and full of questions. I used to hang with Mike Mitchell because he was cool, with a bike I could barely mount.

He laid the bike down one day, as he took to talking to one of the neighborhood brood. I said, "Is it all right if I ride it?" "Go for it," he uttered.

"Auwgh," I thought, as I gushed at such a profound statement. I picked up the hunk of metal. Its handlebars were bent wide. Body was rusty, and shaped like a beach cruiser mountain bike hybrid, that was 15 years old.

My years of six and seven in the dusty, rustic streets of Edwardsville Estates were in want of a leader, one who was big and male. Mike Mitchell was as good as any. He had an attractive quality, so definite. He could have done a variety of things, and I would have followed him.

His cousin told me recently, that even to this day, he is living in the former Edwardsville Estates (now Stone Meadows) with his momma.

Every time I saw him he would be waving around that dirty (we were filthy), long (for a guy) hair, down to his shoulders. He would have a cute new saying it seemed, every time I saw him. "Rad," "Gnarly," or "Totally," I listened to every one.

His mother used to waste precious daylight playing Contra on Nintendo, passing down her skill to Mike. Ms. Mitchell taught me the code to get free men > up, up, down, down, b, a, start.

She was like a dad to me. Mike's mom was tough. Her attractive features lay behind a rugged appearance. Mike listened to what she said. And I listened to her, because I believe mom would not have minded had she straightened me out with a spanking.

But Mike and I got away from both our parents one day. Mike and I rode way over to the other side of the court, to a trailer catty-corner to the park's entrance. We stopped at a mutual friend's house, a girl my age. As we entered, her mom approached us, scooting us out. In a private meeting, the girl's mother explained I could not come over. It's okay though. My child mind I did not understand what the problem was between poor white folks and poor Afro-Americans.

Momma and Jose

Momma taught at school during the day and usually did not get home until aboput an hour after the darkness set in outside. I resented then a little. I really wanted to know where she was. I figured she was with Jose, or at some Parents Without Partners (PWP) meeting. I felt isolated. I think Jharmel did, too.

Mom wanted someone her age to break up the monotony of taking care of a six and nine year-old, it seemed. I waited for her.

I really liked it when mom let us skip school. Skipping school meant you got to watch multiple episodes of Saved By the Bell. Those cool Bayside kids were great. They got life. Everything, even despite conflict, turned out rosy. They must have had something special. They could do no wrong.

Ya' know, too, they showed me an amazing thing. They showed me the power of the mass media. They showed me how far-reaching television and radio can be. People can use it for good. Then again people can get lost in it, giving power to, literally, a machine. I tried to soak up whatever redemptive principles it had in store. That and Kelly Kapowski from Saved By the Bell was smokin'. She stood about 5'8", smiled something radiant with straight black hair just past her shoulders. She was a bubbly cheerleader on the situational comedy.

Television taught me a great deal about human behavior. The way people do things, especially in conversation. Conversation is often nonsensical. Some things about conversations ruffle my feathers. I completely dislike when a person asks, How are you? and then walks right by, without waiting for a reply. "How are you?" "What's going on?" are the same way. When somebody says, "What's going on?" this means the person needs or wants to know how you are doing. Idle conversation is of no use. Why talk in the first place?

I thoroughly enjoyed watching "Saved By the Bell" on TV. Zack Morris, the excellent, handsome, smart aleck who always had whatever he wanted to put in his room, was good at sports, smooth with the ladies, and every guy wanted to be his friend. He affronted Screech occasionally. But he eventually, somehow, let him know afterward he was just playing. Zack and Slater, the jock, put their arms around one another in a friendly way. Their affection made me figure this is how friends behave with one another. Slater called Zack "Preppy." Initially it caused some friction between the two. As time wore on, though, it became more a term of endearment. They argued. They endured conflict. In the end, however, we, the audience, knew they were tight. They hung out with one another. They joked with each other. They could do no wrong. I saw the levels of human interaction on screen—the laughter and good times exhibited in Zack and others gaining employment at Malibu Sands Beach Club as well as serious moments such as Jessica Spano's dependence on pills to stay awake.

Reflections

Asking meaningful questions, inquiring of the person's joys, likes, foibles and so on is utterly commendable. Any conversation that can further mold a relationship is great. Working hard at making a good conversation is super. Genuine connection, which does not come in every instance in every conversation, is what it is all about. When the speech lends itself to understanding, this is the focus. Talk should be used to praise. Talk should be used to give thanks.

Silence is one part of the vocabulary that should be utilized in a person's daily walk. Men serious about discipline should be completely familiar with this concept. Quiet reflection is fundamental to self-control. Making one's thoughts in line with God's thoughts is the purpose of human existence—disciplining the body—subduing it to the mind and body connection, in which the soul is interwoven, to form complete unity. Only through daily intentional silence can this be achieved. I have no qualms about being silent in conversation when sitting in a car with a friend. Caring about my friend, I hear his warm voice, and cherish the interaction. But, in fact, some of the most meaningful interaction between two individuals can be nonverbal. My hands can work. My feet can move. So when I want to make myself of use, my course of action is often, and should regularly be, through action. Action of mouth here, means lack of action. You can speak words out of nervousness or anxiety. People often speak leading up to panic attacks.

Through speech, we simply utter words that make the mouth move, which requires little work. And work should be each day's bread. Making oneself useful is the very essence of action, of being, because when we effectively learn to serve others, we are engaged because, in doing so, we no longer have capacity to worry about self, but we are absolutely capable of caring for others. When I was a child I wanted to be famous. With all the rah rah in TV land nowadays, this is what most people see. But now I have increased in wanting to serve others and decreased in wanting to be widely-known. I estimate my joy has increased in due proportion.

Even when I did go to school (which was most days) I came home and watched Beverly Hills 90210. It was so intriguing to see who would date Kelly's boyfriend, and the conflict resolution. I watched their mannerisms. I noticed voice inflection. It may have been a cheesy teenage soap opera, however, it was all I had.

Then Nick at Nite featured Mama's Family, my very favorite situational comedy. They reminded me of my family. They were not polished like so many of the newer television series. I appreciated the set designer's choice of antiquated rooms. He or she set the mood quite nicely, and most everything about the show was highly reflective of rural Midwestern family life. My grandmother was not abrasive like Ma Harper. Neither of my uncles were slow like Uncle Vint. They dressed, however, the same as my family dressed. Vint and Naomi lived in a short trailer in the back. Grandma and grandpa owned a trailer similar to it behind their property. And Mama's family used the same words.

"Uh-uh. You what?" Ma Harper said.

Vint, this man of middle-age, would droop his shoulders, letting his arms hang down to where it looked like they would fall to the floor and say, "Momma..." in a drowned out tone similar to that of a seven year old. This is what I fell asleep to.

So cable television made a significant contribution to raising me.

I abstained from television once. Oh, how much better the world would be if each person put upon herself some limit. Television is, for the most part, a distraction. The vast majority of it is not worth watching. Discovery Channel, History Channel, A & E, these stations are all worth watching.

My experience was that of watching simply from boredom. All

through high school, I plopped in front of the set, with brother, my mother, whoever was in the room. There is this sense of spoon feeding, a person has called it. A large majority of television has no interaction. Video games at least, are interactive. People can bond when playing Super Tecmo Bowl on Super Nintendo. Friends bicker with one another. Some may even discuss the effectiveness or ineffectiveness of offensive formations against certain defenses. Internet is not only interactive; Internet is one of the greatest educational tools known to man. From essentially all city libraries in the United States a man or woman can access the Internet, also known as the worldwide web. Tens of millions of homes are equipped with this capability, the Internet. But even the Internet is no substitute for just moments with people in role model positions. Conversations are always going to be better than Internet, when someone who has been there teaches you mano y mano.

Writing

I have been blessed to have the ability to write. No matter what, I have the ability to jot down notes and ideas on paper. On some occasions, I think about where I would be without the gift of writing. As one fellow told me recently, "Writing is the purist form of self-expression."

Pondering. I am unbelievably blessed to be able to type on this page. I have the notion that if I were not able to type anymore some day, I could just bang my fingers on my legs and act like I was typing and this would suffice.

However, I do get to type. Writers have ideas. I admire writers. People who write for a living are cool. Even the people who are not required to write for a living who write, I admire that. Public officials, who write much, are admirable. Simply putting words on the page, emptying the self to add something to perceptions, reaching for new perspectives; this is wonderful.

My mom received her undergraduate degree from SIU at Edwardsville. Importance permeated the campus. A desire to attain knowledge was instilled into me from those, my formative years. Mom took me along as she searched for materials at the campus Lovejoy Library. A giant, 9' statue of a man stood at the entrance of Lovejoy library which continually fascinated me on visits. His bronzed features captivated my attention. Light would beam down onto the bold figure. A natural light reflected from a large opening in the middle of the room pouring down past the third and second floors, radiating students' books as they studied.

Living paycheck to paycheck at the trailer court was a trip, and our living room floor was littered with clutter. Trash was all over and, picking up the refuse was not required. Patrick was one of my best friends. He looked at our newly cleaned trailer one day and, in shock, said, "You can see the floor!"

We had this constant dichotomy of having enough money to live on, and even enough for mom to send Jharmel and me to a private school, and living in the cheapest neighborhood in town, across a major route, Illinois Highway 157, and miles from the main, affluent city neighborhoods. We were nearly as close to the rough streets of Granite City, nicknamed Gritty City, as we were to the bright spots of Edwardsville.

Some of my formative years were marked by my brother always being there for us, a strong, sensitive person, who showed me the type of person I was. Jharmel was an excellent blessing from the Lord. He seemed like the most humble person on the face of the earth. He was always a person of subtle encouragement, doing silly impressions of sitcom characters. He ate chips and danced around as if he were having the most joyous time in the world. There is nobody he would have rather been around than mom and me. We were a team.

One day, Jharmel forgot to take a book report to school. Mom had worked so incredibly hard on the project with Jharmel. She probably did more of the work than he did. For goodness sake he was only in the fifth grade. Mom would go to Southern Illinois University just up the road over and over to get materials, to do research. Jharmel had already forgotten to take the project to school once, so mom was a little mad. After hearing he forgot a second time after school mom became extremely mad. I stood in the side of the room as she yelled. Mom tore her vocal cords with the yelling, as Jharmel was getting lashed with words.

Mom built up such a tension, I knew something was ready to break. Her words became stronger and more volatile. More volatile and she started cussing and next thing I knew Jharmel was on the ground. Mom completely lost control of her emotions. She kicked him repeatedly, cussing with every thump. Jharmel was not a big boy, too small to fight back. My mom was a big woman by then, strong and overweight. She laid into Jharmel like I had never seen before.

DRUGS AND FOOTBALL

Our hamster's cage got turned over, he got loose and Jharmel lay there crying, not as much as I, however. He took the uncommon instances of rage easier than me, for some reason. Just trying to be tough I guess. Jharmel was tougher than me as I have said before. When something went wrong he knew how to handle it. I just broke down under pressure more than once as we grew up together.

Patti Dudley, host of the Radio Talk Show, What Matters Most on Family Friendly 91.1 WIBI Radio in Carlinville, Illinois, said when we feel bitterness toward somebody else, it is always hurting us more than the person who caused the hurt originally. When we let the bitterness lie inside of us it festers. She said, when we carry around bitterness we eventually explode.

It's not as if my mom had a vicious plan to hurt my brother or me that day. She made a mistake. Whatever we do unto others, well, those demons have to be exorcised to be gotten over. We sure hurt the ones we love—sometimes without even realizing what we are doing. I realize better now, the hurt I've caused by checking out mom's mistakes.

Being a parent is rough. I have been working with this saying, Knock, and the Door shall be opened unto you. Ask and ye shall receive. Seek, and ye shall find. This is absolutely important. Whenever we are persistent in whatever we are doing we get a reward. We get rewarded big time. No matter what we do, when we continue, and press on, we are rewarded. Somehow we can press onward and put traumatic events behind us.

Despite the home front dysfunction, we went to school like all the other little children. All the other little children had dysfunction at home too. We were not alone, I learned later.

I wanted to look like all the kids on TV during those years in Edwardsville Estates. My goal in life was to be like the children in the YMCA Judo classes, the ones who were clean, well-kempt, and had life figured out at an early age. These children spent considerable parts of their lives at YMCA, whether it was Judo, or playing basketball in free gym. This was what I wanted to be like. These boys and girls had beautiful parents, who drove around in BMW's and SUV's. I wanted to be just like that, with a pretty, successful-looking mom, who always knew when to pick me up from YMCA classes. She would tell me when to read and check on my homework right after getting home at night. All I wanted was evident in the lives of youngsters there at the YMCA.

But one thing I could always count on was on the first and the fifteenth of every month, mom bringing home the bread. We knew on those days mom would treat us to whatever food we desired. The former Bonanza restaurant, which is now Ponderosa Steakhouse, used to allow children to eat for their weight. If the scale read 67 pounds, then I would eat for 67 cents, simple as that. But eating was just an excuse to hang out with mom and Jharmel.

What a Wild Surprise

Mom surprised us with a great announcement that summer. We had talked about it. We had spoken of the vacation of a lifetime, as if it were reachable, but the trip somehow never materialized—until that one glorious summer.

It was the season before my third grade year. Mom told us we were heading to Disneyworld, located in the heart of sunny Florida. We were going to see Mickey Mouse, and Goofy! This was the gang who made you feel like a kid. It was absolutely great. It was fantastic. We hopped in our rented, new Dodge Shadow, a four-door, mid-size family car. The vehicle was more spacious than anything we had in the past. And it had air-conditioning. Our Dodge Shadow was the first auto we rode in together that had cool air-conditioning.

I sprawled out in the back as we set out from Illinois. I was soon fast asleep. I peeped my head up in Atlanta, just outside Fulton County Stadium, home of the Braves. It was a landmark experience, and contributed to the high regard in which I would eventually hold major league baseball.

We stopped off at a Denny's restaurant when we arrived in Florida. A mother and her little girl, who were from France, ate breakfast near to us. The little lass looked up, and said, "Mummy, this is some good French Toast." I thought to myself, "This *is* some good toast," and "this girl has a funny accent."

We then drove to Ramada Inn, as this was above and beyond anything we had done up until then. Mother was giving us the royal treatment. We walked along a bridge leading from the sidewalk to our hotel with a four foot wide creek beneath. We were confident, that even if the bridge did give way, we would be all right. Really, we would be.

Mom drove us the short journey to Disneyworld. I remember seeing these different towns that were representative of different countries around the world. Every five minutes you would walk up, and you had another country, from China to Russia, and India and Mexico. You had the sense these were authentic cultures. So we were blown away by experiencing other nations.

We would look up at the stands from which people sold items. Mom bought us some knick-knacks. But the treasure of the experience was seeing in a tangible way all the different people, and how they complemented one another. They actually gave me a better understanding of how blessed I was to be different. Visitors would travel from far and wide to experience this culture of different ethnicities, this myriad of individuals who lived in harmony.

We then took a ferry across the way to be with another culture. As we exited the boat, a belly-dancer from the East greeted our crowd in song. She chingled and changled. The woman was forward, and danced almost into our laps. She got closer, and closer, and chose me out of the crowd to dance with. She took me by the hand, a lad of seven, and shook her cymbals from the belly. Her hips swiveled in an exotic motion. Round and round she went, back and forth, and I thought, "this is 100 percent woman." She was more experienced than me. I was awkwardly pleased to dance with her, even so far away from my own manhood. What she showed me made me enjoy being around women. Shaking with her made me see how physically beautiful women are, and how graceful. The way in which she moved, slithering, and shaking in motion, made me see different people through a different lens. She was graceful and stunning. I could not get over the gaze in her eyes. The way she looked at me set me almost in a trance. She was beauty.

After all our excursions over the week, the rides we had ridden and the people with whom we conversed, we were excited. We felt extraordinarily special.

DRUGS AND FOOTBALL

Being so worked up left me extremely sick.

The day we were to leave Ramada, I woke with puke on my bed, urine in my pants, and feces in my underwear. I had partied too hard. All the excitement had become too extraordinary. It was too much in so little time. We did too much. We had seen too many sights.

Mom made sure I washed up, and we left inconspicuously. As we spoke later, we pitied the maid who would have to clean up that mess. We felt bad as a team about that; the rest of the day, I felt even worse. My stomach soured. I felt as though I had drunk two-week old milk, in the midst of rotten hamburger. I tasted death in my mouth, and as we made our way back north, I asked mother to fetch an orange juice from a convenience store, to alleviate the stench of it. It was just something to drink. It made me feel better for the simple fact mother was willing to comfort me. There was nothing else. My body would not accept any food for the whole day. I was so very ill.

Nonsensical Words

In my most formative years mother always knew how to comfort me. She always knew the right thing to say. She was gentle with me.

She would say words which sparked my curiosity. She made up sentences and words that rolled off her tongue. Her command of grammar was instrumental in shaping my linguistic desire. It made me say, "some day I am going to use words to say what I mean."

"Tinkerless" she said, meaning tiny. She would say, "Sweetest of days time." Wonder filled me when one of her new words or phrases would arise. Phrases were simple, such as "shortest of days." Her unusual phrases were endearing notes to my ears.

English was mom's forte. She used it to her advantage. Mom taught English before instructing people in Spanish. Her gift was instrumental in developing my language interest. Language was a gift, a remarkable talent. Mom's fluency in two languages made me want to search out my language. Mom's desire to communicate with people of a whole different country of origin, made me want to seek out my own people. I wanted to become better acquainted with my blackness, lest I miss out on half my life.

I could be comfortable with black people and white people.

Angst

My fingers type here as I try to picture angst in my life. Watching mother suffer was tough. We were living in Conroy's Trailer Park, back in Staunton, where most of my family was.

One day, though, on a cool summer evening near dusk, my brother and I sat under the St. Louis Arch not far from mom and her boyfriend Dwayne Cosey. I sat away from him. He came over and said, "Brett, I love your mother." The comment was like a sour slap in the face. I felt as though mom was bringing men into Jharmel's and my life. It seemed as though she was trying to tell us, "children, you're really not good enough for me. I will need to get someone to make up for your inadequacies."

An annoying problem with mom that influences how I view broken families even today was how she would put these men into our lives, and expect everything to be okay. She began dating him to provide Jharmel and me with a male person to emulate. But that usually just made us feel uncomfortable and less wanted.

Dwayne was a man six feet three inches in height, 210 pounds with exceptional athleticism. Dwayne had a competitive spirit and playful disposition. He used to take Jharmel and me to watch him play in softball leagues and basically run over the competition. He was close to being a professional baseball player, as he made it all the way to Triple A in the Milwaukee Brewers minor league system, one step away from the big time. He was an absolutely blessed baseball player. However, Dwayne

Cosey threw all the influence he otherwise may have been able to salvage in my life in one day. The day he completely lost it.

Dwayne and mom were arguing one morning as Jharmel and I were preparing for school. My brother and I began walking to the bus stop, a block away. Dwayne started yelling. I looked back. Dwayne kicked my mother's limp body as she lay on the ground. I froze. My little self did not know how to react. Jharmel began to yell. He proceeded to tell this man to get off my mother. I cried. I violently sobbed. I went to my knees and shook in a pathetic whine. Jharmel continued to yell.

I stuttered and stumbled. I stumbled over to the nearest trailer, directly to my right. I could barely speak any words to the man and woman at the screen door. I was finally able to relay the gist of the situation between tears and mucus. They proceeded to call police.

Danny, a high school janitor, approached Dwayne. He continued to beat my mother senseless.

"I think you should get off her," Danny told the much larger and physically imposing man. Dwayne, shaken up, as though he had been in some alternate world for the past 90 seconds, backed away. He entered my mother's car.

Dwayne Cosey sped away and we never saw him again.

An ambulance arrived. Medics put my mother on a stretcher. They strapped her into a neck brace. She looked like a mangled puppy that had just been attacked by a pit bull. They lifted her up into the ambulance and drove on. She suffered a broken collarbone. Mom could not lift one of her arms for weeks.

Dwayne was not the answer. He did not do the trick, and neither did another man Terry, who she put in our lives (though he tried earnestly). But mom was all I needed. Sure, it would have been better if we were born under steady circumstances. It would have been great had Jharmel and I lived with two biological parents in the same household. However, this is America, and that's our luck for lack of a better word.

Frankly, mom was all the dad I needed. I wanted to be just like her—strong, witty. She made people laugh with her off the wall humor and gestures. Mom would even attempt at playing catch with me sometimes. That is more than many mothers do. Mom was great and still is.

Influences

Many, many men made constructive contributions to my life as I grew. Times were tough growing up in Conroy's trailer park in Staunton. We had moved back to be closer to grandma and grandpa, not to move out of town as a family again. Playing outside, we'd hear people yelling at each other inside their trailers—this was a regular occurrence. Orange gravel had been scattered across the trailer park separating trailers from each other. My brother and I would roam around with the neighborhood kids, walking on the gravel, hearing it crunch beneath our little feet. The trailer park was actually like a big, happy family. We got into softball and kickball mostly. Sometimes we would play with nine people, sometimes three. When George Worthman was around, though, everything was all right. George was my mentor from as early as the age of seven. He stood 5 feet 9 inches, had straight black hair and a smooth complexion. He was the most constant man in the trailer park community. My responsibility was to hang on his every word because I wanted to be like George Worthman.

He was making it, even though he was out of work much of the time. Hey, no cheating, no stealing. He was not a drunk and actually never picked up a beer when around me. Chewing tobacco was his vice. George also cussed—not terribly much, but it was there. He used French, as people called it after they cussed, sometimes remarking, "Pardon my French." George would let me follow him around and along the rock-strewn sidewalks at Conroy's (now Raylynn) Court as we would jaunt to and from the trailers bound close together. He lived with his girlfriend,

Hazel, at Hazel's mother's trailer toward the Country Market side of the park.

I attempted to find a purpose, looking for strong men of character to emulate. Being around such a man made the choice natural. He was strong, albeit, of a coarse nature. He would initiate games of kickball and other sports. George enjoyed watching National Football League games and rooting for the Washington Redskins. Man, I wanted to be just like him!

George was dependable, equipped with a will to survive. George enjoyed life, too, spending time with us kids in the neighborhood. We never really got into any deep conversations, however, George showed me consistency, how to get up in the morning and make use of a day, even if it meant coming over to my home in the summer to see if I wanted to come out and throw a baseball. George didn't have a lot going for him as far as employment, but work he did in this boy's life.

George was excellent. He didn't *have* to be around me; but he was. George used his talents to edify me, if just by hanging around me. But George was bigger than life to me because he wanted to be around me. Li'l me! He gave me purpose, my whole life at that time, because he chose to give me direction. I knew from him that you are supposed to get out of bed and go and try that day. George gave me the courage to try. George and I kept up with each other a little through the years. I saw George up town a few months ago. He leaned out of the passenger side window of a woman's car on Main Street. He said playfully, "What's up, dog?" I told him I had been traveling the country, and it was great how we used to play kickball with each other. I let him know what type of a fatherly influence he made upon my life. It was people such as George who made the difference in my development.

Jason Fassero was my contemporary, and always made me feel better from his unabashed clumsiness. We were close friends, more like brothers. We spent so much time with one another in those days. We were together after school, or on the weekend, or in the summer, at either Jason's house or my house half the time during those years. He put me at ease through his unrelenting avoidance of fashion. He was slightly heavier than the rest of us, with freckles and dark black hair. Jason wore his hair over to one side almost always, with an uncanny reserve to never care about his appearance after getting ready. If one single jet-black strand stood up like Alfalfa, as it often did, he would be none the wiser, and if he was, would pay it no attention.

Through his manly rough ways, I learned what it was like to be tough, to dance with white girls at school without reserve, because, after all, they danced just as badly as we did. I was barely masculine in this—the third grade, like the rest of my peers. Because when it was all said and done, I was a black kid, and just like the rest of the school children at St. Michael's lost and afraid.

In those days at St. Michael's in Staunton our parents gave us some great loving care. Enter Allen Fassero, Jason's dad. What a man. Some men in my life inspired me to do more and loose. Allen cared about Jason and me so much he would allow us to go at it tooth and nail.

Jason Fassero rocked back and forth with me, in a grappling position with me in the first floor of his Pearl Street, two-story house when we were in fifth grade. Green plants taller than our adolescent bodies hung over the rather large television. The foliage was healthy, but sagged, like a middle aged man dangled over the side of his bed after entering his home following an extended noonday run. A bookcase stood in the northeast corner of the room. Jason's room was to the southeast of the living room, with a doorway as wide and tall as a very large man.

A reclining chair set in between Jason's room and stairs ascending upward in the middle of the room that led to his parents' room, an area off-limits to me at least. The corner of the living room was a doorway which led to the kitchen, where Jason's mom was rumored to have thrown a butcher knife at Jason, missing his head by not far, before the blade stuck plum in the side of the doorway to the back door. On the northwest side of the living room was the doorway to the front of the house. Gargantuan plants decked this foyer area also. Walls were tan-colored, a wood shade, that did not have people convinced. A short coffee table stood in the center, and slightly staggered in the living room. A comfy couch was a step to the west of the coffee table. A smaller, couch was on the north side of the room, with plants behind, plants that were as green and lush, so full of life they could have come straight from the

Amazon rainforest. Two cabinets flanked the north corners, one on the northeast, one on the northwest, the former where Allen had his large gun, which Jason showed me for giggles, although I was scared whenever he mentioned the thing. The carpet was originally white but had turned gray from use. The ceiling was of an average height. An entertainment center stood just shorter than me between the TV and Jason's room. A big window was behind the TV. A window of comparable size was just behind the smaller couch. A fun ceiling fan hung from the center of the whole scene. This is my friend's former living room catty-corner from Wareco gas station in my mid-childhood.

Jason, with a pug nose, freckles, jet-black hair with some streaks of gray, used to fight me. We danced like puppies. In other instances, Jason and his temper, when tussling, as erratic as a torrential tropical storm, took me out. Allen stood back often, giving consent to all we were doing, many times rooting me on, as I was less overtly aggressive, but with more utilized technique. We both got to our knees in the middle of the carpet, Jason's tongue stuck out as a German Shepherd pants for water. My stance was more out of submission, as I realized for Jason to be a man, he had to take our wrestling seriously.

"Go!" Allen said. Immediately Jason's face turned red. "Is that all you got?" Jason muddled.

"Derr. Dehrr," I replied. He slammed me in a headlock, as my eyes felt as if popping out of the sockets. "Tui. Tui," I replied, with blood rushing to my face. It wasn't enough yet. I grasped his arm with my right, squirming as a chicken futilely flaps its wings in the clutches of a boa constrictor. Fassero's grip was menacing, taut, with no room for remorse. He was dreadfully calm in his torture, as my submission became less. Fassero's right arm went over my eyes.

"I can't see," I said.

"Sleeper hold. Sleeper hold. I got you in the sleeper hold...go to sleep," he hissed. Often in these fights I felt my neck muscles and many other body parts losing circulation. But what matters of blood circulation anyway. As soon as a person lets off that blood begins to flow again, I thought.

Tapping with my arm, I felt the carpet, I patted the floor.

"Tui. Tui," I mustered. I couldn't see. My pulse worked up, and a wild beast raged inside me. I could hardly contain it. What was more, Fassero, after he felt my relaxation period, knew what was coming. His determination at subduing me made my resolve all the more firm.

He pushed and I prodded, squirming like the chicken that had to stand up for the baby chicks back in the nest. Jason was moving with me, taken to and fro, as a wave moves in the high tide of a sea storm.

"Go to sleep," he said, twisting my body, though his grip loosening with every turn of my torso.

"Tui," I said. "Tui." Grabbing both his arms, I slithered up from underneath, making my way to the floor. As I stood up he, with a red face and mine nearly cherry, he knew what was coming, laughing at me. He laughed, and I laughed, 'cause he knew he was going to get it. Jason, pointing and pontificating, with snot bubbles welled up in his nostrils, felt—"Boom!" I zoomed across the room, toward him, near his bed room, grabbing Fassero by the arm, as he started busting out laughing, as I held his wrist behind his back and threw him to the ground. Wrenching him by the mid-stomach as we were both near the middle of the living room floor, I let out a guttural growl.

"Brhhh." Again, I continued. "Rehhhhr." There was no avoidance for Jason now. He was in the clutches of one so animalistic, like he had never seen before. By now, he could hardly control his laughter, unable to hold up his arms high at all. My iron claw was in tact. "Terr," I growled. "Terr…Rherr. Dherr. Thhhhheeeeeee. Miiiimmmmightttttyyyyyy Bbbeaaaaaaarrrrr!"

There I went, as bees invading a honeycomb going for Fassero, growling, moving from side to side, attacking him with simultaneous headlocks and iron claws, slapping him, patting him with forceful and somewhat playful precision. Standing up, I came back down, only to give Fassero the shoulder straight down. Fassero could not help himself from audibly, erupting chuckling at this juncture, and the fight seemed wholly unfair, as if a laughter interference call was in order.

"Rherrerr," I said. "Breeerrhh," was the sound, hovering over him with all I had, touching base here and there, frequently tickling and tussling, picking him a little off the ground and throwing him down, Fassero laughing all the way, and Allen pointing in amazement, looking away periodically, and grabbing his mouth, then laughing again, giving clearance to the spectacle.

Jason and I would play basketball in the blacktop driveway behind his white house for hours on end. We took far shots, shots from the side, shots straightaway from the garden, in the neighbors' rock driveway, elevated by a couple feet.

Jason's mom Jeanine would make us gooey, stringing mozzarella cheese sticks. Scrum-diddly-umptious. She would often encourage me, and often insist on my coming to Thanksgiving dinner and Christmas Dinner. Jeanine always gave me the feeling their home was my home.

Allen and Jeanine were as parents to me. They inspired me with loving words, showing me I could do anything. Allen told me one time, and I think facetiously, I would make a good president.

We need people in America who give other children somewhere to go; we need men especially. I suppose I am biased in this regard, however, men stand for something so strong in America. Men give other people work; they give little boys a chance.

I have picked some ruggedness in this life from Allen, as he taught Jason and me how to slap box in the living room. He also showed the faith to challenge me with political discussion, even though I was not halfway through elementary school. Allen said he thought the beating of Rodney King was justified, even though I believed L.A. police used excessive force. Allen said, "He was so doped up." And I could see his argument, however, you can see clearly on the video many officers hovering over one man.

Through all the education, all the teaching Allen made an indelible impression on me, providing a young kid with no father around, somebody to look up to and confide in.

Life was more rewarding when it was just Jason Fassero, Tim Kershaw, me and a ball. There was nothing better in those days. We could just have a basketball over at Nick and Nathan Rothgangle's house and the court was our oyster. The grey, short driveway worked past an adjustable rim and backboard. At seven feet as the lowest setting on the goal, the three of us were slam-dunking by fifth grade. The whole collection of sports paraphernalia was completely heaven for us. They kept hockey sticks, pucks, waffle ball bats, baseballs odd balls, Frisbees. Nick and Nathan's was like Christmas every clear summer day. Wrist shots, slap shots, knuckle pucks (from the Motion Picture *Mighty Ducks*). All of these shots were regular and tried. We shot against that metallic white garage door and after missing the net wide in the air got a ding! As Garth Algar said in the film *Wayne's World,* "Game on." Just playing was all we needed to do. Playing was what made us click. We could play every day no matter what our parents were up to—forever and we'd have been in heaven. Just the three of us. We were together at least twice every week from third grade through sixth. We shared four solid years playing Tecmo Bowl in Fassero's basement, eating fire chili in Kershaw's kitchen and throwing John Elway passes on his green lawn. In Kershaw's backyard, when he lived next door to Fassero, we ran loose. His backyard, approximately 80 feet long by 50 feet wide, was the site of many a match of receiver/ interceptor. One person was all-time quarterback, another was receiver, and another was defensive back. As the leaves fell on those autumn days, we threw into coverage and pulled out passes diving, stretching jumping. We tested our bodies feverishly. We loved the game. That was all we could do—play the game.

Another Side of Life

It was not always roses and daisies, however. No, no. I had been through serious frustration. Few people in town looked like me, yet they looked at me often, funny, I thought because I was a different skin color. Maybe just because of my age. Maybe because of my financial standing, or living in a trailer. Whatever it was, their comments and behavior somehow made me stronger because of the perseverance it took to withstand. In the Bible, the prophet Isaiah says in the 48th chapter and 10th verse, "Behold, I have refined thee, but not with silver. For I have chosen thee in the furnace of affliction."

We developed some wonderful relationships through sport. I collected baseball cards with my school buddies. We would talk about baseball. We would speak about which of us who got what card out of what series. We would speak at recess about who had more homeruns. Someone had the more steals and so on. Then we would talk about professional football. Later we would dabble into the NBA. We would just talk and talk, and even though the comparisons were inconsequential, we all had fun. The love of sport got me through twists and bends in the road on the mountain of life. I became infatuated with the Chicago Cubs in seventh grade when the coolest classmate at St. Michael's, Matthew Stein, began talking about collecting baseball cards.

One day a few of use were supposed to go to the Alton Mall together for a trip to a baseball card shop. Abby Neuhaus, one of the sweetest girls in school, called and spoke with my mother. I came in the room shortly thereafter, asking who had called.

"Abby called," mom told me. She was asking for directions to our home and mother said she gave the directions to her. So, I grabbed my stuff, ran out of the door past several trailers, then to the front of the trailer court where these storage sheds were. After getting to the street, Abby's mom's van was about ready to pull in. I was terribly embarrassed. Cute girls from school knew I lived in a trailer. "Oh…my gosh," I thought. It was shameful to live in a trailer. How would I go on? What would the girls think?

I ended up getting over it, and I, who resided in the humblest of environments among classmates, could get over it. I had to, and they didn't seem to care one bit where one of us lived.

Men in my life were highly contributive but even though mom and grandma were of the XX chromosome, rather than the XY, they were like fathers to me. Even though I enjoyed playing manly sports and watching manly sports, somehow this dedication to vigorous activity never seemed to rub off onto grandma and mom. They were always overweight during my lifetime. I had the problem for a brief period in my life, and my brother Jharmel, never. This has to be because of the love of *playing* sport. Allen and Jeanine, Brian and Tammy Kershaw, and mom, encouraged us to get *out* of the house, somewhat because they needed a breather from our high activity, but also because they realized the importance of activity.

Jharmel and I goofed around. I kicked Jharmel. I punched Jharmel on the side, as he was usually 6-8 inches taller.

We sat on the couch inside our trailer.

"Kick me up," I said. Jharmel giggled. I positioned my buttocks squarely onto Jharmel's small, taut feet. Jharmel positioned his feet. He coiled the toes, drawing back his little thighs. A smile beamed from one cheek to the next.

"Flluuump!" He flung me all the way across the couch. I touched down safely.

We laughed outstandingly. We laughed some more.

"Do it again," I said, losing self-control in laughter. "Do it again." Yeah, he did it again.

"Ppluumbp!"

When we went out to eat we would sit down and, Jharmel and I were filled with joy and laughter, because our momma simply enjoyed being in our presence. We liked the former Bonanza buffet, but McDonald's was another favorite of ours. If we did sit inside, the place would often be packed, making our communication a little fuzzy. But being with each other was the main thing. There was nothing better in all the world.

Mom struggled with food in her lifetime, and, it is all the story of excess. I came to realize the food binger is in just as tough a battle as the weed smoker. A binge eater craving French fries when nearing a fast food restaurant is comparable to a smoker desiring a cigarette when passing an ashtray at the entrance to a mall.

Food, however, is all around us. We live by food. We need food to survive. Our bodies require food for sustenance. Need is the main factor separating a Whopper from a crack pipe; a Big Mac from a heroine fix. We Americans are hesitant to call for doggy bags and wrap up any leftovers. Finishing a meal is a way to say, I did it, I can finish all that's on my plate; I am a man. Our portion sizes are out of control, and this is something sociologically we must overcome. To restrain our bodies we must work incessantly to control the palate, which is chief of all the senses. And when a person puts half that meal into a tak-hom-a-sak at the meal's outset, she can surely boast, by the grace of God. Mickie Dee's has some great tasting burgers, chicken sandwiches, milk shakes etc. Whoever is given much, though, of him will be required the more.

Fast food restaurants must behave responsibly to earn the general public's respect. Some people have a weakness. Some have a tough time passing on a meal that looks delicious, and there is little nutritional value in a double quarter pounder with cheese. Restaurants would be good to shrink their portion sizes voluntarily for the better of mankind. A company's first obligation is to serve the public: reducing any temptation would be of noble value to the consumer. Some people find solace in fatty treats. Their sorrows melt into sugary desserts.

"Food doesn't talk back," grandma said.

Grandma is excellent at kitchen duties. She always has been. Other than the kitchen duties, however, she would often leave the rest of her house in disarray.

Grandma washed dishes in her white, solid sink, with silver, shiny faucet. The view directly above and outward from the sink is quaint, homey. Any viewer can see where the septic system empties in the far part of her small back yard. Grass is vibrant in the summer on each side of the tube from which the refuse spills, a shiny hint there is something fresh in the crisp breeze. Grandma scrubs dishes. She stacks cups facing down so water does not sit inside. Grandma puts bowls face down, so as to drain. When there is another helper, she says, there is no need to rinse. A person can dry, while she washes.

When grandma was a girl, she and her family could not afford to run the extra water it took to go for a rinse. Grandmother empties the gunk-filled sink stoppers, because if stuff goes down the sink, Uncle Louis has to come over and clean it, she says. Grandma soaks the stove-top black metal pieces above the burners. She scrubs them with soap, and puts them back.

I remember when grandpa was still alive in human form, when the table was clean on occasion. Grandma would wipe in circular strokes, flab hanging from the thin apron dress. She was in her element. Though the other grandchildren would make fun of me because of my inability or apprehension to sweep, grandma had patience. And at least once grandma chided me in her demanding, yet comforting tone, explaining plainly how to fold and "rinche" a dish towel. Simply twisting was not enough. The rag had to be folded, to get the towel closer with itself, dispelling more water each time. Grandma's expertise definitely lay in the kitchen, what with five children under her belt.

Grandma and grandfather would get into some horrendous arguments occasionally, however, beginning in the bedroom, and spilling out into the kitchen. He would label her fat, sheltering his own insecurities inside the verbal lashings. He was gonna make it clear to grandma, he was loud.

I would leave the room holding my ears when he got that way, which was, fortunately, not often. He never laid a hand on her, and was very caring, a gentle man.

But, when he went off on grandmother, his hair sticking up from his gray head, I knew grandma was in for it. She cowered back, after having received the treatment for so long. Grandpa, at six feet and more than 220 pounds, stood heavily over my warm and affectionate grandmother at 5' 1."

He started to yell, and I took cover, as grandma took the abuse to both her self-esteem and dignity, demeaning her self-worth with each deprecating comment. I would scurry underneath the wooden, white top door border, and over the brown, wood bump in the doorway, and into the living room, wishing to hear no more. Maybe I would sit down and anxiously watch some television. Maybe if the chatter got loud enough, I would step out the white screen door, past the descending steps and down the walkway in the bitter, summer air. Grass tossed in the wind leading up to the swing with wooden flat beams spanning across, able to bear the weight of a boy with storms inside, buffeted by waves, crashing, caught on by larger currents. I would sit down. Waiting was all I could do…Jharmel, my cousins Amy and Christy and me could only hang on. Our place was nowhere near the crashing waves, as children need stand well upon the shore, avoiding the gale force winds. Grandma and grandpa were two fronts—grandpa hot and grandma cold, meeting up to create a whirlwind, bringing a raging twister upon the house, testing its very foundations…it was only sometime. Grandma found solace in food sometimes, though. Food never talked back.

Food is so very plentiful in the United States. The human body eats because it wants. When we incorporate water, however, there is only a leaning of purity. Water takes up room in the stomach, and drinking enough of it makes a person feel full faster. Water is a cornerstone of any successful diet or eating program. Water is essential. Humans are made up of water. We are water creatures. Quality water causes the body to flush out impurities as a river cleanses itself of twigs downstream. We have to drink water. H2O is the most awesome substance we have. If one is ever exasperated, anxious, panicking and so on, she should find a tall glass of cool water and let the human body utilize the most effective form of relief…and then get more water and drink that. Physicians suggest at least 64 ounces daily. Water brings us life, when we thought we were out to dry.

DRUGS AND FOOTBALL

When coming up I was cautious, not necessarily racist, against whites. I had a certain apprehensive fear of whites in Staunton who were outside of my family until about the age of 11. It may have been because I was younger then too and just smaller, but racism was widespread in my hometown at the time. Someone once said we fear what is different from us.

Once my grandparents took me to this hotdog cookout at Schlecte's gas station. My grandpa won a prize when—he said for me to go up and get the prize. I went up, reached for the prize and a man snapped at me, asking who I was. Now, it could have been that I was younger, at ten, or he just did not know who I was, but his tone was scary nonetheless, and I was shivering. So I quickly worked my way back to grandma and grandpa's table, I was so scared. I warmed up to grandpa, grasping his large body. I was shaken, and eventually told them how the man frightened me by what he said. So someone from our party walked up and got the prize. I always remember how that made me feel. I remember the man's words, and his inflection, the tone of his voice, what he looked like when he said it. He seemed harsh, irascible and insolent. I felt as though he didn't take my feelings into account.

I remembered vividly also the warmth of grandpa's large, strong arms as well—how when I got back to my grandpa he would not let anything or anyone harm me.

Grandpa and grandma grew up during the depression in Bunker Hill, Illinois, a small farming community just north of the St. Louis metro-east. Grandpa's dad died when he was only a young teen. One day, after grandpa and his father had worked in the fields, grandpa went out to see what his father wanted him to do. When grandpa arrived, he found his father, dead from a heart attack in a field the two harvested together.

Grandpa dropped out of high school to help with the farm. He was resilient and always sturdy. It was grandpa's sturdiness which made him a more than able grandfather and, basically, a father to me. Grandpa was dependable, and more than any other man, his contributions made me appreciate the importance and dedication it takes to provide for a family. His steadfastness was highly respectable. What Grandpa had, and what he provided, we need sorely in these United States.

He did so much more than just come home after a hard days work. I mean, grandpa was a legend. He was a rough man, and an honest man. But he had a rough side, too. He would lean against the counter with a bag of chips in his hands, and watch me watch him eat those chips. He would then move onto the pretzels, and then the wafers, like an assembly line. Grandpa was lining his belly with more calories. Even so, I can't hate him. The cliché "nobody's perfect" is quite applicable here. He wasn't textbook but he gave me direction for my life, because he listened; grandpa was around, and I knew from four years of age to the week my grandpa passed I could speak with him about anything. I knew it wouldn't be easy, may be uncomfortable at times. But I knew he would always be there for me with those big, goofed out ears and thick sideburns.

Grandma had a more privileged upbringing until her father died when she was ten. Grandma and grandpa were "hitched" in the early 1940s. They both had to stay with grandma's grandparents for a spell as they were too poor to buy a place of their own. Grandpa took off for World War II when grandmother was pregnant with Aunt Lois, their first child. Grandma had to hold down the fort by herself. Aunt Dolly came, and then on December 14, 1950, the sunshine brought my mother. The war was a chance for America to show the whole world what kind of military power we held. Upon arriving back, troops were in a position of comfort in the world, with one of the mightiest physical forces in history. Post-World War II brought the baby boom, a period where soldiers, after coming back from war, were making babies faster than people at home had been making bombs shortly before.

When people feel both safe and comfortable for an extended period, they are quite susceptible to overeating. And eat we did. Since 1960, the rate of childhood obesity has doubled. With prosperity comes the hardcore temptation to become lax in all we do. This temptation must be fought, and resisted to the utmost if we are to be of any service to each other. And service is the very best of what we can do on this earth. "Whoever is greatest among you will be your servant." I thought about self-discipline from an early age. I considered all grandpa did, how people in the community respected him, and the organizations he was active in. I wanted to be like grandpa, and, in some way, I wanted to be better than him in the area of self-restraint. I indeed understood later you are the best leader when you serve others. You try to obtain self-restraint, and at the same time reverse this downward trend.

At certain times people afflict themselves, and test themselves with trials too heavy for them to bear. Fortunately, through the grace of God, I got through such circumstances.

I did some *stupid* things growing up. I sat on my bed inside my meager house on East North Street. I could not go to sleep. I heard a tapping on my bedroom window at midnight. I rose, got my clothes on and exited. Jason Dugger, Chris Dugger, Terry Murphy, Tim Kershaw and I wandered all around town. We walked around, feeling like no one wanted or needed us. We yearned for acceptance. We each knew the need within each other, even though never spoken, so we tried to be there for each other.

Our parents were mostly caught up in what they were doing. Felt like we were not the primary focus inside our respective dwellings. So we walked. 12:45. 1:30 a.m. We looked around the vacant Staunton streets in the hollow, crisp winter air. We looked up and…silence. People slept in their comfortable beds. We felt like rebels. We were on nobody's watch and just fine. We accepted that we were imperfect beings.

"Care about me!" we cried out in our breasts. "Someone save me. Give me someone who will tuck me in, or at the very least ask where I have been during the day. Give me someone! Let me be who I am…different and liking it. Give me someone who can discipline. Give me someone who will straighten things out in my chaotic world. Show me the way is through the way of our forefathers. Show me there is such a thing as standing *apart* for good!"

But though we yearned for the good, we stood for the bad. We walked around laughing about it, proving to our adolescent minds this was what we could do, because our parents approved. We had freedom. So the streets we roamed.

We cut through dozens of dewy yards, moisture clinging to our sneakers. We walked our dirty streets. All we could see was darkness, save for a light on the top of a phone pole. We searched for light. We wanted to find light in one another, wishing to see in each of us what we knew we were each capable of—to a person. But tobacco and alcohol and pot and all the other substances that threatened at our vulnerable age, got in the way. We were looking to each other in an alleyway, looking for the light in the eyes of one another. Where was the light? We searched for the light. Where was the light? The light was absent from us because we chose darkness. Had we stepped into the light, we would have had no concerns of where is the light, because we would have been children of light.

We climbed to the top of the grade school. We looked out onto Deneen Street. A vehicle rolled up two blocks away. We knew what to do when a car neared.

"Get down," I said. "Get down. Car. It's the cops."

No matter what was the matter you seemed to get more response from the guys that way. We were nervous. We were anxious because, we wanted to be close enough to see the police, and far enough away, they could not see us. We wanted to control the town. This was our neighborhood. These were *our* nights. Their attention was all we wanted at that juncture. City officials who warranted our attention. I looked out. Night was clear. I was more than ten feet above ground, on a school we entered during the day.

We would be owned by nobody. We nervously breathed, knowing we were better than this whole scene. This was not our scene. We were better than this whole chain of events. Though we did this often, we knew we were better. We walked to the lower grades side of the building. We looked out to Miller Drive, the most wealthy neighborhood in Staunton. We saw the lights. We saw something that shined. We failed to see, however, what shined in each of us. We yelled. Some spoke as though responsible, commanding us to keep quiet. But this was no time for accountability. We had run amok. This was our night.

We threw caution to the wind and quietly exited the roof top, jumping from higher than a basketball rim. We asked each other for cigarettes. Smoke entered the lungs in a satisfying gust of burning leaves. Its flavor made you want to eat the thing. We then exhaled in a calculated way, one that seemed to make our words roll wisely off our stinking tongues. It felt like being in the Marine Corps on some mission where you have no guarantee of safe return. We cut through private property, crossing yards as dogs barked through neighborhood lawns.

We got back near my house on the opposite side of town. Large trailers used for hauling rock had set on a wedge of an industrial-type lot, decreasing from 120 feet between a street leading to the tracks, and the tracks themselves. One by one we hurriedly filed into the trailers. We laid down, invisible to the traffic that intermittently passed by. We lit cigarettes. We joked silly sayings, our hearts racing. It was a thrill. We sat up, and took rocks the size of golf balls and hurled them at traffic. We didn't really want to hit the oncoming traffic. Maybe we did. Maybe we wanted to come so close to where it felt like someone cared.

But the police and us had a special relationship. We stood. Then we heard the sound of cars. We heard them as they approached. Then our hearts pumped. See, the thing about police officers was, they had to pursue us if they saw illegal or unusual activity. So we were just making their jobs more interesting, if for the wrong reasons. Police had authority. And we desperately wanted the attention, if it was fleeting, and vanishing in the bitter cold and lonely street lights, from someone in authority. We craved that discipline. Somewhere in us, we so desired the attention our parents raised us without. We grabbed onto each other, hoping to hold on for this night. Just this one night. Things would be okay if we could just hold on.

B.J. Leaser and I used to walk like there was all the time in the world on and over the five-foot wide tracks that cut through Staunton. At age 13 we sat there, above the creek with solid sparkle rocks on both sides. We met together with regularity this way for a year to a year and a half. Tracks were above and a hollowed out area of ground was underneath. We used to sit up there and smoke cigarettes. B.J. and I spoke about running away from home. We just talked, though. Main thing was, we wanted to bounce ideas off each other. We wanted someone to listen to us, and to listen to each other, in that order. We wanted to be there for each other. We wanted to know each other in a meaningful way. And sharing our deepest longings helped in this process.

On another occasion we had sleeping bags out on a mild night beside the train tracks. B.J. brought one of those portable heating cans, no larger than a jar of peppers. We ate warm food off the heat that fire emitted. We lived day-by-day and that was fine.

But find that someone you can get next to and just hug, no matter if you are a guy or a girl. Whoever it is, people can hug. Feeling lonely does not have to be something that holds onto people. The body is only a vessel for us to provide service to one another in; this is my firm conviction. This is the meaning of life: to serve others. Each of us is a brother or sister, or mother or dad to the rest.

Grandpa was a dad. To me he was mentor, advisor, counselor, dad, grandfather, role model, leader, steward, strong man, and friend—all in one. It was just this silence he commanded when he stepped in the room. His steady, thick voice brought out the gruff in the gray, scruffy sideburns. All his parts were integral. After retirement grandpa would lean back, with glasses loosely resting upon his nose. Grandpa would sit. He would wait. If nobody spoke, the man would nod off. Well, he achieved silence that way. Nobody wanted to wake him up! But then again, especially when grandpa was present, sometimes we would all be sitting in the kitchen and there was this deep sense of warmth, just because each of us listened to the other before he or she said something.

An orange gleam off the kitchen light was beautifully reflected off grandpa's face, illuminating that wisdom, mixed with a hint of intelligence. When he talked, the room listened. Though I was different looking, grandpa accepted me because he saw a person. Grandpa lent his ears during my most frustrating moments, and cared enough to provide food and shelter, exhibiting love unconditionally.

In the third grade Allison Ringo told the class she was afraid if a black person rubbed against her, the color might stick. I was comforted in the fact she would actually get close enough to me to let the black rub off, if that were possible. At least I had that thought of, what if she *did* rub against a black person, what would her perception be then?

Ringo and I danced with one another at dances, and lucky for her, my tone did not turn hers into a milky caramel. She was still white as fair snow. There was no room for her to doubt any more the efficacy of singular pigmentation, as we all had one hue, with us individually, for better or for worse. Allison and I danced under those spinning, multi-colored balls, in a mutual gaze of adolescent wonder, and, I found out she was okay to be with, even if she was white, though a bad dancer.

In friendly settings even, racism was common. I guess the anxiety that came with it growing up left an immovable mark upon my immature awareness of my small community. Joe Randle, Jason's middle aged uncle, was over at their house one day, when Jason and me were in elementary school. As we discussed the million-man march on Washington D.C., Randle said of the march, "Look, there was only 400,000 people there. They can't even count."

Randle, 5 feet 9 inches in height and with wide, colorful eyes, often wore a smile that had to stay, a grin that took no vacations—ready to spring up at any given moment, as a good friend would, without hesitation, be right by your side during times of crisis. He was a strong man, with hair on his face, and pretty much every other place on his body. Jason, Joe and I just sat in the living room, living with the television on and we were comfortable.

It always made me feel suddenly awkward and then easily accepted to be in a room full of white folks and feel welcomed to the point they were unwilling to mask racist tendencies; they were unafraid to expose to me their prejudicial leanings. Anyway, they were just words—and friendships are forever.

People are anxious, at least initially, around people unlike themselves. It is comfortable to be around people who look like you, talk like you, act like you. But, still, for some people, it is another thing entirely to look at someone whose ethnicity you have rarely seen in person, or maybe just on television.

I met Erin James at Jason's mother's interior decorating party. We saw each other in the living room. Our eyes connected. It was like magic. This girl was my age, from Bunker Hill. She was a stunner—5' 6", slim, trim, a cute little smile, and I was done for. She knocked me to the ground…in my mind. Later we got to talkin'. I spoke about baseball. We spoke about small things. Our hearts fluttered, as if they were one. I stood on the ground outside Jason's first floor bedroom window. Erin sat on Jason's bed, inside. I asked if she would kiss me. She said, "yes."

She said, "Go ahead."

I reached across the moonlit sky. I said, "Okay." Our lips met, and it was like, "Pow." Her lips were moist. They were right there.

"Mchhwue." Mine were there for her. All God had created was there for us to see, in each other. We opened up something in each other that was completely special. Our relationship was unique.

We both made each others' hearts flutter. We began dating immediately. Mom drove us to the movie. Mom drove me to her house. We had some excellent times together.

I stood on the second level of St. Michael's, in the Seventh Grade. I looked out the window onto Staunton's Main Street. I looked across to IGA. I then looked back onto Main Street. Erin was on my mind. It was a cool, autumn day. I thought about her deeply. I think she was thinking about me then. I stood there at the end of class wanting *to be so close.* I wanted to be with her every second of the day. I wanted to know where she was. I wanted to know what she was doing—because I wanted to be doing those things with her.

But we were living fast. We started making out every week. We wanted each other, and the damnedest thing was the carnal attraction. We desired each other physically. This is where we went astray. Had we been mature enough to handle one another, we would have made it. But Erin and I were into each other in the worst of ways. Had we had the patience to be together for the sake of being together we would have made it. But oh well. We went far carnally, giving into temptation, and I did not know where to go next. The Catholic Church raised me to develop a conscience, to understand between right and wrong. Then I transgressed this law, making flesh my vice. I called Erin on the phone. I told her it would be better if we were no longer boyfriend and girlfriend. I got scared. She cried heavily. I did not know how far I had wronged my body, my heavenly Father, and I was a bit confused about the whole deal. I was 14. Erin was distraught. I was emotionally twisted. Courtney Wood, a friend who grew up in Bunker Hill, said Erin is now married, and lives in the Chicago suburbs. I hope she is a compassionate wife. I hope she gives her children excellent guidance and wisdom. I loved it when Erin listened to me. She gave me an understanding of how important I was. She was the best girlfriend I ever had.

I believe the best of what married people have is the desire to be with one another. The very best of what a marriage is capable of is two people enjoying each others' company. They love each other; they *just like being around each other.*

An occasion that just would not quit came in the seventh grade at Staunton public school. I had just transferred from St. Michael's grade school because of tuition cost.

Our seventh and eighth grade classes were walking back to the school building from the cafeteria after lunch period. Jim Mosser was a tall eighth grader with blond hair. He kept pushing me from behind, saying, "Nigger."—Push—I'd just talk to someone along side me, trying to keep my cool…"Nigger."—Shove—

Finally I got sick of it. I turned around, raging inside, saying internally, "He isn't going to keep on antagonizing, tearing at me." So I got tough and punched him. He punched back and before we knew it we were in front of a teacher, both crying like little girls. Maybe we were crying because punches from the each of us landed. Whatever it was, at that juncture I thought I had to fight with fists to stand up to Mosser. It is completely ridiculous, though. I got him and I could not even feel where my punch landed.

By hurting him, I hurt myself, because I let him and everyone else know I then had no control over my emotions. Author Maya Angelou said she can be changed by what happens to her but refuses to be reduced by it.

All the pain, grief and anxiety I felt translated into some false feeling of inferiority, as Martin Luther King referred to it as in his Letter from a Birmingham Jail. In lashing out I gave the anger a chance to breathe. Such is the case with all acts of violence. When nations war against nations and kingdoms against kingdoms bitterness is an end-product. Nothing good comes of violence. A peace may result, but that peace is only temporary, a tense stillness harboring resentment.

Teen angst was a companion of suffering. I was shunned, left out in the cold by some peers. Maybe it was just the bad choices I was making, for the apostle Paul said in a letter to the Corinthians, "Do not be misled: Bad company corrupts good character."

Terry Murphy and I stood outside Nicole Ziglar's house one sunny day. Ziglar was the undisputable, most good-looking, cheery girl in grade school. She was about 5 foot six inches—in junior high—tan, dark brown hair, a mole near her mouth, a slender face, and a good rapport with nearly everyone she met. Most girls wanted to be like Nicole. Most of the guys wanted to date Nicole. For some reason, she had an invite-only party. I was not one of the chosen, and stood with Murphy just outside of her house. She pulled Scott Billings through the doorframe fast. Billings was the starting point guard on the basketball team and Billings was Nicole's boyfriend. We waited for him at Nicole's front step, standing there wondering how a guy like Scott got it all—left-handed and original; good looks with a sweet basketball jump shot; bashfully sensitive in front of women at just the right moments and gregarious on all other occasions. He made us look like school kids. Billings was inside that door with girls such as Brooke Pintar, Robyn Painter and Abby Fritz and I felt oh so inadequate for a moment. Tha's puberty fa' ya'.

All in all I hope to build people with this piece. Whenever someone is down I hope to help bring that person back up through encouraging words. Let me show a person what to do before telling him. Uplifting comes from encouragement. Encouragement comes from I don't know where, but it is not from this earth. The world is used to words of defeat, so why not encourage people until it hurts?

Wherever we go to there is a janitor somewhere in the world scrubbing toilets. Recognition can really bring a man up when he is down in the trenches every day. A person can simply tell a man, "Good job," or even better he can relay a specific encouragement such as, "Strong arm rotation while cleaning the toilet. You were going at it. You were totally committed to getting that bowl fresh and clean." This lets the man know what he is doing right. When a person is recognized for doing service he is uplifted.

Sincerity and humility in recognition are huge. Respecting another man means complementing him without expecting anything, such as a,

"Well, *you* did a good job on the stock market the other day, Bob," in return. When a man has discipline to the point of not expecting a complement for his complement, he has something special. Somebody said a highly profound statement about love. Love is doing something for another person when he cannot pay you back.

When a man can simply pay a specific complement to a guy or point out pluses in his work ethic with sincerity, that man has achieved something. Uplifting an individual comes from respect because when a man is respected he gives respect. A man who respects another man without expecting anything in return will win over the man's heart because considerateness in him is unshakable.

Men look at each other with weirdness when they have received complements, like, what was that? Indeed, complements should be commonplace, given freely *because* we are men and, if not friends at least, then brothers.

Encourage a man to do better the next go 'round. Speak words of encouragement to your brother. Know that this is the great land—a land of promise and reward for those who work hard, sacrifice blood and sweat for gut-level service for others and don't whine about it in the end.

Americans are the uplifting type. September 11, 2001 was a time for encouragement and renewal of our commitment to an idea rooted in the American Dream, that we are all brothers, created equally. People converged on the former sites of the World Trade Center and built America back up again.

Ordinary gentlemen lifted a red, white and blue flag that day in New York. Oh, what a beautiful sight.

Uplifting comes from helping someone perform something, even if performance is menial, such as taking out trash. Simply being willing to serve makes a world of difference.

Uplifting comes from serving; indeed, uplifting *is* serving. When a person serves she is rewarded with a gift—knowing she has created something nobody paid for, but because she did it out of her willingness to uplift her community, and, the human condition.

My grandfather Louis Wesley Brackman would go to schools and speak about World War II. He did not have to, but he felt this was a service to students and his community at large. Usually grandpa talked about the technical aspect such as the deck or wake-up time. One time he said about how his crew was in a battle zone and guys were so afraid they were peeing their pants and such.

Failures make us stronger, but in showing people you maintained faith throughout the ordeal is where a person becomes inspired. Without a rock and a hard place to come out of we would lack resilience as people because we would have come from unremarkable circumstances.

Grandpa's Inspiration

Grandpa stood with grandma beside him before a football game during our successful 1997 season. He watched, just 15 feet away from our warm-up practice near the gate entrance.

A player would bust across at medium speed, picking up the other player at the waist. And there grandpa was watching. He finally saw me get into something I was good at. Football was something I could get a hold of. He knew this. Grandpa saw this desire welling up within me. And he supported me with all he could. I knew he thought I was important because of that; he needed to say nothing. Everything between him and me was all right. It was as if we were out there on the boat once more. It all made sense again.

Grandpa had some serious challenges. Grandpa bought 160 acres in the country on credit just after the second world war. He once did not have funds to pay the bank, but told them he would make the payment as soon as possible, so they said they would go ahead and let him keep the farm. This taught me about dealing with all aspects of life. When you are upfront with people they will give you mercy. Grandpa, grandma, Aunt Lois, Aunt Dolly, Mom, Uncle Louis, and Uncle Gene—they sweated on that farm, worked it, planted the seed, harvested their food, and grew up, sharing memories of pain, joy, happiness, and sorrow with one another. All because grandpa taught them—and me—the lesson of honesty—even when you've nearly spent your last dollar.

Challenges toughened my grandfather's demeanor and brought him a strength to overcome adversity. He shared of himself to his community as, after he retired, grandma said he joined any club that would have him.

Grandpa was a soldier even after the war from the challenges he'd met in his time on this earth. I remember the good things.

Grandpa was America, no matter how cliché that sounds. Grandpa would have preferred to be associated with all this nation stands for, besides the wars… He did not talk about the war too much.

Grandpa asked to hold the flag during parades uptown. He believed people can get along with one another as he made friends with people of all cultures and was not persuaded by bigots. However, it tore me apart when my grandpa would call Japanese people nips. That really made me mad. He was in a war with Japanese people, where people tried to take his life and the lives of those on the ship with him. But I knew toward the end of his life here on earth, he became more resistant to ideas such as bigotry. And the best thing he said to me the night he passed on was better than anything he'd told me in the two decades before—Follow Jesus.

Grandpa was like a shelter. No matter what was going on in my life, there grandpa was…he gave his all. When I was intimidated at the bigness of the world around me, he would have those big arms to just melt into. I always knew he was there to listen to me when things were going sour. He showed me how to go out and go to a job day in and day out. Grandpa was an excellent provider. He could have gone crazy trying to make ends meet and being all he could for each of his children and grandkids, but he maintained. Grandpa was challenged by us, the ones who depended on him. Through what he did by just being there, he challenged all of us to be better human beings and, in the process, sowed a seed in my heart to continue the American dream he planted so long ago.

Rapper Ice Cube once said, "Life ain't no track meet, it's a marathon."

Persistence takes patience. From patience and persistence come endurance. Challenges cause a person to endure through all the strife life can throw at a person. Challenges bring endurance.

John Kennedy was always on people to not stand still. Kennedy wanted people to be in motion, because, when people work together, we can get much accomplished.

DRUGS AND FOOTBALL

Mostly we *did* stand still in Staunton after we arrived in high school. We were scared a little just as most children are at that juncture.

Staunton has a sign stating "Staunton 5100." My hometown had just three police cars and a volunteer fire department. Original businesses could usually get going if they were straight and put up a large sign in the front of the store, or made a unique advertisement in the *Staunton Star-Times*. A choice roadway lined with bricks for two city blocks can be found behind Russell's furniture, just off Main Street. When riding inside a car, a person could feel the bumps on the roads, vibrating the whole automobile.

"Sometimes you wanna go, where everybody knows your name," the song goes. "And they're always glad you came. You wanna be where you can see, the troubles are all the same, you wanna go where everybody knows your name." Just like on Cheers.

Staunton was what my grandmother called a bedroom town. People went to work elsewhere, but made their homes in Staunton. Grandpa would lead me into a room filled with stale smoke at the VFW (Veterans of Foreign Wars) hall where gruff elder men would talk about women. Hunting. Fishing. Hunting and Fishing; their wives, what types of guns they would use when hunting and fishing.

My stomach would growl on Main Street in Staunton. Cavataio's restaurant would feature pizza by the slice special at lunch time in 1999. One large slice of pizza, along with a soda at the drive thru window only cost $2.25. The only way we got that lunch was at the window, which was quite all right. After getting the pizza from the window, we would cruise the strip. Nothing was quite like it. There we were, a group of us, and we'd be kicking up a hack, or we'd be wrestling with one another.

Best times on Main Street, just on the side of Subway, down from Russell's furniture store, was when just a few seconds would pass. Everyone would just stand there, embracing each other's dignity and you could barely hear us breathing, but we were living, all of us. Some of us had the provision to a better life. We could dream. And it was those dreams that sustained us.

I guess I can think of few specific instances because of all the THC resin built up in my brain. It was crazy. All the motivation I lost smoking that bud. It's crazy. There were various other drugs, as well, but marijuana made me stupid. It was my favorite one—and it made me forget about worries, and some of the years I shared with friends.

This woman at the Staunton Public Library had a memory of what I would do when I was a whippersnapper one day. Kay, who used to work up at Fashion Lane on Staunton Main Street, and worked at the library, said she remembers when I was a boy and would sit on her counter eating French fries. Her memory of the Fashion Lane pleased me because she remembered the good.

Many an occasion would my high school chums and me hang in front of McKay's Auto Parts and kick a hacky sack to one another. Cracks on the rocky walkway made the games more of a challenge, but we were quite ready. We would pop that hack up in the air. It would land on the roof several feet up at a slant, before descending upon impact down to our awaiting, happy feet. Once every person kicked it into the air, this was called a HACK.

Even earlier childhood was great. Boyhood was a time to cut loose. Grandma would take me into Dime Store on Main Street. Shelves and boxes of candy littered the front left aisle. Children stood there in an adolescent glaze, I mean gaze. We were all part of the same dream. It was surreal, the whole atmosphere. Most candy cost around ten cents, but some was only a penny. Chick-O-Sticks were my favorite—peanut butter sticks with a coconut topping (I have discontinued eating them recently after finding out the most plentiful ingredient is sugar). Dime Store moments were guh guh guh guh great.

Sullivan's Drug Store on Main Street was a treat as well, as we would look to the candy on the left side of the store. The Sullivan's pharmacist stood customarily elevated above the customers.

Grandma and grandpa would allow me to drive uptown with them in the pickup. They would both make me feel snug and secure. Both of them emitted this warmth. Grandpa was abrasive to grandma from time to time, but she had grown a tough skin. The two were as two peas in an affectionate pod.

Grandpa knew how to talk to me. He also knew how to be silent. I guess it was his German heritage shining through. We went to Hillsboro for a trip to the tractor store. He was so stern that, as we were entering town, grandpa broke a ten-minute silence by looking out at a truck approaching us on the country road ahead, up over the dashboard and past my five year old frame, saying,

"FODE."

Something about it—"FODE." The Truck was all he saw. Trucks were all grandpa saw a lot of the time, except this was a fond memory. And you got to take pleasure in the simple things when you're married like grandpa was. For whoever becomes married, I encourage you to have children and grandchildren.

More Male Influence

When parents play with their children, they can enjoy all the pleasures of childhood with their children. This may sound weird, but it is true, for whatever I know about truth. A man and a woman find hope by kicking around a soccer ball with their children. When the children are kicking, at the same time they are having fun they are activating muscles and tendons. Aside from activating the human anatomy, the kids are becoming disciplined. And the parent is helping, in playing with them, encouraging the good physical behavior.

Encouraging people is important. When a man is down, and you give him respect anyway, he gives his heart to you. One of my friends told me the other day of his journey.

Bill, a white man, grew up in a black neighborhood in Mt. Vernon, a small city in southern Illinois. Bill has no distinction in appearance. He has a full black beard and thick voice. Bill is down-home bluegrass; He is from the country; Bill is country. The man is like a father to me. He can sound intelligent when he wants to: he often enunciates during Bible studies but saves the brunt of his focus for the road. Bill is a truck driver (Fortunately he is home to be with his family and the rest of us at church during evenings).

He was the toughest of his few male siblings. His mom did not do drugs but ran with men who did. She would get him up at night sometimes when he was in the third grade, to be there for her when she would go over to a boyfriend's house.

DRUGS AND FOOTBALL

Bill's dad wasn't around much. His last year in school was the seventh grade. He did not enjoy school. He did not even learn how to read or write up until middle age. When Bill was in his teen years, he began moving around the country. He had no place to go. So he literally lived on the streets for ten years.

Somebody had to have encouraged Bill all along the way; maybe a man bought him a soda at a gas station; possibly a stranger paid his bus fare. Whatever it was, good thing Bill got through. He's a wise friend, and he can control his temperament. Bill is my brother; he has been a father. Bill has helped me in many ways. He is great. He's got a real heart for kindness. He even let me stay with him for five months in '05 after I got back from college. He let me live with his family because of his generosity. He wanted to confirm my dignity. Brother Bill was like a father; he was a brother. My own brother was also an influence. My blood brother has been a person of titanic importance in my life.

Jharmel is nearly three years older than me. He has an angular body, chiseled facial features and high cheekbones. His hair is wild and unruly, like that of the electrifying Pittsburgh Steelers' Strong Safety Troy Polamalu. Jharmel's wrists are strong, and he stands about 5'9", 130 pounds. Jharmel has the ability to string words together better than I can; he was a motivating factor for my getting into writing. Jharmel is definitely gifted intellectually and can wax philosophical with a wide-ranging vocabulary. When he speaks with laughter, a person's heart quickens with excitement at the joy he brings to a room. Jharmel is a big reason I am alive right now. He is creative, kind, and has compassion. Jharmel plays the piano from time to time when he gets in the mood.

Classical is his music. He listens to some Bach and Liszt. He can actually play Liszt on piano. Jharmel plays more frequently nowadays, than he used to and when he wants to play, he can do so with desire, giving a room of onlookers delight and awe.

Jharmel has always been a role model for me, because of his humility, probably his best attribute. I can say about Jharmel he is great as a brother. He holds some mysterious quality to me. He is sensitive. I often want to be like Jharmel.

Before all in the world becomes right, as Gandhi told people, you have to be the change you want to see in the world. And this is consistent with Christian doctrine—Do unto others as you would have them do unto you. This is a principle of constant action; a tune that never rests. Where you need to treat others in the manner in which you would like to be treated, therein you find a challenge every day, to recreate yourself, and therefore the world around you. No matter what level of propriety people try to put upon others, the only way anybody can see significant change in neighborhoods is to see an alteration in themselves. So I can picture my brother as I would want him to be, and continue to ask God for the grace to accept things I cannot change, the serenity to change the things I can, and the wisdom to know the difference.

Jharmel is now living with my mother on West Henry Street here in Staunton. He attended University of Missouri-Columbia, and was preparing to study communications in possibly the best journalism school in the nation. And then something changed. It could have been his grades, all the pressure could have beaten upon him like tidal waves beat upon beach house doors.

He came back, when I was still in high school. He would stay home, and smoke cigarettes. Jharmel would smoke pot with my friends and me. It was terrible, because he was unemployed most of the time. I knew my friends, and, I knew myself, but, felt like if Jharmel gets into drugs it will be hard for him break the habit. This was my thought, even though my insight had not manifested then—I was in love with Mary Jane. I continued to regress into myself until about Junior year in high school, and Jharmel started to show signs of slowing down, though he was still spunky and lively, just a little more dull. He was creative still, but just soaked up that whole culture more than most people who use drugs. It was crazy what my role model was doing—inwardly decaying before my eyes. It's crazy the relationships we had after we both began experimenting with drugs.

The fact I am still standing makes me jump for joy sometimes. Sometimes it just makes me throw my hands to the sky. Getting up is a challenge some days, however, because it is hard to tell what the day has in store. I get afraid from time to time because I am not sure what to expect from the day.

DRUGS AND FOOTBALL

That's why, in the day's beginning, it is necessary to be able to roust out of bed and move around. After this is completed, more than half the battle is over with.

People need to get started off with a bright spot and nothing prepares a person physically compared to a suitable meal. I found that *Total* cereal has 100 percent of the recommended daily value in no less than ten vitamins and minerals—amazing. As I eat this breakfast, my body is basically taking in the equivalent of a multivitamin and then a satisfied stomach to boot. *Total* is healthy, and filling! Filling the belly is good! I feel physically equipped to tackle the day after eating *Total*. This cereal is great, helps me see and function at a much better level.

Facing the problems we are dealt with is important.

I smoked a lot of marijuana when going through my mid to late teen years. I would toke up and crash my system. I was too stuck on self.

Tackling the day's issues are important because there may be a weaker or a poor person in life who needs assistance. Being stuck on self means being stuck on personal problems. Family, whether biological or just by association, will always be there. Family deserves attention and our graces because we have been so very blessed by their presence in our lives, even if we don't realize it every day. Being there and facing our problems, telling people about them, being vulnerable in front of people, is what makes men "humen." Emotion is normal process. Should we deny that, we are denying the way we were created.

Picking another person up takes thought about that person. What are his Pet Peeves? What are his good points, his pains, his fears, his background etc. How can I show him consideration and serve him? All these are beneficial and pragmatic questions.

He may be hurting inside. Maybe his girlfriend just broke off the relationship. In any circumstance, a good friend will lend an ear. Best people can do is listen to one another.

Seeing weakness in ourselves and relaying this incompleteness is one of the bonds males have with one another. We as the human race share this sacred commonality. We are social beings, we thrive off being with others.

Best times are when we can actually share the doubts in our lives as well as the joy. In this world, each person experiences pain and joy. The more we give, the more joy we receive. Do yourself a favor, though, and always keep in mind why we do things. We share out of *love*, for it to be worth anything.

In our very best moments we share unconditionally. Seek ye first the kingdom of God, and His righteousness, and all these things will be added unto you.

One day in my adult life I played basketball with some guys at the Edwardsville YMCA. Their unconditional love put things in perspective. One dude went up for a rebound and he came across with his elbow, which struck me smack on the upper left cheekbone. I was shook right after taking the hit, but I recovered and ran down the court and I was fine.

Not long after somebody told me I had blood coming down my face.

"Man!" I thought to myself. I left the court and went into the restroom to wash my face. Three guys came looking for me in succession, inquiring about my physical health. I assured each of them that my status was okay. One of the guys told me band-aids were available at the front counter. I went up and got one, applied it and people called me Nelly, as in the rap artist who made wearing a band aid on the face stylish. They made me feel extra special.

Pain I felt momentarily was overshadowed by the concern of others. Sport is important for this reason. Pain is pain in life, because it hurts, and if there are any good sides to it, it wakes us up to the good stuff we weren't paying attention to, like that line off the film *Good Will Hunting*. People talk about pain like it's so bad and death like it is so terrible. Okay, both pain and death are bad.

However, when we experience pain ourselves or death of a person fairly close, it stirs something which says, man this life es muy importante as the Spanish say. Pain lets us know we are human beings. Emotion lets each person know he is not just another product in a long line of machines filing out of the house each morning to earn a paycheck. Each of us is important. We, sadly enough, realize that most vividly through pain and suffering. Whenever one of us suffers, another person is there to pick that person up, a special exchange. Coaches are people who pick people up. Coaches are very special people. They teach, mentor, and inspire.

Joe Ehrmann was a defensive coach for Gilman, a preparatory school in Baltimore, Maryland. As chronicled in the book *Season of Life*, some of the main things he teaches his student-athletes are to love each other, build relationships with one another, and include people other than football players.

Ehrmann shows his guys principles and they respond. No Gilman player should let another person in the school sit by himself at lunch.

"How do you think that boy feels if he's eating all alone?" Ehrmann asked his players. "Go get him and bring him over to your table." he said. This is the stuff that makes champions in all of us.

When someone would be talking to friends at school and I would come over to talk I wanted to be part of the crowd, to fit in with everybody else which is important for anybody growing up. Sometimes as I would stand there, listening to someone speak, a person would turn his back to me and face the other two or three guys who were there which made me feel like dirt. But Ehrmann taught his players to be better than this mentality. He taught his players to be above haughtiness

Sean Price, one of Ehrmann's players, said he was blown away at first. All the stuff about love and relationships—he didn't really understand why it was part of football. He said after a while, though, getting to know some of the older guys on the team, it was the first time he had ever been around friends who really cared about him.

I looked upon Coach Tonsor as a type of Joe Ehrmann.

He made maybe the most difference with me quitting smoking pot than anybody. Coach called me into his office my freshman year and sat me down informing me of rumors flying around about me possibly being into marijuana. He looked at me like a human being and said plainly, "If you tell me now," he said, "I won't ask you again."

He would take my word for it. Coach looked out for me. I could tell he cared. Football was sacred for him. It was later sacred for me.

You only put on the football pads for so many years and then you start working a job. But I lacked discipline in both character and subsequent action.

"No, I haven't been smoking pot," I said. He never asked me again, after I had just lied to his face.

I looked up to Sean Price, and, he was indicative of what I wanted, what I was. I was, I wanted to be, at the age of 15, better. I wanted to be a better person for my mother. I wanted to be a team player. But I took to druggin' and thuggin'. But, I wanted to let everyone know about goodness, what it meant to be some sort of role model.

This guy Sean Price let people know, even though he had grown up in tough situations, and then got help from the preparatory school to attend Gilman School.

But weren't mine difficult? I was looking for someone. And then I get to these ugly reminisces. Because I wanted to search for people who weren't there. I wanted men I couldn't see. "Whatever doesn't kill you makes you stronger," my mother said. But this tore me up inside.

Every day I went out into the streets and yelled in my breast, "Where is my man? Huh, where is my guy? Where is my dude who is supposed to teach me the right ways to speak, the right ways, the correct ways to address your teachers, the nuanced versions of communicating with females.

"Do I give her my phone number? Nahh, put it away. Is it like that? Do I have to put it away? Or is this just what myself tells me? Just what my religion tells me? I can tell that by those at my church…" Where is my father?

"What do you say, dad? What do you say? Where is your hero?"

"Why weren't you around?" I asked of the little man one of the few times we ever spoke together in any conversation of meaning, or in any one of the few opportunities we had to do so.

"My dad didn't come around us," was his reply. And that was a smack in the face, wasn't it? Wasn't it worse than a shot to the jaw? I saw people who hit on their children when they were growing up, and the children later on made up, and revered their father for at least being around. And I call him little man, because of the depth of hurt he made me feel. It got all blocked in, inside.

"How can I complain, dad?" I cried within. "I got no one to complain to! I got no one to feel this!" I would say, tears twisted on this face, and so longing for someone to feel me, to be me, to be a part of me. On my bed at home at 13, I would cry. Like a little boy that didn't grow up. "I didn't grow up dad! What is it like to be black in this town? In your town what is it like to be black? Huh? Show me, man," I thought.

"Are you a man? Are you a man? Is this how men behave toward their offspring? Or, is this all I am to you, is offspring? Is it just sperm in a bottle to you, and let go? Do you let go of me, and not even come to see me graduate from anything? Am I inconsequential to you? Where are you?" I lay in bed, covers up around my neck. A soul-reverberating moan, just something that puts twisters in your heart, that makes fishes in a pool of resentment swim around, or so I felt.

"Is this the best of what the human species has to offer?" I thought in feelings, feelings that then felt distorted. So I just keep it all jumbled up inside. So I just keep it all inside dad! I just keep it bottled up like a worm who wants to escape, and leave that bottle, because that bottle is not his home. He wants to go back to the green grasses where the prairies grow, and he knows there he can hear the birds sing. He knows there he can move through the earth and feel the deep songs an Indian girl chants on the other side of the hemisphere. He knows this is his home, where he can feel the earth beneath his slimy body, his wiggly worm self. This worm is inside. He is ugly, and squirms. He wants to get out, though, dad. And I had no one to complain to but you. In my heart I complained to you.

I stepped outside every day and said within my breast, "Where is the lion man? Where is the lion who will show this cub how to roam. Who is gonna show me how to be one of the guys? Who is going to show me how to communicate in a world not my own? This world knows defeat, and I know no defeat.

"Therefore, I must remake the world into my own."

"Yes, father, if you won't listen to my cry, I will have to make this world into my own. There is far too much darkness here! I can hardly find my way, father. I can hardly find my way in this dark room. But, yes. If you won't show me the way into a brighter day, I must step inside, shine the light, and make this world my own. I mustn't let you defeat me father, because this world knows loss. No, father! I must turn the searchlight inward, and make this world into my own. I must give you a son. I must let it be shown. If you will not show me father, I must shine this light, and make this world my own."

Men want to do what is good in the inner most parts. We have simply been stuck in this rotating cycle of violence since we became men physically. If we really become men, men who are able to utilize our minds to bring *forward* the United States, and by extension, bring *forward* the world, we will surely be the greatest nation.

We are great as we go about our daily jobs, life's activities. We are not a great people because of our nuclear capability, our weapons, even our economy per se. These things are all tangible. The United States is great because of the bedrock of this nation, the fruit which flows from "All men are created equal." How beautiful the sound. We can look at that and other echoes throughout the history of this great nation.

Ask not what your country can do for you, ask what you can do for your country—John Fitzgerald Kennedy. Let us not get overburdened with our own sense of pride, however, because when pride swells up, other nations in need are not reaping the benefits from the seeds we have sown.

C.S. Lewis wrote for his book, *Mere Christianity*, "There are also occasions on which a mother's love for her own children or a man's love for his own country have to be suppressed or they will lead to unfairness towards other people's children or countries."

He said, "The Moral Law tells us the tune we have to play: our instincts are merely the keys. So we have this pre-programmed within ourselves already, how to be right and wrong. And deep within us we want to be right."

Lewis points out all these instincts go on within us, but we choose the behavior which is healthy as the right choice to do. When we choose not to take more than one newspaper at a newspaper machine (virtually all of us, I think…!). This is our conscience doing its job.

We all aim to do what is right because we have these keys programmed within us that tell us what is right.

Strictly speaking, there are no such things as good and bad impulses, Lewis said. Think once again...of a piano. It has not got two kinds of notes on it, the 'right' notes and the 'wrong' ones. Every single note is right at one time and wrong at another. The Moral Law is not any one instinct or set of instincts: it is something which makes a kind of tune (the tune we call goodness or right conduct) by directing the instincts.

People aren't born with prejudice, as someone said. Racism is taught. People also fear what is different from them. So when a minority comes into a community, there is speculation about that person, at least in Staunton.

Some people around here wonder because they know little about the person's particular race or ethnicity. People around here just haven't seen the wonders of a community that is a rainbow of color. We are a species made up of different backgrounds. All of us look different. That is why we fight. We want to be accepted and when someone is different from us in any way, we have to guard ourselves so they won't hurt us because we are not sure of their customs and beliefs.

So some people try to get with people who look like them, talk like them, act like them. But being different is what makes us Americans. Being dissimilar makes this nation the best in the world. United States of America was founded on the saying, "All men are created equal." I always wanted to be considered equal with others around me. When we were accepting immigrants left and right during the industrial revolution, we embraced this saying, "Give us your poor, your weak, your huddled masses."

I didn't want to be denied anything. When it came to getting something I wanted the same rights and privileges afforded the rest of my high school friends.

Terry Murphy was talking to somebody one time outside a car on Main Street in Staunton. I was sitting in a car across the street with Greg Wittman and Dustin Bramley. We had been cruising. The sun was shining. It was sticky outside and I was hot. My window was down. Murphy looked back at me across the street and said, "Hey Luster, Let's go pick some cotton."

I had played basketball with him. We smoked pot together. The two of us were buds. And then he pulls racism on me. I felt like slapping him. I stomped across the street, picked him up by his neck and lifted him to the sky with his back up against the car. I was completely furious and lost it. But my error only lasted for a moment as the guys pulled me off him. That was not how you are supposed to deal with discriminatory attitudes.

You walk away. You take some deep breaths and call him on shortly thereafter. But—you don't punch somebody in the face because you got punched in the face. It is childish to disrespect someone because you've been disrespected. Gossiping about another because you heard a rumor they supposedly told about you makes you about as morally strong as a debilitating disease.

When a person gives into rage and anger all that person surrenders to a visceral reaction to something he already knows is bad. S/he only highlights lack of discipline by giving in.

I knew Murphy's comment was wrong. But by letting him get into my head I only let it fester. Well, we learn from our mistakes and life goes on. Murphy and I were buds after the incident. We spoke just a couple months ago. He wondered how my life was going. He paints for a living now. We are friends. I hope he is my friend until the day I die.

Racism is like a virus. Once caught it can be contained by addressing the error in someone's ways. All it takes is a friend to pull someone over and say, man, that's not right. It's been done before. I've done it. The remorse that shows up in someone's eyes after he realizes he was being racist is like changing a bad light bulb and installing a new.

You tell them the "n" word is a sickness not because it's just a word and white people can be niggers, too; not because we're not talking about you because you're only half black anyway, but because it hurts. Emotion pain is a terrible feeling. When that pain tears at your heart it is ten times worse than a pain resulting from an elbow scrape; at least a person can see the elbow heal. When a person *forgives*, however, this is the greatest miracle the world has ever known, according to my Shakespeare teacher, Mary Lamb.

Bigoted attitudes can only be cured by people facing what is alien. When people begin working alongside others who are Asian and some

DRUGS AND FOOTBALL

who are black it registers as special to see someone who looks physically different.

One important avenue in my life, one of the best streets I traveled, was sports. Sports helped me to relate; athletics allowed me to connect to people even though we were different. I longed for something to be good at. I wanted it for momma. I wanted to be the very best son. I wanted to be so respected like Jesus was, and give that respect to my mother, like Mary could tell everybody with dignity who her son is. That my momma could be satisfied to know her son was doing something. So she could tell people I wasn't no punk. So she could let others know I was on my way to doing things. But then is this struggle. This internal angst-ridden crooked path, because I didn't know how to cope.

"But I'm different!"

At a mid-teen age I smoked weed. That garage brings back memories of emotional pain, sex and drugs-bad stuff for a 15 year-old. At that age I was hanging out with Melvin. We knew the people in school. I had just transferred from St. Michael's to the public school a year and a half before. Anyway, Melvin and I were uptown one night. This other kid, Heath, was near the local Subway. Now I never liked drugs at all. I even told one of my friends a year before I would stop hanging out with him unless he stopped smoking weed. But Melvin and I went behind the Dollar General Store in a dark place between a shed and a Main Street building. There was glass and the resin was as dark as the alley. The residue was like soot. I tried to inhale. Soon I couldn't feel my mouth at all and that is the first time I was ever stoned. Melvin rode my bike as I balanced on the pegs. We traveled to his house. The two of us ate Potato Chips with French Onion dip. I wanted to know what smoking weed was like; what people talked about. When I decided to find out it was arguably the worst move of my life.

I can definitely see why people call pot a gateway drug. It opened me up to a whole new culture, I didn't fully understand until I began using it. And even after beginning I didn't completely comprehend the best parts of the lifestyle. Because Marijuana stifled my growth. Weed opened up a whole new world of possibilities for me, but they were internal, and I could never seem to bring my inner yearnings to manifestation. Though more options were open to me outwardly, on the surface, I could only dimly see the limits the drug was placing upon me. It had taken control. After about a month I had set adrift on memory bliss. Bliss was in memory because I could only now grasp what was once a living, breathing, growing creature God had created, was now developing self-inflicted malformities My whole mind had been sabotaged; the plane had been hijacked; I was no longer the pilot. What I wanted to grasp I could only dream about now. Effects of euphoria lasted in some way for a few months, and as they persisted, in an equal measure did my lack of focus and decreased motivation increase. I went to school, high out of reality. My buddies did not take school seriously. Neither did I. Bad company corrupts good habits.

We would often go in my backyard garage. Now the garage was a place where we had few rules. If you came over, you came over. People would enter the garage when I was inside my house. They would go in the garage without me knowing it when I was out with friends. I did not have the resolve, the guts to say anything about it. They were my friends. I wanted it to stay that way. I was a "wuss." often when it came to these things. I sought to be accepted.

The front part of the garage was a sort of normal looking part, with an electric garage door, and windows to the outside. Even the piles of trash bags gave it the feel as though this is someone's Midwestern home, where they are a little overloaded, and have not taken out the garbage in a few weeks. But, after passing through a small entryway to the back you could see this was nothing like a normal garage. A urine smell wafted up through the 10' X 15' space. Graffiti in cuss words and a marijuana leaf bedecked the plywood walls. On the forward ledge you had old beer bottles and cans. To the right were two wide wooden doors we had deemed off-limits. A stale beer smell hung in those after school days where that doorway hung open slightly allowing a shaft of light to pour through. We sat on a couch with tear holes on the surface and inside. The couch's canvas had burn holes spotted, like the stars across the night sky. We would throw cigarette butts on the ground. WE would sometimes urinate and some of us had defecated on the left side of the space where the bottom wood on the wall had rotted. You could see weeds growing there.

We would often leave Old Yeller, our water bong, out in the open. Yeller was a wide, plastic, yellow container similar to a peanut butter jar. My friend B.J. shoved a hose into the top. We inhaled from there. The wooden bowl was about 1 inch in diameter and 1 inch high, where we put the weed in.

Just us—the buddies—hanging out, telling crude jokes that would linger in the stale air. We would cough. We would laugh. We would listen. The lifestyle was passive, a respite from living. We were only half-living. We breathed. We did what was required of us, enough to keep parents off our respective backs. All the rest was on auto-pilot.

Though I was messed up I tried to look out for guys younger than me, the same way older guys looked out for me in the awkward transition from eighth grade to high school (isn't this transition awkward for everyone?). I wanted to do it for the right reasons. However, the lifestyle I had grown accustomed to was anything but worthy to be emulated. Quite the contrary.

Our lives were often filled with hazy dreams and a puff of smoke—the kind of smoke that numbed the head, and slowed emotional reaction. This was *not* the environment you wanted your grade school son around.

I invited a very young guy to my garage as we walked with some of my friends one day. He was in the sixth grade. I was in the ninth. He had not a care in the world. He was a large boy, 5' 10", with strong athleticism even at an early age. He was one of the three best male athletes in his class. He was special, set apart. He came over and we smoked weed one night. He sat there on the ripped up couch, in a euphoric daze. He couldn't remember his name. "Oh, my word. He can't remember his name," I thought.

"What is your name," I asked him. He looked up, slouched over with glossy eyes, and said, "Uh...uh." It was scary. It was like a football injury, when you are trying to see how serious the condition is, but you see white as his eyes roll involuntarily in front of the brain.

"What is your name?" I looked around, not knowing what to do. I was out of answers. I was ashamed. I had given this boy connections in the worst of ways. I opened him up to a world of darkness I did not want to be part of, nonetheless someone else with such promise. He had a good head on his shoulders. And I thought I had corrupted him. I felt as though I had sent him on a road to destruction.

He respected me. I grew to respect him. He was *my* little guy. Wasn't nobody gonna lay a finger on his head. Uh uh. He was my person. He was my project. I gave him life in a way, protection from a rowdy crowd. If he flourished I helped him do it. He was *my* guy.

When he was in the seventh and eighth grades I watched him play basketball for Staunton. He soared and often outmatched the competition. I wondered how much influence I had upon him when he played. I wondered how much of it was beneficial.

Another guy benefited me. I was *his* guy. I was *his* person. He looked after me the first half of high school. He made sure I was taken care of. The man stood 5' 10" and 190 pounds, with short black hair. He had a short, up-and-coming mustache. He was an influence.

I needed someone, someone who would give me the time of day. I needed someone who was older. I felt out of place, like no one else at times.

But he was special. He made me feel unique.

I'd see him on Main Street. I'd see him cruise the strip. Our Main Street was somewhat of a Mecca for cool people in the area. People came from Highland, Edwardsville, Gillespie, Litchfield—all so they could drive our Main Street.

I peered out an apartment downstairs door window just 20 feet from Subway Restaurant as the rain came down. It poured. The precipitation landed upon my so-called teenage existence. My whole existence was debatable. I looked out the window, during that year, not wanting to know about what the teachers had taught. I didn't care. I wanted to know where my father was. I wanted to know who I was. I wanted to be everything I was put here to be.

"Let me be who I am," I thought to myself, as I watched the traffic pass by—**in** the deluge. The guy pulled up in his brown Camaro with smooth down-sloped rear. I walked up, water pouring down my face.

DRUGS AND FOOTBALL

"Get in," he said.

I got in, no questions asked. I leaned back. People all over the place had rode in this car, who were, I then thought, far cooler: Nathan Leaser, Chris Johnson, Julie Young: all upper classmen; every one accepted. I wanted to be accepted. I so sought their approval. I went along, like always.

I traveled the same low stream with them trickling, drip, drip, drip.

He and I had a good relationship. I always felt safe around him; protected. I felt as though, through the bad news we were into, he always had my best interests in mind. He looked out for my well-being. And he got me high.

We cruised the strip, with no particular place to go.

"Take this," he said. I looked at the metal pipe, marijuana leaf hanging loosely out the end. I took it from his hand, picked up a lighter, and smoked. My cares washed away as the rain continued teeming, flushing out our fears, our lonely unmet expectations. Water streamed down the window, atop my hope, dousing flames of aspiration.

But he kept me close. I wanted what he had. I wanted to be accepted. I wanted to be wanted.

We pulled over into the other half of the trailer court my family had just moved out of. His Camaro came to a stop. We stepped out, and walked up to the door of a man's home who I'd seen few times before. He was a large man, 6' 4", a little over 300 pounds. My role model walked in and stepped into the living room. I walked a little closer, like his sidekick—the two of us loose on the Staunton streets. He loaded up another hitter.

"Take this, nigger," he told me.

"He just called me......."—I thought.

Blood rushed through my face. I breathed heavily, excited. He looked at me with acceptance, as a general would look at an unseasoned recruit. He glanced at me, then gazed into my eyes quizzically.

"What, my little nigger?" he said.

He was so much bigger than me.

I sort of sighed, and looked around to the larger man, whose home we were in the midst of, then I looked at the hitter. I grabbed it and smoked. I didn't like what he just said though I had heard him call other people that. I took it as a term of endearment in this, surreal of surreal moments. He was influential in the school and I so longed to be a part of what he was about. He was my guy. It felt like a marriage. I would be connected with him for the first half of high school, for better or worse.

Good thing there was football. Through all the chaos I faced off the field, the game was a quiet in the midst of the storm. The sport opened something up inside me. On the same level as the drugs had detracted from the good things along my journey, football in an equivalent measure added to them. Had I not had football, or Coach Tonsor, I may very well have been put in jail serving a long sentence before leaving high school.

Finally here was something I gave into. Not like drugs, because this required action.

I needed something to fit into with others. I needed something I could do well. Wait, did I say that? Did I think, that? Where is my football? Whoa. I thought that, about my football… Wait, football is becoming a part of me? I am giving into this game, and it is becoming the air I breathe, the wind breezing across the school lawn at lunch time… And it wasn't in any idolatrous kind of way. Football was just becoming everything I knew. I got serious about training. It was becoming everything I cared to know about. All I ever wanted to be a part of. I wanted to give my whole being to this game, so it would never leave me.

Coaches have some giant influence on youths. I believe men in America need to stand up, and seek to build up our children.

Coach Larry Caldieraro was our varsity Defensive Line Coach. He laid it on the line for his students. Cal taught drafting and construction.

He had a burly, hairy frame of a body. He always made space in front of his desk for students to come and speak with him. There is no substitute for face-to-face time.

Coach's eyes lit up when a student approached him with concern. He spoke with a gruff, but reassuring voice. He had a way of commanding respect, however, when people got out of line.

DRUGS AND FOOTBALL

"You keep this up we're gonna have to go out to the wood shed," he said.

As I began playing football my freshman year, I saw other guys hitting one another across the ball. I wanted to do the same thing. I enjoyed playing football so much. Coach Legendre wrapped up one of my scrapes after practice freshman year. Just a small hurt, as my leg was bleeding. Next day my yellow bandage stretched all the way around my knee, hanging off in tethers, dirty from practice. I had also slept with the tape the night before.

My bandage loosely hung from my leg as I stood in our usual congregating area in front of the high school building, with shorts on. A good portion of the sticky was still attached to the knee.

Our school was towering to a freshman, two stories high, with a brick façade. In front of the back drop, Fassero, a friend of which I had none better, yelled, "Bandage boy!"

I was stricken, as having hardly realized the wrap was still on. Football, by the short experience I had, was a part of me as was the bandage. Fassero, with his pug nose and be-freckled face, bent down and howled laughter at me, as he often did.

"HaaHHaaa," he lamented. "Luster's got a bandage on his knee. Check out the bandage boy! He's got a bandage on his knee." He made an idiot of himself. Fassero was laughing so hard his larynx was ruffling with mucus, his mouth agape, reveling in an onslaught of my adolescent humiliation. I could not control the man. He could hardly control himself. What a spectacle he made of me, and all because my devotion for sport was so great I did not mind the whole world seeing my hurt.

Dustin Bramley, one of my buddies, smoked a pack of cigarettes and a joint a day during football season. He was a big dude, too, six feet tall, 230 pounds with these blonde sideburns and a round smile. Bramley was clumsy and did not attempt to hide it. He was an Illinois man, a monster on the field. Bramley could throw two defenders off the line of scrimmage.

He drove a roughed-up golden mid-1980s Custom Deluxe pickup. We would drive around in his machine and get high. But drugs and football did not mix. We would never bring intoxication onto the football field.

This was an unwritten, seldom discussed rule. You didn't show up for games either drunk or stoned. The game was too important. I'll give a synopsis of this sport I cherished for great times and hard hits. Football consists of two teams.

A team is on offense and the other is on defense. Offense has 11 players and the defense has 11 players. An offensive line usually consists of six players, lined up along the line of scrimmage. Their jobs are to block the defensive players out of the way, so the quarterback or running backs can run down the field with as little hindrance as possible. In the middle of the line of scrimmage the center hikes the ball, passing it between his legs to the quarterback, for the play to start.

Guards line up on each side of the center. To the other side of both guards are offensive tackles.

In most cases, the tight end lines up on one end of the offensive line. His main responsibility is to block defensive players, but he also catches passes occasionally. Running backs begin behind the line of scrimmage. The quarterback can either hand off the football to a player, normally a running back, or pass the football, normally to a wide receiver. All offensive linemen besides the tight end are not allowed to catch passes.

Purpose of the offense is to get the football into the other team's end zone. If the offense brings the ball into the other team's end zone, the team receives six points. A defense's job is to prevent the offense from scoring that six points.

The game became a part of you; football lived in your blood. As a player on those playoff teams, you thought about football day in and day out-in practice, in the shower, in the car. This was a man's sport. I wanted to be a man. We were a match made in heaven.

You could sum up aspects of other men on that field. You knew a man's work ethic—how hard he has practiced leading up to the game—by his quickness and agility off the snap. A person could tell how much weights he lifted by checking out his size. Size often mattered, but sometimes could be a hindrance.

When men did not carry their weight well, or failed to train well, they would carry their excess around like a backpack filled with so many bricks. And this extra load would weigh these players down.

But then again you've got football players all over who *did* carry their load, and with a bounce even. When they would put a load into you, they "hit you like a ton of bricks." Their determination was admirable, fire unquenchable. These guys were not only endowed with the physical size to play a physically demanding sport, they used this advantage to their utmost capacity.

They separated themselves from the rest through the individual effort they commanded from their bodies through the season. They got to know their bodies, bringing them under subjection, even when the rest of the coaching staff or players were not around. When walking to classes they would practice a reach step, and imagine getting lower than the defender. Tight ends would at lunch, in the middle of the day practice making a cut and turning their bodies toward the quarterback to gather a pass. These players were a beauty to watch, with the grace of a white tail deer bounding across the meadow.

When playing on the offensive line, it was just you and him. My position was tight end. I was the last lineman. My junior year Dustin lined up next to me at right tackle. I never played with a man who had more passion for the sport than Bramley. Football was *such* a physical game. And though very cerebral, he was an extremely physical player.

People would toss others to the ground play after play. It happened to the best of us. We would shake it off and keep playing. You respected a guy who came across and hit you solidly. No matter what team you played for, you were all brothers. Whether kickers (who kicked field goals), cornerbacks (who tried to keep other guys from catching the ball) or linemen, you were connected. It was this feeling of sacrifice and you all gave of yourselves collectively.

Come game night, you knew the guy across from you had busted his chops in practice to play against you. He not only showed up to practice every day after school, he pushed himself to be picked by his coach as the best at his position. After the ball was snapped there was little dialogue besides grunts and hollers.

The instant before every play, however, we would get ready. We would put the hand down and set. You both laid it on the line.

Scott Tonsor was our head coach. He was a large influence in my life, like a big brother. In all my days, there was never a man more frank and passionate about teaching young men the game of football.

Coach Tonsor was a father to me. He taught me everything I needed to know to be something good. He really gave me what I needed to succeed. Coach was the first male with the same interests as me, and expected discipline. He was brave, an oddball in our town because of his insistence that we give our very best.

Coach was the best at what he did. He was the first man I can think of, who reached for success, and exacted that desire from those who followed. He took us under his wing. Tonsor prepared us to overcome. We were his soldiers.

Courage means stepping out to face challenges, no matter how daunting they seem. Coach Tonsor came to Staunton High School as a head coach, starting in the 1994 season. He was only 23 years of age, stood 6 feet two inches with blazing red hair.

He was relentless. Just after he accepted the coaching position he brought all freshmen who came out for football into his office. He let them know they were *his* bunch. Tonsor wanted to win, and wanted players to write out some goals.

His team wanted to go undefeated their senior year. Tonsor, with his fiery red head of hair and thick mustache, yearned to win.

He exuded courage, taking Staunton football from long-time bottom feeders in the South Central Conference to contenders—the team to beat.

Coach Tonsor brought a unique atmosphere to our program. He did a lot of what Bob Shannon did, just at a smaller school.

Always some people will be out there who will disappoint you, without fail. But we need to search for people such as Scott Tonsor and Bob Shannon. These are men of commitment. A book featuring Shannon actually changed me in high school. I wanted to be more like Shannon. I sought to be more like Tonsor. I wanted to be what the book title stated, "The Right Kind of Heroes."

Shannon coached the legendary East St. Louis Flyer football team throughout the 1980s into the mid-90s. Those teams won two national championships and six state titles. Possibly never before in the state of Illinois has a large school put together 15 years of such classic football.

I wonder at how many times Shannon had to tell his players to stay off the streets, or to go to school. Through Shannon's years at East Side, he coached NFL standout Bryan Cox, and All-American Dana Howard, and many more standouts. Shannon obviously had the respect of his players. And respect is what drew me to Tonsor and Shannon.

I was in awe of the respect, the discipline these two men demanded from those under their care. It gave me goose bumps to read what Shannon told his players, and how they came together as a cohesive unit *only* after they endured the subjugation under which he put his players.

There *was* a higher authority. And they'd better learn it sooner rather than later. Especially on the inner city streets of East Saint Louis

I always wanted to be the type of guy who Shannon was, or Scott Tonsor, for that matter. I wanted to be one who had patience when 22 men would cling to your every word.

"I am only as good as my word," Tonsor said. I adored listening to him preach to us. It was great. He was all I had. He was all I needed. He behaved as though he enjoyed being around us.

Tonsor heard the parental complaints. He trudged through the muck. Tonsor was a recipient of yells from the stands. They instructed him how he should run his team. He did not mind them.

"They don't come out and practice with us," Tonsor said.

He would run the team how he would run the team. If people did not like it, should he get fired, he told me, "I'd have a job by the morning." I knew he was capable of that, too.

Tonsor was the stock of man other men were apprehensive of being. He said what he meant on the football field.

Tonsor would bend over backward for you, which many men can relate to. He was willing to step outside the box. Staunton was electric when he was there. Those teams of the late 1990s were minor miracles.

He was, I guess, a mentor. Outside of family, and next to Coach Legendre, he was probably the first mentor of my life. He had all the qualities of a role model actually—faithfulness, punctuality, honesty, a clear sense of right and wrong, loyalty, courage, passion, enthusiasm, optimism and a will to win.

Winning isn't everything, but wanting to win is. I suppose being a mentor and role model are inseparable. You have to have one with the other; they coexist; the two inseparable like peas in a pod; as Archie and Ethel.

I suppose I wanted to be a role model, but my gears were in idle. I felt stuck, on the road to nowhere, wondering how far I had fallen. I wondered how I would get there from my erratic lifestyle. Through the course of history man has felt and endured pain from his mistakes.

President John Kennedy said war has always been the rule rather than the exception. Men have been fighting physically and killing each other for thousands of years.

Kennedy wrote a book entitled *Profiles in Courage*. The book is stories of how some of the most courageous men in the history of American government reacted to adverse conditions.

I skipped school one day, which was a normal occurence Just me at home with a much used pipe for smoking weed. I scraped, trying to free some resin for one strong hit. I lit it. "Tssshheee," the hot metal felt as it burned my upper lip. I sat on the couch unmotivated, empty inside. I looked onto VH1. Duran Duran came on with the song "Ordinary World." I heard them sing,

>As I try to make my way to the ordinary world
>I will try to survive.
>There's no time for yesterday
>In the ordinary world somehow I've got to find
>Where's my world

He keeps saying this last line over and over as the song comes to a close It lingers there in a sweet, high-pitched, desperate melody.

I sought after God that day. I looked for someone I could not describe. I missed being in church, and the cleanness of being there with the Savior. I wanted to *be* clean. But all I felt was dirt and mess.

I got down on my knees. I prayed. I felt something come over me. I felt some presence through the haze clouding my mental sky. I cried for a world not my own right then. I cried for a world that I could call my own some day. I knew from then on drugs were not me. They were something that gave me pleasure, something I would do to pass the time with friends. But I was then on a quest to find something that would define me. I would search for something other than drugs. I sought to find the path I'd strayed from. I wanted to be like Dwight was. I wanted to be the clean boy who wanted to be everyone's hero.

Close Encounters

I knew where I needed to go. I knew where I wanted to go. But I was headed, nevertheless, in a bad direction. The drugs stayed with me. My poor choices held me down, like ball and chain.

Though I had wonderful male role models, I was failing them. I fell short, over and over.

It was hard growing up, but, I made some terrible decisions with women. I had all this expectation. So, I never looked back. I had a passion, a deep, burning desire to be the very best I could be at football. So, I worked at it hard. I became stronger, physically solid, and more a member of the team. On top of a blessing, however, this was a terrible curse.

Being a football player at any school is a privilege. It is an honor, a distinction. But, it comes with some not so expected advantages, which seem like benefits at the time.

Plenty of beautiful, young women, just growing into their bodies, show affection to you. If you are not careful, they will show too much affection, and you will be wrapped up in a terrible state of guilt and shame for months and years to come...all until you have the courage from God to admit this was an error.

Such was the case with me. I would be remiss to go without speaking of intimate relationships I had with women my age.

A friend and I were at a party in an apartment just behind Mancell Music on Main Street one night. We partied hearty. We loved it. It was fun, because we were inebriated. This excitement within our bodies, and we were only 16!

But worse came to worse. I snuggled up next to a girl on the couch. I had known her before from associations with a mutual friend. This girl and her friend would come over to my friend's apartment and hang out with us. But tonight was different. It was boring, and I felt, like, this girl and me are here together, and there are only five people here. I thought, "This girl and I can go somewhere and get to know each other better."

I expressed as much to Luke Wittman, and through his big heart, and a wise concern far beyond his years, he stated emphatically—"Luster, don't go to her apartment."

I said things would be okay and would not listen. My mind was set. The young lady acquiesced, and there we were—headed to her apartment just a block away.

We walked slowly up the stairs. My arm was around her. We got to the apartment door and entered in.

We smoked, and talked. After a short while we lay down together, lights off.

I was 16.

I put my arm around her, she warmed up to me, and the rest was history. I completely gave myself to this woman physically.

It was not the only instance.

Situations similar to this one happened three other times, where young ladies would just "give in" because I played football. Or maybe it was because I was so young, and they were too, and they wanted to know what it felt like to know each other in such an intimate fashion.

Possibly they were starved for love. They didn't know what it meant to be loved, or give love, so they gave love in the most entire way they could think of.

Whatever the case, I think at least some of it was these women were in need of attention, emotionally, and physically.

I was no different. I longed for a "good" woman to snuggle up to, to put my arms around, to caress, to touch and not let go. I wanted a woman to be there for me, and me for her.

It was a damned sequence what happened. I would ask, or just begin. They would give in, usually without much resistance.

It was a hellish way to go. It was horrible, because of what the intercourse led to.

My Pastor preached once about sin's two twins: guilt and shame.

Nothing could have been more accurate. As I began to see women as vessels to be used capriciously at my whims of lust, they became less of people to me.

I became desensitized to what the best things women have to offer— a proclivity to caring, warm personalities, sensitivity, thoughtfulness.

All this was going out the window, the more I gave in. The more I gave in, the more my relationships with women in all other areas of life began to decay.

I walked by girls in the hall at school, and, those females I used to easily walk up to and begin conversations with, were awkward, and forced.

I no longer saw women as of use, but to be used. Indeed, I could hardly communicate effectively with women. When I tried, the thought of my misdeeds came creeping in to my subconscious, haunting me, like a murderer armed with dagger. I needed no nightmares. I was living bad dreams in relation to women in the light hours all through the day.

Around mom, I just was not the same loving son. I moved in the room a bit more calloused, an little more cold. Whatever I tried to do, it had more to do with me. I lost sensitivity to what women were capable of. My relationships with the opposite sex became less meaningful. They became the one half of the human race I wanted to very much to be close to, but could not get close. I tried over and over. Brick wall. Thumm! My lack of sensitivity to women coupled with frequent drug use made into a volatile combination. I was in essence, on auto mode. I walked around.

I looked for what I had before. But it was lost.

Personal Role Models

"I am not a role model," former NBA superstar Charles Barkley said. He was right. I looked at Barkley in his playing career, and, at six feet something he was awesome.

But why in the world would a professional athlete or TV personality be the mold for your child? *You* should hold the distinction. Parents should live the honor. Television needs be an educational tool: informative; thought provoking.

Children can see crack addicts on television or a promiscuous rock star. Strongest role models in any household are our parents—for better or worse. A nine-year-old can ask Jay Leno what to do about drugs in his school through a letter but the more practical thing would be for the parent to turn off the television and educate. Even if the adult fails in some so long as he is there. At least the child has the opportunity to ask how to approach the situation. Greatest feeling in the world is mentoring. Mentoring lasts.

Coach Tonsor was an exceptional mentor. Class was starting. We would learn our lesson eventually.

Crowds were small before he arrived. By the time we started winning, the place got nuts.

But his first year roughly half his players were on drugs; the team's motto may as well have been "play hard, party harder." I heard they were on cocaine, pot, crack etc.

These guys had as much talent as any team I was ever a part of. These guys worked hard, not necessarily as a cohesive unit, with what Vince Lombardi referred to as a coordinated efficiency; the squad of players was immensely talented person by person.

They just faltered as a team. As erratic molecules in a drop of hot water, players scattered and moved in various directions. Coach Tonsor, however, was up to the challenge of making men of boys.

He came from the old school in Jerseyville, a town with football tradition. Winning was not everything in Jersey, but *wanting* to win was.

Coach Tonsor tried to whip his Bulldogs into shape through exhaustive two-a-day practices in the summers before the regular season. He introduced Tonsor Time to us.

We would have to be on the practice field by 5:50 a.m. We then jogged around the far soccer post and back. A player had to be on the practice field before we started, even if it was 10 minutes to the 6 a.m. start time. If a player was not on Tonsor Time he would be required to do ten green bays for every minute he was late. You would have to drop to the ground and push back up to a standing position to complete one green bay.

If a player cussed, the player would have to do 15 green bays for every letter of the word. If a player missed a practice, he had to do 125 green bays and two suicides, which were grueling running drills

Tonsor would then send us to our positions where individual coaches taught us for an hour. That was the easy part. We would then run conditioning drills called agilities at the practice's end. These exercises were feared year-round.

Our entire team, freshmen through varsity players, were divided up into seven groups. The first station was ropes.

You had to get your legs up between six inches and a foot through each rope, high enough not to trip because teammates were coming up directly behind one by one, like train cars in succession. See, if you tripped this means the line would come to a halt. If you chose to be lazy every person who followed would suffer.

Ropes were timed. When players on the ropes were finished, the rest of the team would move on to the next station.

Coach Legendre put us through bags next.

DRUGS AND FOOTBALL

The point was to jump over a series of bags in a line running laterally, each bag standing about a foot and a half high in the highest part of the bag.

"Heght!" he'd say. "Heght!#! Heght!#!"

Coach Legendre carried this wad of tobacco around in his jaw throughout practice. One day Bramley spit a loogey. It landed smack on Coach Legendre's shoe by accident. Coach looked at him coldly.

"Haaaaach*—*Thweup..." Legendre said and shot all his chaw upon the tongue of Bramley's spikes. Yuckie.

Season practices were difficult; Coach Tonsor displayed the same intensity he must have lived during the four years he started at Illinois College in Jacksonville. This fire burned inside him. Every time he would write an e-mail to somebody, attached to it was a little saying—"Winning isn't everything, but wanting to win is. Do you Yahoo?"

Staunton went 4-5 his first year at the reigns, then 3-6 the next season with some talented individual players, and in 1996, we made the playoffs for the first time in 20 years with a four-game winning streak, the last game of which over no. 1 in Hardin-Calhoun. I watched from the sidelines because I was ineligible to play. I had failed math a year before. We lost by more than a 40-point margin in the first round of the playoffs to Decatur St. Teresa, a school with the ability to recruit.

But our team accepted me back, players welcomed me, and we were filled with joy playing the sport we loved together.

I tried to just not think about being white or black on the football field, or with friends. That made it easier. If I could be like a mirror to them, reflecting whatever good character I could understand of them, there would be no need for unnecessary distinction. My best friends, white or black, understood the silence. Sometimes, I had to soak things up, however, and submit to the fact I could not solve everybody's problems. I wanted to. Really I did. I felt like I would get depressed if I thought about others' setbacks over and over. I felt selfish, and utterly incapable of doing well with both these gifts—of athleticism—and another gift I began to dimly recognize—being different than others in ethnicity.

On the field everything was kosher. The game bound us together. When we players were together with a coach of Tonsor's character we could do no wrong, it seemed. Sometimes it felt like we were invincible. But then off the field, away from the team, things could get a bit hairy.

You have different people, with different attitudes. And not everybody got along, all the time. I pulled alongside Jason in my black Chevy S-10 truck, a junky ride estimated at $600. He was rolled up in a black, plush, envy-invoking 1980-something Firebird. The car was sweet and we all knew it. Everyone in school wanted a ride like Jason had.

We were parked on the West end of town, on the side of Main Station liquor store. We started talking. And when I pulled away in the S-10 with no power steering, I wedged even closer to Jason's car, which was now dangerously close to mine—less than two feet. I pumped on the gas of the stick shift truck, letting out the clutch ever so carefully, when the expression on Jason's face blew up. His eyes became like razors, shooting to the back of his ride. I let off, let off—after all I had to act as if there was no trick to getting out of this tight spot, as I was only 16, and knew how to do it all. Cranking the steering wheel with all my might in the next instance, with anticipated fear of Jason's breathing, panting, pug-like nostrils, I whipped it, turned, oh, oh, crunch! I swiped the car. The front bumper of my mom's petty ride weightily smudged Fassero's dream machine. A horrendous smashing of metal upon metal precluded an outburst which was automatic from the notoriously hot-headed Italian Fassero, my dear friend from preschool. "Youuuu Nigger!" he said.

Rancor was not a worthy description to match his tone. His baby had just been assaulted, and I, his chum of 12 years, was the culprit. He maneuvered his car around, sparing no crunching from the weaseling of the two autos, and, stammered out, face as red as the day he fell on Michael Kellebrew's back tire, that put a literal skid mark on his rear-end. Oh, he was livid. But, after realizing the magnitude of what he had just said, he, in shock, was taken aback, not so much at what I had done to his vehicle as what had just come out of his mouth.

His head, looking like it was about to explode, freckle-faced and red as a cherry pop, directed the rest of his body back into his car, opened the door, and sped off. No exchanging insurance information, no saying when to get together again to hang out. I was just stuck there, in between Main Station and the new location of the Dime Store, like a man with a shaggy beard and wide, wandering eyes, hanging on a deserted isle, with nobody to save me. Well, there was boar meat on that isle, I thought, and there were bananas in dozens of bunches. He told me later, like the gentleman he had matured into…that he was sorry for saying such words. I know now the sorrow he had for saying those words hurt far worse than the gash on his beautiful ride. It was a triumph for my white brothers to be going to school with a mostly black man. I always felt considerably cared for also, when, after folks would say the "n" word, and they were acquaintances with the perpetrators, buddies would say, "Oh, well you're not black," or, "Anybody can be a nigger. There are white niggers, too." The "n" word became familiar, but never comfortable; common, but never accepted, as the words of grandpa repeated in my mind, "You're just as good as everybody else."

Friends brought me relief, friends considerate for me and my social standing. Lucas Wittman was cool. He stood about 5 foot 11 inches, with blonde hair and freckles. He always spoke in an assured tone, even when he didn't know what he was talking about.

Wittman hated the "n" word. When he was growing up in Jacksonville, Florida, his mother let him and his two older brothers know she would beat them if she ever heard it coming out of their mouth. This was reassuring to my safety, because he let me be his friend—Lucas— who the girls thought was attractive and the guys wanted to hang out with, or, you could accurately say, who everybody wanted to hang out with. He simply did not speak about color often. Wittman kept quiet about the subject, making me a firm believer in his tolerance of people, regardless of what they looked like.

When people tell folks, "I'm not a racist. I've got black friends," and so on, this may mean they are hiding a prejudicial leaning. If you got to say it, come on, aren't you looking at their outside? In this day in America, doesn't it make you look good if you are white and you've got black friends?

But then there were those great, fantastic parents. They made me feel at home in their home. They made me feel wanted.

'Twas always great when parents would go out of their way to make me feel comfortable by making gratuitous comments to try and assure my acceptance.

Janey Best's mom Linda was a graceful woman, beautiful in speech, radiant in appearance, and utterly charming. She had blonde hair, a good tan, pearly white teeth, and a laugh that rolled out as if she was always walking on a red carpet. She was high class in a backwoods town; someone to be both cherished as a friend, and admired as a choral singer. Scott Billings and I waited at Janey's one day and upon my coming in, we were talking about race relations somehow. As I lived in Staunton as a rare child of African descent, this conversation was common. She told those standing in the room, "Well, we even allow purple people into our house." I was flattered and awkwardly comforted in the same moment. She did her best, and I admire her for the effort.

Rick Warren wrote in his book "The Purpose-Driven Life," sadly the ones who hurt most of the time are not wolves, but other Christians. The same even goes with close friendships to people who do not necessarily believe in my faith.

Folks can be interactive, learn how to be a teammate, and develop communication skills, all while getting meaningful exercise. Everybody should exercise. People can have fun doing it, and learn things about themselves by sharing with others in the process. But ironically one of the most sour instances of angst from a dear friend came from a basketball game. This was as a slap in the face.

Getting made fun of is where the angst comes from. I worked a job at McDonald's in Troy once. I was enveloped by the aroma of cheeseburgers, French fries, and, quarter pounders. MmMm. Mc—double Donald's on the circle tip. Those two buns, melted cheese, pickles, fresh onions, ketchup and mustard were enough to make my taste buds jump, hip hip hooray. The celebration was over after I would settle down in my bones. My body came to the realization this food was not good on a regular basis. I began carrying around more, loose weight around the stomach. My boobies felt flopping. I felt a laxity in my step.

DRUGS AND FOOTBALL

Luke Wittman and I were on the basketball court, playing hoop, and as I squared my hips to box him out for a rebound, he cried, "Foul." There was no reason for the next comment. He called me a Fat %#! The comment was tougher to take *because* he was my friend, like a close brother. If he wanted to tell me something about the health implications of being overweight, he could have said—"Luster, have you been eating your fruits and vegetables?"

I struggled with my weight thereafter only briefly, as football season was starting. People in my family have consistently had problems with weight, though. We, as a nation need to take what we insert into our mouths seriously. Nine million American children are overweight. We could blame fast food, or other external influences. However, when it comes down to it, self-control is key. Self-restraint separates us from the beasts. That's why controlling our urges, and appetites is essential, and sports can help us do so. When we get out onto that field of play, we are doing great things for our bodies, and this is a healthy environment to take part in.

The *game* is one of the uniting factors in America today. When we score a goal, we are elevated. When a team wins, that is a win for the whole team. This is a building experience. Even through competition, fun must be the center, the essence. I learned more from watching sports than reading about them. Playing the sports, however was where I learned the most.

I read a quote on the back of the YMCA sports director's shirt.

"Sports do not build character. They reveal it." Getting into the game brings out the qualities within a person which were before unrealized.

Scott Tonsor considered his players *people*. He referred to us as men. Life was not a throw away for the man. His order was: Faith, family and football.

We connected because he rose up. I emulated that. I wanted to be like that. I could feel him. He was my kind of guy. When he spoke, all of us listened to him to glean determination.

I felt as a current of electricity on some occasions in those games.

Discipline. Discipline proceeded like a magnet to a wire bail. Coaches said, "Hit!" and "Set, Go!"

We obeyed. We hung on Coach Tonsor's every word. Those were days when a man with a sizzling red mustache, burning flame in his eyes, and a plan for the boys under his care, instilled discipline in every one who would listen. Faith was a part of Coach Tonsor. Coach possessed it. He had belief in things hoped for, but not yet seen.

Our community was already built on the football mentality. Giving what you had was imperative and that was enough.

George Moore used to discuss our opponents in his barber shop. You could participate in the same talk at NAPA Auto Parts up the street. But come game night on our central Illinois field, we put talking aside.

Hopefully you won that day, but life was about how much you gained in wins *and* losses. A beautiful aspect of sports are the small things you can learn you weren't even looking out for. All sports have this quality, but football I think has this unique significance to everyday life.

Coach knew the atmosphere; he experienced a working-class environment in his hometown. He possessed endurance. He bore a class abounding with alcoholics and drug addicts; vandalism to his home; people calling to his players from the sidelines and more. But Coach had belief in things not yet seen. Coach was *the man* around because he came in with a purpose.

Coach came from the outside. His otherness was what I probably admired most about the six foot two, 210 pound lightning rod. He spit fire when he gave instruction on the dusty lawn of a practice field. The man was awesome and I feared him. We all feared him a little.

Our team had to be on the field by 5:50 a.m. for two-a-days. Dew still glistened on the lush green blades of grass. Air tasted fresh, untainted, as a flower uninhibited from its growth into maturity through a summer of change.

Jason Steinmeyer led us as our pre-practice warm—up run would start us off. Steinmeyer stood six feet tall, 230 pounds, with the accent of a gentleman. Steinmeyer carried a refreshing demeanor, as people loved to follow him. "Come on, guys," he would say, with his blond hair blowing in the early morning breeze.

Dew settled, and then glistened, as he told the team to pull our feet in together. We stretched one by one across the field. In unison, like a group of soldiers preparing for a war, we called out—"One, two, three, four, five, six seven, eight nine, ten." He was a senior, and considerably effective as a team leader.

"Right leg up," he said.

Then everybody followed, "One, two, three, four…"

Football got us pumped. Staunton was completely alive those sweet summer mornings, when air just hung in the vast expanse across our precious acres there, while we worked out.

"—Skell!" Coach Tonsor would call out in a hurried voice. When he yelled it through his orange mustache in that burning sun, players in skill positions were supposed to go with him.

We played Gillespie Junior year. Coach called the play, Pro 59 Levelle. I was pumped. A pass play going to me.

"This is great," I thought. I got down in my stance, putting my right arm down to the ground. The sun had just set in Gillespie after red covered over the mellow Illinois sky. It was beautiful.

I put my hand down. I thought subconsciously, even though we were within 15 yards of the end zone, and I probably would score, I could do this for me. I would be the one walking down the hall, people talking about my touchdown catch this early in the season.

Frank snapped the ball when I hopped up and bolted out of my stance. Within a second my hands were up, five yards from the line of scrimmage. I was ready to receive Bennie's pass. As he released it with a soft touch, we were 10 yards apart and the play seemed like slow-motion. The ball fluttered in. Just before the ball got in I looked up field as the leather thudded off my hands. There went my glory.

Learning comes in some mysterious ways and, as someone said, God works in mysterious ways. I did not deserve that catch because looking to the future up the field to the end zone was more important than realizing what was right in front of me.

My life meant far less if I was not playing football, I felt. Football was a drive, a passion. Hitting people was excellent. This may sound violent, but I possessed a strong desire to stick my helmet into a person's chest pads and drive him back. When I got the first two steps in before my man, short and choppy, he was beat. I knew it. Especially if I was lower, he was done for, even if he was stronger. A person can play sports with speed. Physical strength hardly makes a difference if your person can get around you.

Strength and speed matters, however. Oh boy does it matter. Strength and speed gave me a headache one day.

We faced Southwestern two games later in the season. I lined up in-stance and this guy came across with his hand against my helmet.

"Thughh! Thuggh!"

Every play, he was clobbering me.

"Thuggh! Thuggh!" I had stars in my vision. He sapped my strength. I kept coming and he continued to deliver, with unmatched force.

"Thuggh! Thuggh!"

He left me dazed and confused after each play. At halftime, we sat in the locker room with a close game at hand. Coach spoke to us as we sweated. He talked and talked and my head throbbed. I remember leaning on a table in the locker room, with a bench laid across. Coach spit with the words that proceeded from his mouth.

"Get your butts in gear! This game's out there waiting for you to take it. So go ahead and take it!"

A surge of electricity shuddered throughout the room. His words changed the atmosphere. A helmet hung in my right hand as I tasted salt in my teeth. Shoulder pads hung on, with sweat occasionally dripping off my brow, head a bit dizzy and ears ringing.

Autumn air was sticky when we went back out and hung in the balance with virtually no wind. Temperature was a balmy 85 degrees. Second half was a mean treat.

"Thuggh! Thuggh!"

He continued to pummel my head like a short, spurt jackhammer. I got up in my stance, but too weak to execute.

"Thuggh! Thuggh!" I had just enough energy to extend my arms to my man. But *we* executed well, and ended up winning that, the third and most pivotal game of the season, 20-13. My bones burned. My brain felt like a battery which lights up the flashlight only after several shakes.

My junior year we played Bridgeport Red Hill for the first round of the playoffs in Staunton's friendly confines.

DRUGS AND FOOTBALL

Stands were jam-packed. For a normal game we, a school of only about 400 students had just one side of bleachers at our field. Come that Saturday though, that entire side was full. People stood all the way around the field gates. People brought portable stands before the game to accommodate the boisterous fans.

Spectators came from all over the region to watch undefeated Staunton take on Red Hill. They were right along side us out of the gates. Through halftime we were neck and neck. You could hear the long-time Bulldog faithful fan Carl in the bleachers yelling, "Get 'em dogs!"

Cow bells were chingling and changling. Now, we had nine wins and no losses at that point and it was not like we were in the business of letting some guys come to our house and feed us our lunch. We weren't playing tough, though.

Steve Wilson, mammoth of a man, was head up on me. Wilson played head up on me head at defensive end. This cat was huge—6' 5" inches; 230 pounds; solid. He caught a 50-yard pass and you could hear the air come out of our crowd. He had this graceful gait and was quite poised. But I took him. I blocked him successfully. I was big for some standards, 5 foot-11, 175 pounds, but not on that talented line. I was probably the smallest guy. The crowd started getting into it, and we ended up winning a defensive gem, 13-7.

Next Up: DuQuoin

Coach Tonsor said, "if you want to go to the state championship you have to go through DuQuoin." The Indians consistently made playoff appearances in the 1990s. As we rode into the DuQuoin school parking lot nestled in the heart of Southern Illinois a sign of their greatness—literally—was displayed for all to see across the outside of the locker room. An Indian with tomahawk in hand was exhibited, complete with playoff years, and indicating advancements to the quarterfinals and semifinals.

DuQuoin's success was intimidating to say the least. Music blared next door as we got ready. Hard rock resonated throughout our room.

"What's with that?" I asked. Coach rebuked me sharply calling me to focus on the game.

Tension was thick. We came into hostile territory, spotless. Nobody had our number the entire year.

As we entered the field, people were all around the gate. Their fan base was amazing as the place was filled to the brim.

Rain spoiled the field. Mud was all over. Spikes would not set into the grass so we could not fire off the snap. Our team was like the roadrunner cartoon where his legs spin in a circular motion before gripping finally, except, we didn't grip.

When I couldn't gain any ground I simply stood there and put my arms out to block. That was my job. These guys weren't supposed to get to Ben Frank, our quarterback. He would often say, "Come on guys," while the eleven of us lined up in the huddle.

DRUGS AND FOOTBALL

Frank had this cool confidence about him. He would wipe his hands on a towel hanging from his waist. He waved his svelte hands back and forth, relaying the play. We tried 50 double ups, a pass play, where another player and me ran up the middle of the field.

We ran another play, 34 veer, the bread and butter of Staunton football, as Tonsor would say. We used what is referred to as a veer offense. We built our game on the run.

Billy Schuette, our fullback, carried the football on the 34. The guy was an animal. Billy was down-home muscle.

But that day in DuQuoin he couldn't get traction either. Whole middle of the field for one hundred yards was like a brown line through a green tunnel. Conditions were ridiculous. We had to put up with the weather, but then again so did they. The whole contest was a defensive struggle.

DuQuoin had the ball late in the fourth quarter on us. They could have punched it in for another score. But they declined to do so out of respect. There you have another unwritten rule. If you're leading and have the ball with a first down with little time remaining in the fourth quarter, let it rest. They could have scored, as Bramley said later, but they did not do so out of courtesy. They were first class. They defeated us in a heart breaker, 14-7.

Outside of parties, this was the most distraught I'd ever seen Dustin. He yelled on the bench in the locker room at the top of his lungs, put his face in his hands and cried.

Bramley yelled. The rest of us walked around in a dumbfounded daze. How could we have lost? We were South Central Conference Champions. It was tough.

We were emotionally spent. This was the best run Staunton football had ever seen. We became heroes within the course of 11 weeks.

It comes back to this dichotomy, however. I mean, I felt like Superman, in a small central Illinois town. It comes back to feeling there was this something missing, a vacuum within my soul. Drugs temporarily filled that expanse. Drugs are horrible. Alcohol is bad. Alcohol is very, very bad.

Next season I bent the rules before a big game, the most crucial game of my high school career.

Before that season began, however, you could see we were missing the leadership of guys from the year before.

Cory Buse was one of those players. He had practiced all year but never played a single down because of academic ineligibility. Cory just loved the game, though, so he went through three hour practices every day of the week with us.

Bramley had graduated the year before. Ben Frank was gone.

We missed Jason Steinmeyer. He taught us in particular, day after day in practices, as well as on game nights. He was a wonderful football player with tremendous character.

Steinmeyer sacked the quarterback 13 times that season. Most important aspect of his sacks was not their ferocious nature, but what the after effect. Steinmeyer would get up from the ground and bend down, offering his hand to help the quarterback to his feet.

Jason would literally uplift another person during a football game. He was in the works of encouraging at the most important point, when he was down. So we missed this attitude, this character. We had some character. But resilience, the last seniors had resilience.

Tonsor said about the 1997 team, players led by actions, not words. They had something *each* high school football team, big or small, could learn from.

Playing football was what I loved. I enjoyed hitting people with pads on. Camaraderie was so tight. But then again, anything can be like that. So long as a team is focused on one main goal and they are willing to follow someone, you see change, and you can get the first down.

I look back, and am glad the team did not follow in so many of my decisions. They would have been the blind trailing the blind. We would have been 70 players walking into the ditch.

I was busted. Staunton police caught me with alcohol. They held me at the station. I called mom. She would have nothing to do with me.

I was stuck. I chose to make a dreaded phone call. I asked my grandparents to pick me up from the Staunton Police Station.

Grandma said they would be up soon. She entered the police station. Shortly thereafter we both walked out. I put my head down. walking to the car as a hoodlum would, hands floating along my sides, head on a swivel.

I stepped into the back seat of their car. For the first three minutes, nothing.

"What in the $%## were you doing with alcohol in your car?" grandpa said. "That has got to be the stupidest..." He banged the steering wheel agitatedly with an open palm. He kept an eye on the road. This was a lot for him then, he was so very irate.

"I come up here and get you from jail for alcohol. You're not of age to be driving with alcohol in your car. This has got to be the *stupidest* _____ you've done."

He then hit the steering wheel with one fist, grabbing the wheel with the other hand in the same way a boa constrictor clenches its prey, massaging it to death.

You could see the back of his neck turning red as the Staunton street lights shone inside. He continued all the way to grandma's house.

We walked inside. Then for the rest of the night he didn't talk about it.

It was the maddest my grandfather ever got toward me. Watching him react that way gave me a sick stomach. I sort of thought, "This is how grown men respond to these things. He looked like a buffoon."

But then I felt shame. I'd let him down.

I didn't see a reckless, unlawful behavior about him—he was a true American hero. I wanted to make him smile in calling me his grandson. Football would revive me.

I began squatting heavier than ever before by the end of senior year. I became then more and more aware of how my body responded to intense workouts. I bench pressed twice a week and squatted twice a week. I worked more serious than ever before. I lifted in the compact weight room with reckless abandon.

I drove my opponent back on a block easier than in years past and I believe squats provided the extra push.

Simply looking at competition is exhilarating. Rivalry between two opponents is downright beautiful, because football is on display, on the line of scrimmage, two men wrestling with one another like bears in the

Arctic. Both people going at it, so hardcore that they don't know what hit them.

Vinnie Sanvi and I went head-to-head in a blocking drill the first day of full pads practice before my senior season.

We both got in our stances. Coach Cal said, "Hit!" and we locked face masks. We both extended arms. It was like a controlled brawl. We were down-low. Our legs churned. We were competing. Then, when both sides meet, two rams bucking in a colossal match up of the ages, release is breathtaking, not just for the person winning over, but for both sides, if they come prepared.

I wanted to get Vinnie, a close buddy, and push him back five yards, to exhibit the proper blocking technique.

We wrestled together in the circle among the younger Staunton Dogs as he sent me back about six yards. He got lower. But competition is fun when two people are striving for something and they each know how to get it. Preparing the self for it is a journey in and of itself. One must beat his body and make it his slave to be competitive in football, and this is what we were after. For, we were chosen, but not with silver, for we were refined in the furnace of affliction.

We would run simple plays without an offensive line. Here and there Tonsor brought over someone to play on defense, to step across sort of as a decoy. I lined up against Doug Guinneweg often. He stood six feet, one inch, with a rugged, solid build. You could not see his hair through the helmet. Guinneweg had a raw passion for the training, aggression tapped into a sport he enjoyed. He lowered a shoulder in a quick collision. This was his work as a defensive man during our drill.

Ted Frank would call out, "Set. Blue 48. Red 50. Go." Doug came across me straight off my pop up, and—"boom!" He was a grade lower than me, but he laid a hit like he was a Dugger brother.

"Boom." The cackling of the pads were like a crunch from a child, who took out frustrations onto a coke can, after his sister made him mad. "Crunch," he would pop. There was nothing quite like it, the hit, the contact: player on player; mano y mano. Doug wanted to hit, and he hit with a vengeance.

We were friendly. Guinneweg shook hands in the halls with me in his hi-dee-ho voice, and then come practice, "crack." You felt a sudden, absolute release under those pads. There was no turning back after a hit, it was just the player who felt that temporary pain if pain is the right terminology. Sure we wanted competitive. Yeah we wanted glory. Accolades were fine with us. But if team was not advanced in our pursuit, there was no reason for I's to play. Our trials came through practice, because, Doug and me knew if he wanted to get better he had to come across and make me a champion. And in between the two of us, 180 pounds on his side, 190 on me, there was no telling who represented better, as long as the two of us came with it. Better made no difference. We had to build up team.

I blocked for Bill Schuette, one of the most feared men on the football field in half the state. When he lowered the shoulder, "Boom!"

Any defender had little chance of much side to side movement. Billy, stood 5 feet eight inches with short brown hair and a stout, ruddy 200 pounds. He had a full blonde mustache by the time he was in seventh grade. Billy was a guy who could knock a defender out of his cleats. Northern Illinois University recruited him, and he was all South Central Conference East his junior and senior seasons.

Anybody would have wanted Billy his football team. Schuette worked hard play in and play out. He did not complain. He made the game through determination. He lifted weights at home even, when other guys were out with their girlfriends. Billy was a fullback, and extra muscular for a seventeen-year old. He had ability to *burst* through the line. When he stepped onto the field, Billy was raw power. Billy spoke with his helmet, right in the ear hole.

Sport was the mold that made Billy physically. During skell, Schuette kicked up dust like the rest of us, reaching his top speed within four steps.

Coach called in his clear, serious tone, "Pro 24 veer." Billy went through the four hole just to my left. We'd go to the huddle.

"Con 23 veer." Billy busts the ball inside, kicking up dirt along the way in the dry dust. Our field was dry as an old Western. We made it feel like dirt.

One afternoon during skell coach called "Pro 24 Veer." So I went to the line, looking to block down on the Middle Linebacker. In my stance,

I breathed hard and heavy, preparing mentally for a fundamentally short sprint.

"Go... Fum Fum," Billy's steps sounded. And then, "Boom!"

He knocked me to the ground. Billy rolled over in one motion, both of us knocked into rings like Salvation Army bells as we lay on a loose layer of dust.

Such instances were *not* fun. But they prepared us for the Friday nights, under the lights, when awareness was crucial.

Football was not always pretty. The sports took an outpouring of dedication. Football demanded a certain toughness. To be willing to hit, and take one, even through protective pads, was crazy.

But a person has to find the discipline.

To play he had to come under control for the game to be any fun. He had to practice and lift weights. He had to beat his body and make it his slave. He had to get under himself, and bring his body under subjection.

It's funny, though, because I would just eat and eat during the season. Then I'd lift weights and sprint with the team, turning the food into muscle. Those extra calories gave an offensive lineman a strength advantage. Strength brought you the ability to shove the other guy back.

But I could not use this skill in our first game against our rival Gillespie, because of an alcohol violation in the off-season. It made me feel bad. Getting caught and reprimanded made me feel scummy, like a first-rate let—down, and certifiable loser. I felt like an insult to my race, like a shame to the school I represented.

I watched from the sidelines. I was a witness to Tommy Bauer, my Gillespie buddy, play middle linebacker against us at our house. He was good. But I could not see what blocking him was like. I could not be on that field when Gillespie's defense zoned in on Billy, which gave sophomore Zack Rigoni a chance to showcase his exceptional athleticism, and score five touchdowns. No, not this year, not in this life. I had to watch from the sidelines.

I *did* let the team down. It tore me up in that game, and even more the next week. It tore me up inside, these feelings of frustration I had brought upon myself. But I was getting better. I knew I had not wanted drugs anymore. I knew alcohol would not mandate the direction of my existence. Even if you could not see it from the outside, I was improving as a human being.

I roamed the sidelines at Carlinville, wanting to get in the game so bad, after we had easily defeated Gillespie.

Rigoni was a short, lightning-quick tailback. He had a stellar game. He moved his feet, shifting weight well from side to side. He read the line's blocks. Zack was in the zone.

He would speak like his brother Alex, one of those *respected* guys from the previous year's undefeated season. Zack would say in a homely tone, "Come on, guys," just like his big brother would.

I paced the sideline, wanting so bad to get in, like an intense heat surges. There was no way this time, however. I had violated the team's trust.

"Come on!" I said to Herbeck, vocal cords unnaturally straining. We had the game in control, but you would have to know the game like I knew it to understand. I wanted to help our guys, even though we had it in control. We were good, about as good as the year before. We fought. We knew how to battle. Our collective team body had excellent momentum.

We found a will to win without me—as a team.

First game I was back we faced the Piasa Birds of Southwestern. A certain stale electricity hung in the air. We played at home in front of an anticipatory crowd. Our team was 2-0.

Our opponents gave me a headache the year before. But I was a whole season wiser.

The defender played inside of me most plays and getting into a rhythm was difficult. I wanted to make contact. I wanted to hit him, and hard. But he continuously lined up so far within the interior I would only get a piece of him.

Billy Schuette kept running into walls of defenders. Their defensive front was penetrating our porous line like a noodle strainer. Schuette was tough like green spinach. He was mobile on the short game. He could read defenses normally. But when we failed to move their guys out of the way, he was stuck like peanut butter between bologna and bread.

By halftime, we were being humiliated. Ted Frank, our quarterback, stepped into the arid locker room with a slam.

"Bam!"

He stood over the sink in front of the mirror, panting like a dog. I walked over to console, and said, "We can win this, Teddy." Our whole team sat perched on wooden benches behind us.

"Tell them that!" he said, tears welling up in his eyes. Even though we were losing badly he was the leader beyond any of us. Ted was cool, he knew what he was doing, but tonight we were just collectively running out of gas. With sweat and water flushed through his face, he could not readily face the group, downtrodden. People's countenances were down; every man on the roster had a heavy weight upon his shoulders, like our minds were telling us this cross was too big a burden to bear. That's what this game does to you.

Football zaps you of everything you've got. Then it asks for more. It takes, and takes. It requires everything, even your whole self. This is the only game where a group of men give themselves to it like this.

Only in football do a mass of young individuals come together to form a unit greater than the sum of their skills. Even when you are losing you feel what the other person feels. You breathe his air. You are stuck in the same locker room, with the bunch of sweaty players you practiced all season with. After a while you become the same person. And not in some drone or robot sort of way. No, you have invested your entire being into what you love. You have given yourself to something better, a cause greater than your own interests. You begin to feel the emotions of other men.

I heard that if women are in the same home with one another for long they eventually get on the same menstrual cycle. With men, when they spend so much time with one another, they begin to feel what the other player is feeling. You see the same things on the field. You can taste victory as one unit. And when you know, in your bones each human being wearing your color jersey is on the same page, you get this sense. Maybe it is dangerous. But you start thinking you are invincible.

You start thinking you can do things far above and beyond that which you were personally capable. Because if you say something, you know the other person has your back. You know he's down to ride for you, he's down to die for you. Football bonds are thick, and you get the same concept in other sports, however, in football the tie is stronger. Hey, maybe I am bias here. Well, I am biased. But you know in football the other guys are with you. You all put on the pads at the same time. You feel the jitters as one.

With his whole body shaking, Teddy walked across the floor, searching. He searched for what was inside. He searched for an answer to all of our frustrations out on the field. *Why could we not move the ball?* Why could we not create momentum—on our field—at our house? We had two running backs who were extremely talented, though their running styles were completely different. Ted, our emboldened leader, a veteran of two full varsity seasons already, searched. He looked for answers. Then coach entered.

Coming back out for the second half, our plays were not near as fresh as they had been in each of the past two games the two weeks before. We played subjected, as slaves to this strong, but by no means superior, Southwestern front.

In our minds, we had already lost the game.

We were down by 30 points and with half the fourth quarter to go. We did not try to pass consistently throughout the rest of the game. We needed a score, and I wondered why coach was calling these running plays.

You taste victory with each other as a team. In disappointment you understand life has an end. All good things *must* come to an end, and our 15-game regular season winning streak was about to come to an end.

Our Culture

Walls in the locker room were painted white. The ten commandments of football were written in black on the wall outside the coach's office. Someone painted a beefed up bulldog near the door going out of the locker room. He stood in Staunton football jersey and pads standing upright, snarling and bloody, holding an opposing player's spine and skull. It was sort of the mood in the locker room, though not quite so carnal. It was take it to the opposing team or get your lunch fed to you, as Coach Tonsor said. The warm waxy concrete floors in there were filled with energy when we played, charged with excitement, because no matter what happened we were together. We were "one" on those nights.

I experienced angst coming up in Staunton

Football somehow made sense, though.

Football made me a better person through simple rules. We had boundaries on the team. Actions had consequences.

I missed a block one Thursday on the game field behind our high school. I hit the man to my outside, the outside linebacker. I gave him a good licking, but he kept on ticking—and it was the wrong block.

"Run it again, Luster!" Coach said. "And stop having brain farts." Even though I was a senior, he was being a bear and instilling discipline. He showed the whole team we would suffer as a unit if I was going to be selfish, and fail because of laziness to learn my blocking assignment.

Next play I got a quick first step into a tight sprint. I had radar, proceeding immediately to the middle linebacker Donnie Nicholas, where I was supposed to block to begin with. I got up under his pads, "Whoa Boossh—" The block knocked him backward instantaneously, leveling him to the ground. The whole sequence was one fluid motion. Sometimes the pressure was wearing.

Sometimes, it felt like Coach expected too much, though. He could be abrasive, when reaching for such a high plateau, it seemed he scraped his arms on the rocks. I went out for a pass play during a practice once and it was the wrong one. As I jogged back to the line, Tonsor said, "What was that?" while walking toward me.

As I looked to Ted, and back to Coach, I replied, "miscommunication," and he was furious. He was lit. "Miscommunication!" he said, and then told me to get back to the huddle.

I was frustrated and mad at what he told me to do sometimes, and the tone he used. I would not let myself *stay* mad at him, though. He was too important to my life. I think I would have let him get away with more things than most men and everything would seem hunky-dory, because, he was special. Coach made sense. He chose to be with us. He chose to give us inspiration. And he controlled my destiny in the game I loved, a sport I was infatuated with, one I felt I would do about anything besides bloody murder to hold on to.

Our season wore on. We did well. We won mostly. Then again we lost. We lost, looking back now, more than we should have.

We went into our last game of the regular season with a 5-3 record against Alton-Marquette. They were 5-3 also. It was for everything. Whoever won would go into the playoffs. We went onto their bowl of a field and defeated them.

We were going to the playoffs!

Illinois High School Association matched us with LeRoy High School in the North Eastern section of Illinois for the first round of the playoffs.

Now LeRoy was a tough squad, with an excellent record, and a stumbling block to small schools up north. LeRoy was not far removed from greatness, as they won the state title two years before. But they played in a weaker league than our South Central Conference. Staunton played stronger competition and bigger schools.

We had confidence we were tougher. All us guys—Teddie, Atwood,

Kershaw, Herschel—we knew what we were up against. We knew if we played our type of ball we'd be singing sweet Dixie come Saturday evening.

We had the faith. Unfortunately, however, the very people who were supposed to have faith even when we lacked it, lacked it when we had it.

Our darling cheerleaders talked about where they would stay when they made the trip to LeRoy. One of the girls uttered something equivalent to steak knives screeching down Mr. Malone's chalkboard.

"Why are we going to go up there? It's not like we are going to win anyway."

It was as though a thunderclap sounded outside, and reverberated throughout the school halls. This would be wood for the fire, however. We were set on our goal—a bull's eye on those LeRoy jerseys.

I had invested the past four years of my life to the game. I loved football. Coach Randy Legendre taught the game to me, who said he would give his left nut to play again. Other coaches concurred they would give their left nuts to play again.

"You only need one anyway," Tonsor said.

Football was something the whole town could get fanatical about. When people finished work of a Friday night, they could go watch the Bulldogs play.

Football is a beautiful sport, one of dexterity, mental agility, and brute physical strength. Coach Tonsor knew what it took to get people to move as one unit. He got jacked up about the game come Saturday. We pulled into LeRoy's campus, about two and a half hours north of Staunton, enclosed by a small town on one side and a vast cornfield on the other.

Harvest was upon us. We were boys of the fall.

Aunts and uncles, grandparents, mothers and dads, watched their kin become what they could on some level reach out to on a stretch of green grass. Staunton had what it took. A vigorous teacher named Tonsor dug into our inner reservoirs.

Leroy's team consisted of Northern Illinois farm boys, corn fed, corn bred; ol' boys who'd take a lickin' an' keep on 'a tickin'.

Skies were partly cloudy, the field was wet. I wore some spikes that fit well above the ankles, and were rubber on the bottom. Laces were so long

DRUGS AND FOOTBALL

I had to tie them around my ankles and back again. My usual Reeboks were obstinate, and would not receive plastic cleats into the appropriate bottom holes.

We brought seniors, juniors, many sophomores, and even some freshmen to LeRoy. We looked around at each other, while we stood crammed in this tiny barn of a locker room, knowing we had a legitimate chance to advance to the second round of the IHSA playoffs.

We knew what beating LeRoy would take. Our team studied them all week through film sessions.

We ran through a tunnel under the home team's bleachers. We took the field, running across to the opposite side. We stretched as LeRoy's crowd throbbed with electricity. LeRoy's players ran out from under the large stands, and the town went wild.

The atmosphere was intimidating to say the least. These guys were dressed like college football's Florida State Seminoles. Amid the roar of the crowd two minutes prior to kickoff it was hard to see they were high school athletes just like us.

But after the first ball was snapped our fears subsided; we loosened, and their crowd settled down. We came to the recognition they were human; our nerves were under control and we played as trained.

We came to see LeRoy as they were on film—beatable. They were our size and we knew we had the upper hand.

You could hear the cheer of the Staunton crowd positioned just behind our sideline. Our fans that day numbered 500 or so, and they helped. The moral support was a boost on account of how up and down our season had been.

But this day we were jacked.

We wore on them all day.

Teddy threw a pass that looked like a lame duck, traveling 5 yards in the air and 20 yards downfield. A horrible pass, I don't know if he was hit or what. Timmie Kershaw, a constant at wide receiver, adjusted in the middle of the field stepping in front of his player, catching the ball, and tucking it in. He proceeded to fall flat on his butt.

Mike Popovich, a junior wide receiver, caught a dandy, too. It was a same caliber geeky-type throw. Mike jumped up with a defender at his back and was pushed. As soon as his feet hit the ground he slipped and fell, still holding onto it, though.

We felt great. We played with reckless abandon. All day we felt as one unit, in synchronicity with one another. The feeling was that of invincibility; we knew the plays to run; we would pound the ball inside. We could not be stopped. It was as though there was no end. All space and time was somehow compressed into a single afternoon. Time was nonexistent. We were in a different dimension. This is what we were created for—to live this day. We were made to be with these guys—with each other on this day, on a field that was an extension of a cornfield, the same surface that nurtured us. This is the ground that gave our forefathers sustenance. This is what they tilled, to make fodder for us, nourishment to make us grow.

This was *our* time.

Today we would go out and give our kin what they had come to see. We would give ourselves to this game, for, we could not be stopped. No, not today. We would not be denied. From all the frustrating times in raising that soybean crop, or preparing the wheat for gathering; in due proportion we were bound and determined to give our parents the satisfaction of knowing we would play with all of ourselves. We would play to our utmost capacity, as one unit. *This* was why we stayed after school. *This* is what we sacrificed so many other activities for. *This* was why so many of us chose not to drink. *This* was the game. And we would play it as the game of our lives.

But LeRoy was good. They were players. Leroy's quarterback was a stud. He was average-sized, about 5 foot ten inches tall, 185 pounds. But boy was he an athlete. He ran down the sideline on one quarterback keeper, and flipped over one of our players, landing in the end zone for a score.

We displayed heart. Schuette ran like an ox. He ran clumsy, but as a bull rushes the streets of Barcelona. Bill had no burst of speed like a Walter Payton or Ricky Williams. He just put his head down and plowed like a Clydesdale. He did not run the safest way, either, using the top of his head sometimes like a battering ram. Bramley once said when Billy got the handoff, he actually closed his eyes as he carried the football. I wondered what the action would look, sound and feel like.

You grab the ball, then everything goes black. Pads crunch and mash, bones crash, as you collide into people like a boulder tumbling downhill meeting other stones at the bottom, grinding into other players with bodies built for punishment, just like yours. Other times you could simultaneously crash into five players, one after another, like a single, red and white wrecking ball headed into stone pillars lined up one next to the other. This is all depending on how fast the offensive line is getting to their blocks.

Schuette pounded the leather like an animal. He competed that day as a champion, a stallion. Billy had to have carried the football 30 times.

As tough as Schuette was, Teddy was vulnerable on that autumn day. LeRoy was after him. They tackled Teddy and he laid at the bottom of the pile. Ten bodies were on top of him. They slowly rolled off. There was Ted. His eyes were red and tears. We knew something was wrong. His voice cracked. He was visibly shaken.

Ted marched back like a soldier, got back in the huddle and called the play to Schuette.

This is the Fourth Quarter:

Here is our time to dance.

Billy Schuette. No. 32 Billy Schuette with the ball…Schuette the ball carrier. Our plays went 22 veer, 20 draw, 24 veer load. We could not have passed the ball more than twice the entire last drive. Billy's legs were like the Roadrunner character, chugging.

Hand off to Billy Schuette for four yards. We'd wait 20 seconds. Then Schuette took the ball again. He was unbelievable on the drive.

South Central Conference saw it all season long. LeRoy had to have seen it on film in the week leading up to the game. But they couldn't stop it.

Every snap he ran for the past three years on varsity prepared him for this. Any strength he possessed on that charged afternoon, he left on the field.

We drove the ball 70 yards deep into their territory. We led with less than three minutes to play. We managed to take ten minutes off the clock in that final quarter. We knew we had the game under control as Schuette broke away for a 15 yarder towards the end. We did not punch it in, though, as we learned about courtesy the year before, when DuQuoin could have scored against us, but relented. So Coach Tonsor let it be what it was and we chose not score on the last drive. Tonsor had been around football for fifteen years, and said we demonstrated the finest he had ever seen.

Lesson

Next week I felt tight, like all was riding on this. All was riding on this one game.

We watched film as we prepared to face the Stillman Valley Redbirds in the second round of the IHSA playoffs.

Night before we played Stillman I went out on the town with Aaron Hainaut, who had been a stellar defensive player the past two seasons. We drove around. A bottle of liquor rested on my lap. We drove past the Super Eight motel where Stillman Valley was spending the night. As I sipped on the alcohol I told Hainaut how it was a shame these guys were coming all the way down here from upstate to lose to us on our field. He shook it off.

We drove around for a little while in his black Grand Prix. Hainaut drove me back to my friend AJ's house where I stayed the night.

Next morning I was a bit hung over. Corn Pops tasted good, but it was not enough. Come noon I was going, but not full on. I would have benefited from some meat at that juncture.

Rucky Babcock started on their offensive line and would later start at the University of Illinois, a major college football program. Their fullback was rough and tumble. He stood there in the backfield, with this barbed wire tattoo. It was a little unnerving, as he had strong arms to match his artwork.

The guy I was assigned to block was either on two feet or in a three-point stance every play, head up on me. They did not play me that

Saturday like most teams. It seemed that virtually every play, the guy would stunt inside and I would just miss him, similar to what defenses Southwestern played earlier in the season. While we were on offense, if Schuette ran to my left, in between the tackle and me, and the guy head up on me sprinted inside; it wasn't any good. We were actually working against each other. I would just push the defender into Billy. The day carried on and we were losing.

By the time halftime rolled around I was running on fumes. I could still block if a guy came at me.

Our team never had control of the line of scrimmage, where games are won and lost, in between the tackles.

Stillman Valley's offense, on the other hand, refused to run toward my defensive position which was strong safety. Basically 80 percent of the time they ran the football to the weak side——away from me. This made me furious. "Come on!" I said. "Bring it this way! Bring it on! You don't want none!"

Game over. Man, I was exhausted. Stillman was physically stronger. But the Redbirds may have been mentally stronger than they were physical. Coach Caldieraro said after the game they controlled us on the line of scrimmage. We had speed, but up front they handled us.

Probably a thousand people showed up for that battle. Afterwards they ate a meal in our multipurpose gym, which we also used as a cafeteria.

Following their victory we received a note of how nice our community behaved during their trip to Staunton, stand-up type stuff. The Redbirds were a great team. They would go on to win the state championship the next two seasons.

You win some. You lose some. But you do not drink alcohol the night before the most important day of your life. So booze was not good for me.

Recognizing my failures as a leader on a football team during varsity was sobering. Then came bitterness in knowing this game would not be in my life anymore, at least on the high school level.

Directly after senior season I took a while to lick my wounds and mope. I was depressed; I would spend hours in the sparse-to-empty Staunton Fitness Center weight room.

I just lifted for boredom and the mourning of what I saw as the temporary death of football in my life. It was as though I lost a dear friend. I would reminisce about the time police pulled over Justin Winslow and I the day of Staunton's first ever home playoff game. I recalled Chad Dugger, then a sophomore, drilling me after a catch I made in practice, the hit sending me to the ground, causing me to wince in pain.

I thought upon Chris Dugger his sophomore year, my junior season, as soon as the ball was snapped, popping me under the chest pads, sending me flying six feet to the side as I stumbled, trying to regain footing… I placed 365 pounds on the bar, a considerable weight, and difficult to lift in the first place. I stepped under the rack placing the bar on my shoulders. I lifted the weight off the apparatus, backed up and squatted down; it would not go back up.

Brett Herbeck, our outstanding middle linebacker, saw my struggle and immediately got under me to bring the weight up. He heaved upward, walked the weight forward with me directly under the bar, as we both placed the mass of iron onto the steady hard clamps at chest level.

Herbeck felt the effects of my lack of planning (I should have placed "catches" under the rack, so after going low, if the weight was too difficult to bring back up, the machine would "catch" the bar) as he walked away woozy from the rack in the small room of free weight machines. He saved my body (and ego) that day of my grief, as I had wallowed in abandon. My [high school] playing days were over.

After football, weights were therapeutic. Weights made you feel a certain way. It felt as though you were in this iron factory. You are the assembler, and your body is the assembly line. But when you choose to allow yourself failure on the last repetition with somebody backing you up, you are developing your body even further. You know, if you do it the right way, people are there to back you up. If you are fortunate, you will have somebody to back you up, all the way.

You find what tools build this muscle this way, what workout torques your endurance another way. I always felt relaxed working out with the guys whether at Staunton Fitness Center or Staunton High School. Pressure releases from the whole body, like a feather falling from a fiction writer's desktop after finishing a tenth novel.

Life circumstances are like that.

I guess through all the sulking after football, it was a release following failure.

The prophet Isaiah said, "Behold, I have refined thee, but not with silver. For I have chosen thee in the furnace of affliction."

Our last game, at least, was a failure. It was a failure in that we lost. But when you get back up again, somebody will be there for you. You would be wise in getting a spotter beforehand, however. And if you want a spotter, be a spotter. If you want a friend, show yourself friendly. If you want a chum. Be a chum. Coach was *always* my spotter. He was around when he needed to be. He was a hero. Coach Tonsor was *my* hero. He was my father. He taught me so much about myself. He rescued me from a young life that could easily have been otherwise spent incarcerated. He demanded. He expected. And as I looked back, challenge was the exact ingredient I needed for the spiciest, most delectable life.

Our team was a combined 23-9 my sophomore through senior years under him. He coached us to the playoffs those three seasons, which is not an easy task in Illinois High school football. Under normal circumstances, a team would have to finish with twice as many wins as losses to make the playoffs. Prior to my sophomore year—1996—we hadn't been to the playoffs since the 1970s. He retired from Staunton football with a very good 8-3 season in 2000.

Grandpa and Jose in grandma and grandpa's kitchen

My beautiful mother. She never gave up on us

Grandma and grandpa preparing for the daily smooch before grandpa headed for work.

Jharmel and I at the Edwardsville YMCA

Me, mom and Jharmel

Me, Jharmel, and grandpa

DRUGS AND FOOTBALL

Football is like an addiction. One time somebody told me weightlifting was an addiction, that a person could suffer withdrawals from going without it. I told the person there is no addiction in weightlifting. But in football, yes there is a craving, an urge to hit somebody under shoulder pads, to spread the love, as it were. Not in a violent sense, not to maim the other individual personally, emotionally or physically. In fact, quite the opposite occurs.

Linemen do somewhat of a tango. Chemistry between the offensive and defensive warrior in the trenches is poignant. They go head-to-head, toe to toe, mano y mano. The giants of the gridiron are creating something good after that ball is snapped. They engage in a colossal battle. They are not fighting one another in the destructive sense.

Even though the two men are on *different teams*, they bond to one another. This dance in unison is similar to the collective *teamwork* an orchestra achieves coming together to perform Rachmaninov's no. 3. All these different sounds make different music.

But the audience hears a symphony.

They listen to the drumbeat: "Boom..." Then a flute in its drawn out melody. And a soft violin creates a unique hum.

Building the body is an awesome feeling, especially when others are around backing you up. Being in the weight room just feels great.

Being up front is definitely uplifting. When another man is hurting, be there for him. Don't simply assume he is tough enough to handle a problem by himself. Root of the issue is most important. Hiding a scar does not remove it. Revealing the scar takes away the sting of what caused it to be hidden in the first place. Then you expose what is ugly, but is going to be there anyway. So, owning up to the original hurt and making it part of you is helpful.

If a man's wife separates from him and he tells everybody he is fine, then he needs to level with himself; he needs a hug from a friend. If he is upfront with the other person, however, he can bring himself out of the bubble he was once in, because now the man recognizes someone cares about what is going on in his soul, deep inside.

Challenges

I was on the road one time, when I looked up to the sky and saw a large, almost completely dark cloud in the sky. The thing was ominous. I used to get scared sometimes when seeing these types of clouds.

They sit up in the sky and hang. Dark clouds say, "Hey, I'm going to try to ruin your time because I am big, bad and scary. Fear me because I look mean."

There is no sense in fearing big and bad and scary clouds, though. By going directly toward these clouds, women and men overcome the wickedness the clouds symbolize.

When clouds, storms, challenges come our way, we can turn around and run with a tail between the legs, or grab faith like a shield, stand up and fight. Challenges make the storms. Challenges are what lingers inside the storms. People need not look at storms and say, "Oh, well, that's scary. I'd better not go there."

But when a person is up against something difficult indeed, say a possible divorce, things get stormy. People get upset, tempers flare. I have never been married, so my frame of reference is limited.

In my experience storms came rolling in, and many times people brought these tempests on by personal effort.

Toward the end of my senior year I stood around at a friend's house with Aaron, a close buddy.

The house was old with brown '70s furniture. About six people in the other room watched whatever show played on television. They were unmotivating themselves, passing a bowl of weed to and fro.

    I hung around Aaron with about eight other people in the next room, a 12' x 12' kitchen.

    Trash hung out of the can in the little room beside us. Dishes were piled in the sink.

    Aaron was threw down a half ounce of cocaine. Then he got a sheet of aluminum foil, put down some baking soda and the cocaine.

    Next Aaron took a straw and lighter. A bystander near the table held up the flat foil. Aaron lit it, put the straw to his mouth and inhaled.

    I never liked it when he did that.

    I suppose it was all those drug-free America commercials I'd viewed growing up, when the woman got ready to jump off the diving board. But then as she was jumping, you could see the pool had no water, just the bare cement.

    When people turned cocaine into smoke I stayed away.

    I did ask Aaron for a line, though. He gave me one.

    I stood in the kitchen, and asked. I asked if Aaron would give me another line. I asked again. I stood there like a stray puppy, pathetic and lost in the puddles; he went on about his business, smoking his brain into numbness, barely acknowledging my plea. He taught me something that night.

    The night said to me, "Cocaine is a better friend to your friends than you are to your friends when they are addicted."

    So I took something from that—to stop putting that junk up my nose.

Recurrent Storms

When you get into a storm—a big gargantuan storm you just see and are terrified of, you want to put your tail between your legs and walk away. Sometimes you see clouds in the forecast, and are not sure quite how to react. But when you react, when you act, you are doing something strong. Passivity is like death. Neither leads. Both follow. Sometimes the thought of challenges are scary. But these are just silly storms. In the center of them you will find the refining quality for which people strive after.

Prejudice was a common factor in relating with people, which complicated my life. Even one of the teachers made me mad.

He discussed music artists with students during class. A half-dozen students and I at a table in a circle. Someone mentioned the rapper Jay-Z.

My own teacher said, "Who's that? Some nigger?"

This nastiness stood like a monster all around me. It was as journalist Joe Klein said, "a gaping American wound." This meanness inside was bogus; the meanness was a plague, reaching our far and away villages and country sides from sea to shining sea. This just because people were not regularly exposed to African-Americans.

People, in small town America, Staunton, did not know black folks aside from the UPS guy who came to the library every week.

That day in the classroom I learned a little on how to keep the enemy of rage at bay. It was by thinking about what I could do and then taking action to not let the wrath turn into a reality.

God shown his grace upon me, because I felt like hurting the man.

DRUGS AND FOOTBALL

I could have got up and strangled the guy. I felt like punching him. My physical body probably could have overcome his physical person. I was at the physical peak of my high school existence. I could have gone completely berserk; that was my hood, my stomping ground—this was just my feeling at the time. But through mercy granted from heaven, I held back.

It may have been the fear of whether he could have physically beaten me in a fight. Maybe it was the collective pot residue inside the cranium slowing my reaction time: possibly I was too high to react.

But life's crazy like that because God works in mysterious ways.

Whatever it was, I stood standing at the end of the day on my own two feet.

I told mom. That's right, you can laugh. I told mommy. But it made me feel better and I am better for it. I was above what he said. I overcame something through all that. God refined my self-discipline somehow. My mom told the principal Mr. Milam. My teacher called me up before the end of the week and apologized.

Racism has been a big problem. When I come back to Staunton and the bigoted attitudes hurt sometimes. Racism does not feel as bad as before. Now we've got several youths of color in the school system.

But I see something, someone, bigger than theses storms. You could figure, "Oh, man, what if I get rejected by Yale. Ah, I won't even apply there." Then a chance is missed to see what you can do. You see, these challenges bring an opportunity to be tried in refiner's fire.

Even if you chose wrongly, failure in a challenge need not bring a lasting sense of dejection, but a perseverance, a toughness. Under seemingly dire odds people can blossom into people better than who they were. We can go out Thursday night and drink seven beers with an impending test the next day Friday, be hung over the next morning, or ante up. We can tell friends we need to study, read ardently over the material, take the test, and ace it.

Accepting challenges wherever we are in life is important, because perseverance strengthens us. Storms are necessary. Without storms the sun would shine—all the time.

What good is that? People need storms, to see the level to which they can elevate. Under a challenge, a man can look up and say, I did this myself while being tested. Nobody else did it but me. That is a unique claim.

Last semester of my senior year I got a good job as a delivery boy for Little Italy's Pizza in Staunton. It was cool. I hung out with the guys who went to Lewis and Clark Community College and all.

I did not know the direction of my life. But I would make something of it. My life was actually going well. A year before that moment, however, I hadn't a serious thought I would be attending an institution of higher learning. Things were cherry.

Bramley, Luke Wittman, and I along with several other people, sat at Wittman's kitchen table. His mother was gone. We had the small, quaint house to ourselves. Wittman's kitchen was new, approximately 10' x 12'. Floor was a light-wood, unhindered by wear. His sink had the shiny faucet, jutting upward and hanging over, as a half zero. Cabinets had windows on the doors. Stove and oven were of a modern decor.

We were having ourselves a little party. Bramley handed me a pipe, nearly a dime in diameter. "Sitghh," was the sound it made as the paraphernalia burned my left arm.

"Ouccrh!" I said. "Bramley!"

His eyes a quarter of the way shut and the color of near ripe gala apples. He singed me bad in the middle of my left forearm.

Maybe he meant no harm. Possibly his crude, unrefined action exposed my limits.

Through grace I am able to forgive friends when they do even silly things, and when they give you that puppy dog look, as though they know what they did was a mistake, without even thinking, without even considering what could make me yell.

Life takes patience, great patience, to persevere. And this forgiveness goes *both* ways.

I was at Wittman's place again. Wittman's mom asked if I knew how to drive stick shift.

"I know how," I said.

"Will you back Greg's car up in the driveway?" she said.

DRUGS AND FOOTBALL

Greg just got a job as a pizza delivery man at Pizza Hut in Godfrey. He was able to afford this sweet, black 90s Chevy Sunbird. I hopped in and prepared for what was supposed to be a simple maneuver. But the 40 feet worth of driving turned out to be one wild ride.

I put the machine into reverse. I started backing, and rolling along. His door hung wide open in the fresh, cool air.

Uhhh... I noticed the base of a tree right, behind,... I let off the clutch, and it, was—too late. "Crunch."

Ahww man. I *knew* Greg would be on my tail. Wittman stood 6'5", 190 pounds. He sported brown sideburns and spoke with the voice of a middle aged health magazine model. He got home and expletives flew. I wanted to say sorry, but...just could not get anything in. He continued speaking four lettered words...he continued to brew. I stood and tried to get in words of remorse. I was sorry. Possibly I should have just told Wittman's mom he could move it when he gets home. Then I would have not been responsible for my error.

I knew he would be upset, and he got not only upset, but what seemed to be utterly livid. I did wreck his car. But I did not understand how backing the car door into a tree could cause him to get into such a tizzy. Life takes patience—like when you are backing a car up into a driveway.

It takes patience to be with a friend, to deal with him, even when you don't understand how his possessions can even momentarily override the bonds of your friendship. Patience is waiting on your friend. You wait on your friend even when crunching his car was not the intention.

Each of us was equipped with feelings that get hurt and the feelings got hurt a lot when we were growing up. Most of us are in adult bodies but the most important lessons remain the same. Forgiveness is our ability to show mercy to others. I don't know if Greg ever said he was sorry. I think he did. But regardless, what he said, two months later was water under the bridge.

We were air tight. Not all are perfect, indeed none of us. But forgiveness takes only a beating heart with intention. Result is the finest miracle known to the human species.

Every day we make decisions which have affects. Taking personal mistakes and owning up defies any sense of pride.

If a man is in a bar and another man steals his drink, the two may get into a fight. Next day the two, saying they both work at the same job site, can bury the hatchet, so to speak, or harbor a grudge which destroys some of the very fiber of each of their characters.

Why live with a grudge when saying, "I am sorry," is so much easier?

Speaking through problems eliminated not enough wars. Saving face is not worth it when egg is splattered over the brow.

Here's another option: Walk up to the guy who stole your drink at the bar the next day. Say you are sorry for fighting him. If you can say you are sorry about anything with utter sincerity, unwavering, then you can stir the sea. Or you could just refrain from going to a bar.

Little Italy's to Big Help

Work was going swell. I called customers sir and madam during deliveries. I felt in earnest I was doing service to the Staunton area. I arrived at the vast majority of deliveries on time. I did whatever jobs they had such as mopping the floor and wiping down counter tops.

Then I received a traffic ticket and my license was suspended. They released me. I was completely sunk.

I didn't know the way to apply for another job. Pride tasted bitter, as I asked mother for a ride to Edwardsville. I applied to Market Basket, a grocery store/landscape supplier. I then asked a tall, large man with grey hair and business look on his face if any work was to be had. He said we could go out to the yard and see. We *both* went out. We walked beyond beautiful plants in plastic pots. I glanced out and saw boulder-style rocks, mulch, and a variety of driveway rock. We approached a man named Jason. Jason sat on a large industrial-use tractor with five-foot high wheels. The man assisting me asked Jason if he needed any help and Jason said he did not. Nevertheless, the kind sir said the job was mine. Turns out he owned the store, and Jason was his son.

Not gonna learn how to handle the challenge until you try. Life is crazy like that.

Icon

Grandpa got sick, and I didn't know the severity. I did not know how to handle it, really.

Martin Luther King said we are caught in an inescapable network of mutuality, tied in a single garment of destiny. Whatever affects one directly affects all indirectly.

When grandpa was sick, I did not comprehend how sick he was. I didn't understand he was living some of the last months of his life. Drugs damaged my motivation.

People came to me from time to time in need of something. When grandpa was sick grandma asked me to come over and change grandpa's oil. Hesitation was my first reaction.

I was preoccupied with my own life. She sensed my hesitation over the phone. "Brett," she said. "If you don't come over here and do this, then, we just don't understand each other."

Then Grace, the unconditional love, was at work. Because at the moment when she said we wouldn't have understood each other, I saw all the things my grandfather did for me—when he took me fishing, or to the Sportsman's Club and made me to feel like a big man, a respected man in a little guy's body, and it shook me in my heart. Grandpa was my hero. He was sick. Grandpa was not getting better. He eventually had to go to the hospital.

He then got really sick.

I sat in a small, private waiting room at Barnes-Jewish Hospital in St.

Louis. Physicians gave my grandpa intensive care next door. They tried and tried.

I sat watching people walk into the waiting room: Julie, my cousin; Louise, my cousin; my Aunt Dolly; Jennifer, my cousin…

People just kept on coming. I began to comprehend the seriousness of grandpa's illness. He was going down. But people just kept coming. Before long, all grandpa's children, and grandchildren besides Amy, who was on the East Coast serving in the Marine Corps, stood or sat there.

After waiting into the evening hours, seeing all of us in a reunion, I was stuck in the sight. I didn't know. I didn't know all this man had done for me. I didn't know fully what he meant to everyone in the room. I didn't know until now. Now I was beginning to find the most significant measure of his impact. And now he was dying. He was dying, and he was a shell of his former self. He was a shell of what he was. He wasn't the strong burly man he had been. He had become weak. He had become what he never wanted to be—weak. He never wanted to be what he could not control. He wanted control. He wanted control over family matters. He wanted control over his cancer. Grandpa wanted all these things. He wanted everything at one time in his life, he did. But now he had nothing. He had nothing and could not do a thing about it.

He was subject to his own mortality. He was finite. He was a mortal. He had to accept it. He was about done. He had nothing. Grandpa had nothing…Laughter. I heard laughter from the mouths of babes. I saw the children playing, my little second cousins, playing with each other—William and Joseph. Julie's little child Joseph crawled along the floor. A new generation of Brackmans, and an older generation, all in one room. Our children played, and played. Then it wasn't for nothing. Then I knew, I heard. I heard something good. I heard something good come out of all this. I heard an excellent laugh. I looked around and viewed. I literally panned my head around the room, where all of us sat, cousins, brothers, mothers and fathers. All of us sat there waiting for him, as though the miraculous was going to happen; as though the miraculous was inevitable for this man who always seemed larger than life; a man above death.

And I considered grandpa extremely fortunate to have such a support system. We were there. We were all there for him. He knew he had support. We had his back—all twenty-something of us. We were there for the man who moved us.

Someone said it was my turn to be with grandpa, ya' know, if I wanted to be. I wanted to be, I just didn't know how I would handle it.

Christy, my cousin, sat next to his bed, looking down toward his body, distraught. I saw him. He was less than what he used to be. The skin was shrunk like a vacuum hose had been thrust into his side and taken out so much muscle. He was beaten down, his body wracked with suffering from a ruthless, unforgiving cancer. He was so thin. I looked down at him, in a position of complete subordination. His eyes were closed. Christy cried softly. His mustache was thick, thicker than his thin lips. His glasses hung, on his smooth forehead. He lay there in a state of subjection. He was a mortal.

I sat for a while in the silence. I soaked him up. Sometime thereafter I exited.

I went to the waiting room.

We rested with one another. We hung there, as a family, for hours.

We were alarmed. Nurses made a commotion. A doctor came through. Something was wrong. Grandpa had begun to jaundice. His skin had become yellow. I somehow gained access to him once more. I walked to his mobile bed. He looked up to me as if to say, "This is it. We are not going to be seeing each other any more. Not here at least."

He gazed at me, and did say the last words I ever heard of his.

"Follow Jesus." I didn't know what to do with that. What could I say? Physicians wheeled him in to a room…behind closed doors…and that was it.

I went to college two days after we buried my grandfather.

Jose and mother drove away in his maroon Chevy S-10 on that first day at Southern Illinois University Carbondale. I was petrified. Mom was going to miss me and as she looked back it was all over her childlike face. They knew, however, the move and the challenge of being in a different environment would be a good thing.

My home was Steagall Hall the first year. Steagall was on the point of a medium size drive overlooking Thompson Lake, our college body of water. Thompson Point Residence halls consisted of three floors, with approximately 32 residents on each floor. Getting used to life there was tough.

School was a completely different world and it made me feel rather uncomfortable at first. Just considering Grandpa, though, helped me. Such a blessing this titan of a man was, a behemoth of sorts. He was definitely a man's man. All Grandpa taught me in the years we had together paid off, every second of it. Every moment made me want to be nearer him, to learn from this man who knew me better than I knew myself. He understood my troubles, my fears. Grandpa understood, he had empathy, through his experience. Grandpa had been there. He had seen some things. And he was capable by a sight. Every day he spent with me was like heaven. It was bliss. And then came college thoughts, thinking of growing up.

College was markedly different from my hometown, Staunton. Staunton was 40 miles from a considerable-size city, it was small, people talked with reserve, and there were only white people (It seemed that way). This bothered me more when I got to college than I had anticipated.

I felt disillusioned to start off my SIU career, showing up for the hall meeting in a white undershirt on my upper body, still reeling from the cries old men could not bear to keep inside, as they sniffled like children in front of grandpa's coffin. Looking back, I could barely hold in the joy grandpa gave me, and the day he was buried was a blessing, as I saw what a man who was close to me, meant to scores of others in our community.

But I got some of the *best* of him. We were tight. One day we stood in the kitchen at our farm on Reservoir Road in Staunton. He peered down into my small, a-bit-past-toddler eyes, and gazed at me intently.

"Don't trust **anyone**," he said. And this stuck with me. He said that, my grandfather, my hero, the man who meant the world to me through the 19 years we had together. He said not to trust anyone, so I did just that.

Jon Kirksey was my roommate sophomore year.

I met him less than a week after grandpa's body was six feet under the earth's surface.

He was a fighter. Kirksey looked like a firm, 6' 1" inch rock of stone, stealthily fast like a cat. He lived and slept less than 15 feet away from me for 9 months, shadowboxing with white strips of linen wrapped around knuckles, rocky under flesh, which made me think of The Shroud of Turin. Jon bobbed up and down, stayed down, and then back up again.

Let this book somehow come through me. I want to be a conduit, and if a conduit, a conduit for love because, God is love. Our purpose here is to love somebody, to be used up as Pastor Rick Warren talked about in his book, The Purpose-Driven Life, to find our shape. Until we find our shape we cannot fit into what our creator meant for us to be. We fit into a shape by finding what we are good at, and identifying it. We have a choice to figure what we thrive at doing. After we know, then we are able to whittle that wood. Or refine that steel. However we work, God has a purpose for that talent. We are good at something. My Uncle Louis said everybody is an expert at something. Whatever the "it" is, everybody is good at something, excellent at something indeed. Each person is made for a specific reason. Fortunately I was at college, in Southern Illinois when the purpose just slowly developed before my eyes. I could see something spectacular in a pencil and journal. These two ingredients were all I needed at the time. Before this, things were more stodgy, disconnected. Finally they had become closer, more intimate because of this. Mom always had a writing talent. But grandpa. Grandpa was the reason for writing something important. Everything I knew in my life was grandpa. He was a strong man. He kept an awesome house. So after his death I just wrote. Writing in that journal with a Chicago roommate was so comforting. I could just jot down whatever feeling, whatever emotion would come up. Journaling was not much then. Maybe half an hour per day. Then as I went further on, exploring this talent, it became more and more. This is growing up.

"Jab—Jab. Pop, pop," his hunched over frame swaying speedily to the rhythm like an eye level punching bag. Punches flowed in succession, "Pop, pop…jab-jabjab." The man was hungry in those days of raging hormones, hormones in all of us really.

His fluid technique was clear. And so skillfully graceful. Was he a prize fighter? Well, he was a prize in the room "JAB-jab-jabjab. Pop pop." Wind whooshed and "wherrp—!"

DRUGS AND FOOTBALL

He regularly did sit ups, push ups, and this was evident in his body. He lifted his shirt revealing a flat, sculpted stomach.

These two men, my grandfather and Kirksey, were completely different. Grandpa was not particularly intelligent, a man created from dust of the Illinois plains. But he made a concerted effort at reading and studying History.

Kirksey was intellectually gifted, quite able to apply knowledge. He *did not*, however, apply himself.

Grandpa cared for no mainline sports. Kirksey enjoyed football and boxing.

Jon was slender, athletic, and spoke with a mildly deep, resonant tone. He often laughed with his mouth in his hand, or away from people. He smoked weed often and was a bad influence on me to begin with. He became less so as the year progressed.

Starting out, however, it was just us, each in college for the first time, fitting in by determination. My journey was fraught with difficulty, and I relied on my own, sometimes mechanical, way of prayer. Jon was reliant on what faith he had and a sharp instinct from the streets.

Kirksey lied like a snake for his victims, waiting to attack. On one occasion, a mutual friend came in the room.

"Brett was watching a gay porno film," he said. He laughed. I stammered and was sp…sp…speechless. I could say nothing. I failed to form words in my mouth. More I tried to speak, the more Kirksey laughed, and, the more, breath that escaped my trembling nostrils, the more, he chuckled. His grin was sardonic. His twinge of spite disgusting. I considered the comments that day and for days thereafter. He got my goat, as we say in the Midwest.

There was no reason for Kirksey to make an idiot of me. But now I am better for it because I was humbled. Latin for the word humility is "humilis" or, to become low. Kirksey made me low that day.

No use in getting mad at someone for something like that.

Kirksey, though, is more my brother now. I was able to forgive him by the grace of God, but maybe it was me who needed the forgiving. People have to be able to control their appetites, desires to be of a benefit to people. Because within each of us is a light that shines. But if we fail to discipline ourselves, our dreams will slip away with the passing sunset.

Kirksey said to me "Man," as in, "What do you know about Noreaga [A rapper], man?" or "Better tell me next time you're going to the lunch room so I can go with you, man."

No person could have prepared me for what was to come better than Jon. He was impressive. He said the most revolting things in a sharp, cunning wit, so much so it made me jealous. But if he can make it, anyone can.

I understood he was rather bright in high school, but his behavior was no indication. He entered our room usually around 4 or 5 a.m. after a night of smoking weed at Felts Hall, or drinking beer, or, smoking weed and drinking beer. He made fun of people, on one occasion drawing a picture of our resident assistant giving oral sex to someone on the football team and posting it on the RA's door for all to see. He was an oddball of sorts, without rhyme or reason why he would pull some of these things. Jon taught me, however, some of the ways I did not want to be in manhood, how to be a man. I hope Jon is doing well at this very moment. He taught me so much.

He taught me so much.

Grandpa's demise was fresh in my mind. The grieving process was tough to deal with, especially being away from the people I cared so deeply about.

I was anxious and sleep-deprived. Sometimes I would just lie on my bed in our 15-foot by 9-foot room at night thinking about grandpa. My role model was alive no longer.

Grandpa's demise was fresh in my mind. The grieving process was tough to deal with, especially being away from the people I cared so deeply about.

I was anxious and sleep-deprived. Sometimes I would just lie on my bed in our 15-foot by 9-foot room at night thinking about grandpa. My role model was alive no longer.

At lonely times in my brick residence hall at Southern, my journal would be my best friend, a channel between me and the creator, wherein

I listed accomplishments, failures, successes and let-downs. My darkest fears could go down in that journal at Thompson Point, depending on my boldness in a given night. As a person is writing, he presses down on paper and that constant pressure—pen on paper—is soothing in itself, a kind of flowing exercise as the hand scribbles up and down the page.

Journals need not be neat and tidy either. They would be best if they expressed the person's whole self. Journaling is *the* place to express your uniqueness. If drawing happy faces on the left side is how to express this on the page, smiley faces are good.

I wanted to write since that semester at 19 when I broke in my first paper journal. The journal helped me to express feelings I could not explain. I soon understood this was giving me a closer walk with God, not knowing *just* how much at the time. I wanted to be more like Jesus. I believe when one person puts whatever down in paper, that is powerful and moving. It is liberating to write down a sincere, unabashed thought. Journalism is awesome because of the good news. We are alive today because of the hope in our hearts. We must learn that art of speaking from our hearts also. I always wanted to find better ways to write.

Journaling was special to me because of the time I spent in Staunton. I felt Staunton. I *was* Staunton. It felt good. All these storied people around. All they've been through made them stronger.

One of the few best things about journalism is reporting on issues. A journalist can give people insight they would have otherwise missed, and important insight, thus capturing the interest of an audience and subsequently uplifting a community.

College was a glorious part of my life. People all over would benefit from some type of education after high school. I was enamored with the learning process at Southern Illinois University at Carbondale and also intimidated. Popular guys who looked like they could have been all state on their football teams scrambled to make friends and introduce themselves to people. Quieter students cut out for Architecture or Computer Science were looking for buddies, too.

Eddie Frey showed up within the first week. He stood 5'11" 165 pounds with wavy surfer-like hair. He was athletic, though not a fan of any of the four major sports. He was the model of health, did not smoke cigarettes and did not drink. He skateboarded and laughed easily. Dude was comfortable and I knew I wanted to be this guy's friend. Eddie was a city kid even though from the 'burbs. He stayed in the Mariana Towers, these tall apartments in downtown Chicago. Eddie attended an art institute in the city before coming to Southern. He was so friendly, with this magnetic personality. When he stepped into a room people were just drawn to him.

We hung outside near the lake occasionally, smoking weed, trying to prove ourselves tough as cowhide. My habit was not broken; it hung on like an abscess a person continues to lick upon, so it doesn't go away. The infected area remained irritated because the person continued to bother it.

But I was on my way, as the habit had gone from an everyday thing to a once-a-week occurrence. Turning back on the drug was all I could do. It did me no good. Mary Jane was no friend to me anymore. She only gave me bad dreams and made me sick.

Eddie, Mike Sanderson and I smoked potent Cannabis in Eddie's room one time when Eddie got his video camera out. He taped us smoking. Mike threw up into the sink. Eddie captured the spectacle. Then he pointed the camera on me and I started freaking. After looking into the camera and saying some words, all that went through my mind was getting out.

So, after lying on the floor briefly, I hopped up and left the room. Sleep was out of the question. I tried, but to no avail. I was so stinking terrified if that tape, should anybody get a hold of it, people would be so terribly disappointed, I could not grasp the dreams, so alive in me, was my thought.

I put up with bad thoughts. I put up with not being able to sleep for what felt like hours. Then a thought occurred. It was though I had an epiphany: there was only one way to get to sleep—a nice, fresh run.

I appreciated that night, in a tremendously significant way, the power of physical exercise in tough situations, even in terrifying anxiety. I could have killed the man. The night was one of the few scariest times in my life. I figured, if people were to see the tape, how could I be a positive, motivating force in people's lives? I would always be brought back to that stinking video, the proof of uncleanness. Fears I felt at Eddie's place and afterward in my room, however, spurned me to recognize, if my experience with drugs is brought into the open, people can be reached, and hopefully changed by the dark valleys through which they don't have to travel.

My experience can reach people. The tape simply adds more flame to the gloomy firetraps I previously fell into, but pits I would now avoid, because the light of truth shone bright. That was my last recollection of smoking weed.

I can see something through that bleak, painful experience. Through all the darkness and aloneness there was something, someone. I believe God was looking out for me. His Spirit somehow guided me along, through the dark. I was in deep sometimes. What felt scary at the moment was comforted by a run; a simple, childish run.

I began to get some footing. I was understanding my body like never before. I sat out in front of our residence hall. I sat there between the building and Thompson Lake, only 20 feet from the water on those warm autumn afternoons. I spread my legs in a stretching position and sat. I listened. I listened to the gentle breeze blow past my ears. I listened to opportunity. All this freedom and new friends. I looked forward. 'Twas no use in looking back now. I could not mope over spilled beans. I could not let my previous lack interfere with the harvest in front. I remembered sometimes, however. I evaluated my life.

Bobbye

Bobbye and I have never had even a decent relationship. I always wanted a dad who would play catch with me because I loved sports so. My grandpa was my surrogate; always there for me when I needed him. A few other men stepped up to the plate to act as male figures for me to follow. In all this time through college, however, I did not see him. Not once. Bobbye, my biological father, was an art teacher in the East St. Louis elementary school system. I often thought about the way his name was spelled. Bob-bye I would think, separating the words into individual parts in my head. He was there for me financially when I got to be about ten years of age. Bobbye, as we always called him, was a man full of promises. I would receive phone calls from him of a year. Bobbye would ask how I was doing and so on. He provided the sperm so I could be a human being with my mother. That is how I used to look at the whole thing.

Bobbye would come by unannounced and wonder how I was doing. We would talk for a while; things would be swell. Here's the kicker—and men never put your children through this because when you toy with their emotions you wrench their hearts also and everyone deserves better than that—he would say he would call me around Christmas so we could get together. This happened often times that he would call and not deliver so do speak. He would wind up and not throw the pitch. Bobbye would call, but not slap on the cheese. One night, the first football game I played in high school, he was there. So was my girlfriend and my mother. Everything in my life was right then. I even got a sack on the quarterback.

DRUGS AND FOOTBALL

I saw Bobbye after the game and he was Bob-bye. I do not want to rag on my biological parent by bringing up all the negatives he ever did for me. Hopefully, what I say can resonate with some guy who is unsure of whether or not to become a parent. Because this sensation leaves you empty when at such a young age. Bobbye left me feeling sick with my situation. I felt at times I was not good enough. My self-esteem was damaged. Bobbye had a knack for not showing up for the game. I suppose I have not forgiven him in my heart yet. I have forgiven him in my mind and I have said I forgive him in confidence to my Christian brothers at Vineyard back in Carbondale. I failed to make a concerted effort at seeking him out and telling him how he made me feel, no matter what emotional scars I still bear. For me to be able to stand firm with my head up I've got to say to him he has wronged me. I need to tell him in person how his actions made me feel insignificant as a human being, how I was searching for a dad and never found one quite like him. How I found men who believed in me. How people saw me through ordeals such as racism when he could have backed me up. Yes, even should he walk away as I tell him these things, he can just as soon listen from my lips the bad things he put me through. Not to humiliate him. I have to see the expression on his face when he hears words that have meaning. He growls at me when I groan for imperfection. This tiny voice inside saying hug me, daddy. I want to feel important, too. I want to be grown up like you some day and work a real job. Then I want to tell him how I wanted to say, "show me how." I want to tell him I wanted to ask him how to wrestle because he was supposed to be all-state at Cahokia High School. He went to state or something. Point is he was good. I want to let him know I am not afraid anymore. I want to tell him I cannot be afraid of a world that was a challenge I had to face when I felt unwanted. I can tell him things were easier with a grandpa who cared enough to take me to NAPA Auto Parts. I knew Bobbye was the thing I most wanted to strive for. I do not write this to put the man down, but to let other future parents know a child hurts when he is let go of. I want to know what comfort a grandmother with warm hands and a steady smile is. I want to let the person, Bobbye, know a steady man is an uncle named Louis who would listen no matter what, even if he didn't say much in return. I want to tell him—Bobbye—

what a mess I felt I was and then realized I was just normal. I would like to let Bobbye know saying bye is not okay in my book. Saying bye is not acceptable when the heart is a child's. Saying take care is much easier. I knew the importance of knowing a dad. I know what it means to have other men step up to the plate and do the job by simply being there; listening to me even when they know their words are not enough to solve all my problems. I know sometimes words cannot express the various things we want to express and I am thankful to the men in my life who stepped up and made the pinch hit. Thanking people; encouraging people is what it is about. This man-Bobbye—needs to know I don't hold this against him, however, these years of pain. They will all be okay if he knows simply I forgive him for the pain he caused in my life if he comes to that acknowledgment. You've got to be willing to recognize you did wrong to accept forgiveness. It's crazy how that works, for it is good to be willing to forgive someone. This is an excellent first step. But for someone to accept that forgiveness he must understand he did you wrong. Letting Bobbye Luster know I am willing to forgive, that is the biggest thing I need to do.

An indescribable feeling brews in the heart of a forgiver. Mercy has a profound way of humbling. Sometimes people do not even see they are in need of forgiveness. Possibly they say, well, people did the same to me when I was in your position. Why should I do any different to you? But I've got to forgive in my heart. I've got to let go even when the person does not see the error. Mercy does not make you less than a man. Forgiveness transcends the petty. A man who forgives with an open heart frees his mind at the same moment. Conviction is like a tiny voice inside the head telling a person the right move to make. An equation has been proven: Forgiveness equals love no matter how difficult this concept of love is to achieve while we are still here on earth, in human form. As words have danced across this screen I have noticed actions, rather inactions which need to be amended.

But enough about personal struggle for now and more about service. More about serving the neediest of us and how this brings us low as well, and that in a good way bringing us closer to ourselves. Because through courage of the downtrodden to move on breathes encouragement into us.

    Sylvia Lawson lived in the Abbey nursing home in Carbondale, Ill. I asked if she wanted to go for a stroll and I could push. Rolling a woman down the hall in a nursing home may seem, well, not awfully worthwhile. When a person sits down and thinks about it, though, a woman in a nursing home lives in the facility for 365 days a year. People perform service for her every day, making sure her bed gets cleaned, making certain she is fed properly. But when somebody comes along without pretense and speaks to her, she is pleased beyond what words could say. When you are having the least fun in doing a service such as this is when the time is most fulfilling too, because you are doing a service which is not required of you on a bad day, when you could be watching the Cubs game, if that's your hobby.

    I sat in there, uncomfortable for a few moments because of the stench of her urine and excrement, but after awhile, got used to it. Ms. Lawson, a small woman, was aged with curly hair and a frail figure yet stately. She still had spunk.

    She did not usually say things I could spin off and have a conversation with her about, but she was a talker. She lowly said things about men in her life or about what she used to do when she was living with family. We sat in her room. We went to the front lounge area, sitting by the debonair flowers. Simply being with her was a benefit to her. You could see it on her face. People can learn a lot just by sitting with someone and not saying anything. When a person has sat through a conversation not going anywhere, fortunate tidings come. That person knows his very self is being put to use as a companion, if nothing else, to the person sitting across from him.

    Americans talk constantly, though. And I believe this is something we need to work on. Oh, I love America, from the pit of my stomach and from the depths of my football cleats. We played board games in a dinner hall during a party one night. It was a hoot. Sylvia and several others of us played and talked how our families were. Then as we continued playing Sylvia moved out of her place a bit, and peered her head over toward the

TV. She was at peace. She gazed across the room, watching the television, everything was all right.

Other days pushing Ms. Lawson's wheelchair was a crowd-pleaser. I came over and went directly to Ms. Lawson's room. I asked whether she wanted a push around the building. She accepted, and there we went, down the hallway 5' wide, with doors to rooms spaced a long way from one another. Residents viewed us traveling. She kept moving while sitting. Wasn't that something? At 1.5 miles per hour we traveled, eyes peering at us along the wing. They looked up, and became interested. We passed by and peoples' eyes lit up. We were a spectacle, dinner theatre, smiling at the on-lookers. It was amazing. Ms. Lawson must have been such a stunningly good-looking woman people were automatically attracted to her. I felt a celebrity status. People looked out, and perked right up. Some peeped their heads out their doors and saw what we were up to. Some asked questions and we slowed down even more—we couldn't slow down much more than that, so we stopped. People were so very interested, and we learned much from each other. The smell *is* a small obstacle. I found, no matter how bad the smell, you get over it. The odor just becomes another of the thousands of smells we take in.

Holding a muttering woman's hand at the nursing home is sobering, uplifting in the possibilities realized that, well, I can go ahead and live my life so I can have complete fulfillment at her age, should the blessing come my way to even get there, for, if somebody was there for each of our Sylvia Lawsons, we would see the Kingdom of Heaven open up before our eyes.

Elderly folks need encouragement, too, because we are all people in this world. We may look different, talk different. But we all bleed red and put on our pants the same way. Well, maybe Americans all put on their pants the same way. The Dutch wear them suspenders.

Encouraging is of the essence these days with too much wrong going on abroad and, it seems like we are really at a loss for good things to tell each other. Simply *pick out something small* about a person. A guy may walk more upright than most, carrying a joy about him. Some other woman always has a good attitude. When people test her, and push her to limits the average person would push back for, she takes it in stride, not being pushed over, but being bold, not resisting the evil person, but killing others with kindness.

Possibly a man just opened the door for an elderly woman and you could comment on his courtesy toward others. All sorts of ways people can let others know they are worth more than any dollar sign, any new pickup.

As far as conversational etiquette goes, a person should avoid asking how another is doing and then just walk away right after asking. A person may have something to get off his chest. We are a people, undivided under liberty, justice, for all. When we see shadows in our own lives, let us root them out.

This book is important to me. Writing is my life, my vocation. Encouragement is imperative because we can build the temple of the body—in others—through encouraging gestures and words. Encouragement. Encouragement must be the air we breathe, the flame that lights our fire. When we encourage one another, we make them strong and we are stronger, too. It puts a special wind up under the sails of others.

Martin Luther King Jr. said we are all bound together in an inescapable garment of destiny. We have found each other throughout the ages, from the first years of man until now. Now does not end after our bodies have gone and passed. No, we must encourage. Whatever affects one directly affects all indirectly, King said.

Degradation is the antithesis of encouragement. Encouragement is the cure to a false feeling of inadequacy. Passing on a compliment means the world to a man who just lost his wife to breast cancer. Uplifting words can be empowering to a woman who has been suffering from kidney disease.

Encouraging words bring us closer, make each person feel like part of a team. Togetherness is the result of encouragement; inclusion, rather than exclusion is what we will all experience one day when the long, dark path of the world has traveled into the light of the greatest roads man has ever seen, roads built by hands worn, together through charity and goodwill, in a truly global village.

We are great as a people because we are free to do what profession we choose. Americans must take full advantage of this. Enjoying work is one of the central keys to life. It is an indispensable freedom we have here in the states. By that I mean a happy life filled with joy, one where fulfillment is the norm. Journalism is enjoyable.

Disseminating information is an important privilege in the current state of affairs. People have the responsibility of putting out facts humbly. Only with a humble heart can men change the world while on TV or during a radio address. A newsperson must train his mind to be equipped to deal with new events in both a timely and a responsible fashion, with tact, with sound judgment and with a humble heart and level ego. He must keep emotion intact with the help of a journal, writing down regularly, his thoughts.

A journalist must keep his *writing skills* sharp, because even in a baseball game, a triple play could happen, or back-to-back-to-back home runs for that matter. The newsperson must know how he views teams he covers and gradually blend in his style from facts. Facts always come first, though.

Humility is required in journalism, because, as mundane as the profession can seem at times one day gay marriage may be made legal, or the Supreme Court may render a landmark decision on abortion. Therein, the journalist must use tact and caution in relaying to the reader in the most appealing way, what he has gathered from his sources of information.

Montgomery Improvement Association was falsely accused of misappropriating funds by one of its members during the struggle for racial equality in the 1950s. Martin Luther King, leader of the MIA, straightened the record about another accusation, that some in the organization had large egos.

The nonviolent movement was highly covered by the mass media. Dr. King said he denied the accusations of bigness. It is true, he said, that some of the leaders received national and international publicity, but only the shallow-minded are excited over publicity.

In going into a news story, the reporter needs to look at the situation as if he were telling the story to his best friend, as a *Daily Egyptian* reporter said.

A basic cordial relationship benefits the reporter as well as he who the writer gets the information from. In essence, the two do become friends, even should they not hang out regularly.

One professor told me at Southern Illinois, The best reporters are those who can put up a wall with their sources. It has taken me years to see the wisdom in what he was saying, though it seemed cold at the time. People do need to look at a story objectively. Two people can, however, act kind to one another even in a newsgathering situation.

Publicity of the journalist may be his largest detriment. Meaning, a journalist is being of the most service when he is like a vessel, carrying information to the audience and his own persona is out of the way.

Going in-depth requires a journalist to prepare himself for the interview. A steadfast journalist must be strong in faith and at least consider focused prayer. By doing so the reporter readies herself for whatever comes. Walter Cronkite reported on the assassination of President John F. Kennedy. As he relayed the information on a nationally broadcast television news station, a tear welled up in his eye, he paused, removed his glasses, wiped his eye and went back to the account.

Cronkite spoke at SIU during the last portion of my schooling in Carbondale and said the tear was a normal human emotion. Best journalists, best whoever, are connected to their own individual emotion, with no switch they are keeping their fingers on in the back of here or there like some dastardly wizard of Oz, waiting to switch off the beat as the difficulties of life arise.

Humility

Humility is essential. Humility means a person allowing himself to become in his own mind and the view of others, as small and low as a snail. Allowing the will to submit to grace is a challenge and when we suffer for a redemptive purpose, we can set people free.

Elijah Lovejoy, former writer for the *Alton (Ill.) Telegraph*, once said the best place for a man to die is when he dies for man. Striving fervently to become completely selfless is noble and one of the great objectives in life. Men and women can live the legacy of being the most celebrated pop stars in music. Dudes can roll around on dubs (flashy car rims), behaving just fine. He is still fine when he remembers the greatest of what this life stands for.

Only when a man humbles himself low to where he will wipe a woman's cheek without hesitation if she threw up in the same room can he be considered selfless. Humility as therein described is actually the stuff relationships grow on. Selflessness. Along with courage and humility men in my life were endowed with a great deal of humility and discipline. They set a standard for these qualities I could endeavor to attain.

Shooting for the stars requires giving of yourself. The more we are given, the more will be expected of us. Serving is the best thing a woman or man can do with time afforded them as giving all of one's self is our ultimate fulfillment on this planet. Service should not be performed, if the *feeling* is the primary motivation. Making the *other* person's day is more than reward enough.

DRUGS AND FOOTBALL

People do remarkable acts in barely noticeable ways, too. Paying for another man's check at a restaurant happens on occasion. Makes me think in myself, "Did that just happen?" Some people are who we call angels among us who do good deeds, making benevolent charity look like it was always meant to be.

Watching Oprah's program makes me want to be someone who has been given much and give more of what has been given to me. Oprah keeps coming up because she is doing what she can with the talents she has been given.

Becoming the greatest journalist you can be means becoming great at serving others, being transparent and selfless. Using the body as an instrument is the way people in any profession use their skills to their utmost. Instruments which glorify the person make for quick rewards that do not last. Moth and rust will corrupt. The same principle goes with ourselves. We only last for so long. We are but dust in the wind the band Kansas said. Each day we would be wise to live as if though it would be our last. When folks use their bodies to uplift others through actions, serving others who cannot reciprocate, they choose to use their bodies as instruments in the *highest* form of service.

Oprah's squad performs as nonchalantly. Nonchalant should be the word to set the standard for journalism. Unassuming. Humble. Giving of the self is what writing for a mass audience need is in its finest hour. Gail, Oprah's friend said about Oprah, she uses television for what it is meant to be used for—to create community. Superb.

Building up the community is what life is about anyway, right?

I was refined by watching a man on one of the worst days in New York City, a day that will live in infamy. I recollect viewing an awesome leader on the scene, visible and concerned about the people of his city.

New York City mayor Rudolph Giulianni makes me glad to be a human being, and an American.

On the morning of September 11, 2001, I was in my bed on West Ridge Street in Carbondale when awoken by a radio report with people screaming in New York City. After considering the whole deal to be some sick joke I just put my head back in the pillows and tried to go back to sleep. I finally woke up and saw the live events unfolding on television. Good and evil collided on 9/11.

We weren't necessarily the good ones either, just the victims. I read this article a few years back. Man speaking in the editorial wanted the reader to forgive the perpetrators of September 11 as, he said, we may never know when we might need forgiveness.

Sentiment was alive shortly after 9/11 to simply be hostile toward Arabs—not a smart move. Comprehending another people is what it is all about. Mohandas Gandhi said ¾ of the world's problems would be solved if we looked at the situation through the view of our adversaries. I believe in that right now.

Martin Luther King envisioned an action-filled peace. Creative nonviolent non-resistance to evil means using the brain to actively think up ways to resist without hurting the one who inflicts violence.

I believe Giulianni acted with extraordinary character, and unquestionable commitment to his people, in agape love through and through, and this, just by showing up. He was the best on one of the few worst days his people had ever seen. Just by seeing him out there with the people, for the people, gave me chills. He could have been in an office somewhere, talking about how to rebound, while his city tumbled. But Rudolph Giullianni walked through the fire, showing the finest courage men are capable of. He reflected a wonderful, deep care for his fellow man. He also went to the funerals of victims afterward. He said his father always told him to go to the funerals. It's *easy* to go to the weddings, Giulianni said, but people *need* you at funerals. The man made it count—on a bad day.

Pain happens when a young boy puts his hand on a skillet fresh off the fire and he jumps back, crying to mom. Pain teaches. The boy will not touch the skillet when it is hot again. Children pick up on pain just as adults do. The older people get, the less likely they are to indulge in illegal drugs. Pain the body absorbs from these drugs teaches a person after a point to slow down before wrecking the person physically, mentally and spiritually. Just because we feel pain and we may experience discomfort in some situation means not that we should avoid the circumstance. It means we should give a try. This risk could be the very step that sets the soul free.

Overcoming some roadblock seen up ahead is superb. This tingly feeling wells up inside a person giving her the ability to shake adversity like a halfback stunning a middle linebacker by spinning off the initial impact and landing into the end zone for six.

We are passing as the wind. Our lives are but a mist. But through the valleys, a person can have strength, even when the world looks stacked against him. Just like when a wide receiver goes a few steps out then in on a three-step quarterback drop, and sees the linebacker playing a little back in the middle he knows he may get hit. When he catches the pass, however, the impact does not matter because he has advanced his team farther down the field. Making the catch was the important thing, not the force of resistance, which was inevitable.

Women go through child labor, and experience considerable pain when the baby comes. But afterward pain subsides. They rejoice because a new girl is born into the world.

Hope is something I wanted to convey. The world is full of idiotic happenings. People are persecuted for their religions, for their ways of life. Parents need to play with their kids. If Johnny is outside playing basketball in the driveway, then Suzy, his mother, should go out and play with him. Basketball may not be the thing to do with the kids all the time, but, sometimes, at least once every three times seeing them play, a parent could go out and play. Playing is important. No matter what it is. Basketball is good, but, any sport, for that matter, will suffice. Grown ups could stand to be not so grown up. Holla, as the ol' bard Shakespeare used to write.

Here at SIU I saw a dream open up for me. I saw things I had never seen. I felt as though I could do anything. The whole world was filled to the brim with different avenues. I could take another street every day and not go wrong. At junctures it felt like a maze.

SIU's campus was like a little town, but with 20,000 residents. It was crazy. People walked by in the morning, in the afternoon. Different buildings held different people, teaching different ideas on different topics. They were all created equal, however. This person sustained a desire for this discipline. This person adhered to another. We were on a college campus. Primary responsibility is to learn. I could go all over the place and try various things I always had an interest in.

Watching people had given me a release. So theater was a natural outlet to give others something choreographed, and well-rehearsed to look upon. All the TV watching earlier had in some peculiar way done a wonder. But I was through watching others with no reciprocation. The tube had inspired within me a yearning to be in front of others—to put it all out there. Hey, I was ready for others to watch me. I signed up for an introductory voice class with Harrison Key.

Harrison was a manly man. He formed sentences well, yet was not a stereotype of theatre. He was bald, with a beard and mustache, slender, and very strong. He was athletic and used to play baseball competitively. He was no namby pamby.

Our class met on the main stage. We filed slowly, most of us uncertainly, onto the black landscape. A significant portion of us had not taken a theatre performance class before that semester. We knew not what to expect.

Harrison told us politely to get on our backs. We got on our backs.

He told us to release the air. He walked around slowly, much like a general would pace around his troops as they do calisthenics.

"Haaauuh!" and we, in a scattered flurry, let a long wind out. It was strange at first, but unique in a free, unhinged manner. Our whole class of about 16 people sprawled across the bare stage. We began to loosen up. The several hundred audience seats were empty. All that shone upon us was a sufficient row of spotlights shining from the top down. Most of us were apprehensive. It was a little intimidating, and liberating at the same time. There we were—freedom. We could yell as loud as we wished.

"Picture someone on the ceiling," he said. "And you are trying to tell them something." He continued to step softly. He told us in theatre our bodies were the equipment, and this concept stuck with me. Body is equipment. I was trying to make the mind, body, spirit connection here.

"Take in all the air," he said. I took it all in, breathing upward, arching my back. "Fill up your lungs." Felt as though my entire system began to refresh. I felt as though in the same due proportion I held the pot smoke in my lungs, the clean southern Illinois oxygen was now working to heal them. There was a sweet release. I was about ready for liftoff "and then release it in a deep exhale," he said.

"Huh!" we said.

Theatre allowed us to let loose. Our main place to meet and make plans was the green room. Just the name alone lent it an inviting tone. Green? Come on. What do you purposely make green? But in theatre, your differentness was what made you. You were fine whether black, white, Asian, Hispanic, Eskimo, non-Pacific islander, all that. Gay folks came in there, strong people, weak people, athletes, dweebs. This is where we were like the weak things of this world—shaming the strong. Like the foolish things of the world—shaming the wise. We were vessels. You could be all you wanted to be—you just had to be different. You had to be different. Then you had to be about it. You had to come to a juncture where you felt at ease with your eccentricity. I was breaking away. I was breaking away from what I had expected from my hometown life. I knew something now. I knew something bigger, something better. I knew theater. These people were odd. And you could be anything to anyone. You just *had* to *know* you were different. Everyone already *knows* they are different. But you **had** to **know** you were **different** and never try to hide it. You had to embrace your difference. You had to grasp onto that special something, and never let it go. Those were the people who were the most gifted. They brought out the best of the talents they had. They were unfazed by risks taken and failed. Because in their risk-taking they had tried. They were the most celebrated. You could be on the Moe Lab theatre stage with a pink sweater and in a wheelchair and people were going to say you had it going on. If you worked at taking this art form to an even higher plane you had the respect of your peers. You had to respect it. 'Cause everybody was different. They could be made fun of no longer. They made themselves the center piece of this weird, sad, bright, encouraging, ostentatious, suave, calculated, and complex little world, where people performed every moment of their existence. People picked up the line and put it down. They had enough of being made fun of. They had enough, and were not going to have it any longer. No. They were going to show the world what they were made of—who they are. Yes, they would show others you cannot make fun of me any more. No, I have this self-deprecating humor. I am in the highest form of physical art. I will not be made a slave to a society's perceptions of me. They made it from where they were. They made it, and they made it everyday, because they were a little queer.

I was a little unusual. I guess I was different like these people. I was a special color. But so many people around here were oddballs and class clowns. Some behaved freakishly. They were rejects and models. All of them were different. They were so very weird, it finally made me feel at home. Their presence soothed me.

Robert Barton, author of *Acting: Onstage and Off*, said we are all actors. But best actors actually forget about *themselves* when performing. Those bold souls use their bodies as instruments to tell the story. We set the body free when we train it, completely focusing on the task at hand, making the body submit to the character.

A Deacon spoke on the Eternal World Television Network one night. He talked about behaving with his wife when they argued. Deacon didn't say a thing to his wife as she chewed at him. Deacon just stood there and took it.

A few days later he was angry. He said he learned to become vulnerable in the presence of his wife. He was no wimp, but a spiritual soldier and I had never seen a more spiritually intense Catholic. A fire burned inside him, fueling a great lesson.

He was a man. He possessed in his character some of the greatest qualities: patience and love. Methodically work at being vulnerable in front of your wife if you've got one. Show her you are the head, but you can be sensitive. A man is tougher when he lets his wife know his feelings.

Women actually desire men more so when they display emotion openly. A man who has a problem being open with his mate will get into more arguments with her than an emotionally uninhibited man. He holds onto something balled up inside, as a pitcher winds up for a split-seam fast ball, holding it in his hand without the release.

People learn how to succeed by failing. **Overcoming** fear—Taking stock of the personal inventory, as Oregon acting professor Robert Barton calls it, is important in dealing with fear, and overcoming it. Fear is just one of those things which *should not* be a hindrance. People just wonder about stuff. People can wonder what happens if...this is wrong. But it has not happened.

People should be concerned, first of all. Worrying never helps. I've heard people say, "I'll worry about that later." Nonsense. People only worry about things if they tell themselves they cannot accomplish the task.

An audition for a play at SIU-Carbondale made me worry one time. I came in there, hopped in the 40-person line, pumped.

Waiting is the worst part about those situations. Chatters spread throughout the line as people singularly filed out of Moe Lab Theatre following the audition. People in line started talking to me. If there are some problems at home then I'll listen, but these guys were trying to make small talk.

This was my big shot. I wanted to dazzle. What I had to do was already in me, but then there was all this nervous energy people passed around like cheap drinks. This was not even necessarily tension, but icky idleness. 'S all good and I even did well at the audition. But, I'm not worried about it.

Preparation can quash that nervous anxiety-type stuff. When an actor dives into a text, or an offensive lineman on a football team intently practices extending the arms on blocks in practice, the only nervousness that may come is before stepping onstage or before the first ball is snapped. I've been in important situations where I would not even get nervous.

People can overcome fear by rehearsal and commitment. Preparation is essential. If we have a strong fear in God, we have no need to fear daily obstacles. Actually, each of us can learn from one another's trials and bring each other comfort in trials of need. Overcoming takes assistance. People must ask for help when help is needed and not have a do-it-alone attitude.

The play I was set to try out for was The Beaux Stratagem—a swashbuckling, sword-fighting, comedy—a rip-roaring good time. I just wanted the challenge. I thought of the movie Good Will Hunting and how the movie's essence changed me.

Best actors empathize, or understand, the trials a character is going through—
the pain and the joy that character would be perceiving in this world we live in. Audience members need to take lessons from movies, as the best movies teach us about ourselves. It is important to know what the director and actors feel about the human condition in relation to subject matter.

Films have gotten me through jams and *Good Will Hunting* used to be my favorite. I've probably watched the movie 20 times. Matt Damon and Ben Affleck considered the audience when they wrote this Academy-Award winning screenplay. Attention to detail was evident.

Movie's synopsis is as follows: Will Hunting is an orphan in South Boston who has grown up with an uncanny intelligence, and in unfortunate circumstances. He works at Massachusetts Institute of Technology, a prestigious college in Boston, as a janitor, and while maintaining the halls does anonymous, intricate math problems on a board outside a math class only elite mathematicians can solve. Hunting, with no formal instruction in higher education, completes the equations quickly and decisively.

Down the road he attacks a man his age who had abused him in kindergarten and meets with a psychologist as part of a plea bargain so he will not have to serve time. Hunting is required to meet with Shawn Maguire, a community college Psychology professor, who grew up in the same neighborhood, but is old enough to be Will's father. A love story is also a major portion of the movie. Hunting looks for intimacy with a Harvard University student, Skyla. He is cautious with her. He wants her to be all he ever wanted.

He seeks out and finds his place in this world as a man rather than a brain; a lover instead of a fighter. The film is intriguing because Hunting is still standing at the end, no matter how much dirt he shrugs off. Though he had friends and spoke with a confident veneer, until he spoke with Maguire, he was unsure of himself. His trials made him stronger.

Damon and Affleck explained even the most discrete details. We understood why Shawn was so stirred up after Will talked about Shawn's wife. The audience could deduce there were demons from Will's abusive childhood, ones causing his insecurity and inhibiting him emotionally.

Even the more subtle aspects came into the open. Will wore muscle shirts frequently because he wanted to be known as a tough guy.

Will walks the room inspecting the collection of books while in Shawn's office for the first time, as the considerably larger Maguire is seated.

Shawn: You work out, huh?
Will: What, you lift?
S: Yeah.
W: Eh, Nautilus?
S: Nah. Free weights.
W: Oh, really?
S: Yeah.
W: Free weights, huh?
S: Yeah, big time.
W: Eh.
S: Just like that.
W: What do you bench?
S: 285. What do you bench?
W: (Looking at a picture)…You paint that?

We understood why the tension between Maguire and his former roommate in college, Professor Lambeau. Every detail in the movie was made clear for the viewer's benefit.

The most compelling aspect of the screenplay was how clearly the screenwriters skillfully pulled the need for a male influence out of Will Hunting's character. You've got a boy, lost, wondering what is the best move for his life, and it took an experienced man to direct him to the right path.

'S so good I had those men who stepped up in my life. I always had men to show the way. Had I not had these men I don't know what would have happened.

I chose Will Hunting's monologue at the end of the movie to give for my audition. I waited outside until they called my name. I was a little nervous, but figured, "What is the worst that could happen?"

Really, what could happen that would be too very bad?

I entered our school's main performance space, the McLeod Theatre stage. A light shown on me from above. I sat down on a single, plain chair in the vast expanse of a stage. I looked out to the empty audience seats. 'Bout 20 rows back several professor-type men and women sat, looking on.

Still.

Waiting for the show to begin.

But this was my first. I had never done this. Why were they looking at me? I felt cheap, like I was on sale. Like a $3 suit. I felt like a Christmas Ham at Wal-Mart Supercenter the shopper looks at, licking their lips, because they will soon devour the well-presented bird. I was on display. I was made a spectacle to the whole world, to angels as well as to men. I sat there.

"Hmmum…Why shouldn't I work for the NSA…That's a tough question…but I'…"

"Why don't you," somebody interjected from the sparse crowd. "Why don't you give your name, and what monologue you will be giving."

Okay. So I would. I *would* give them the name of the monologue.

"My name…is Brett Luster. And. I am going to say a monologue from the movie Good Will Hunting.…

"Why shouldn't I work for the NSA? That's a tough question. But I'll give it a shot." And the monologue went on. My voice had little range of inflection. It was nearly monotone. I don't think I had anyone fooled I could have been someone who the NSA would have *wanted* to work for them. But I continued on. I paused, I re-grouped, and went on with the speech. All the while, I knew I could get 'er done if I took the time, composed myself, and focused on the character, rather than those intent faces in the rows beyond. Afterward I got up.

"Thanks," I said, and walked off the stage.

Next week I got into the green room. I leaned over the swank, late 70s style couch, up at the soft bulletin board for the call-backs sheet. My…name…there was my name! They wanted me back. They liked me.

They really liked me. It was great. I felt like a million. I went to the callback. They gave me the part of "Servant." I was thrilled. I was in theater! Yes!

Challenges make you better for what you could become should you succeed. *Even if they don't the situation prepares you; action through the nerves refines you.*

I tried out for the Southern Illinois University basketball team at 6 a.m. one day. I did not play for my high school and was a bit overweight. If I learned one thing from that unsuccessful tryout, it was to keep moving with the ball and keep it away from the defender, 'cause this guy from East St. Louis stripped the rock from me like I was a first grader.

When a person goes for something, he has an idea what he is up against next go 'round.

Human body is like a flow of streams. The body is made up of about 70 percent water. When streams get low they tend to stagnate, causing such a body of water to slow. So long as humans take care of the physical gifts they have been dealt and treat them like gifts people will be healthy.

I want to use my body for something good. Disabled people who need wheelchairs to function are all over. I wonder sometimes, how they would feel if they had all functional limbs.

I think people would go wild, running like cheetahs through the Kenyan landscape. Rehabilitated people would swim like a salmon in a rushing river. People have opportunities all over the place to develop their bodies to benefit themselves in daily life and above all, the human condition.

I have been fortunate to have used the weight room as a tool to overcome drug abuse.

California Governor and expert bodybuilder Arnold Schwarzenegger one time said he feels comfortable around the weights. Being in a room of iron is an experience. By looking around a person can visualize lifts. Trying is the funnest part, too. Living in there, gazing around at the seemingly indestructible metal, is humbling.

Knowing the body can only hoist so much weight makes a person feel as if she has come down to earth. Feeling comfortable in the weight room lends itself an ease all together refreshing. One might think, "if I can be at ease in here, with all this heavy equipment around, then I can be solid when I step outside." Handling it around the weights means maintaining out in the real world becomes easier. Self-discipline is a fruit of the Spirit.

Swollen in the gym is actually a good thing, unlike when a person gets a bruised lip. When a man swells after any lift he is applying the maximum amount of force on his muscles in the most efficient manner. The man is going through *hypertrophy* where the muscle grows as opposed to atrophy where muscles shrink through non-use. Attaining hypertrophy is possible for the vast majority of human beings.

Governor Schwarzenegger said a person has to work a muscle at least 150-200 times to get the best workout.

But just so long as a person gets out there is the most important part. He must participate to achieve results.

John Kennedy said we are a nation accustomed to spectation. We look instead of play. We ride instead of walk. Our existence deprives us of the minimum physical activity essential for healthy living.

Forward is where this country should be going. Forward is always good. People can never lose with progress.

Reality television, too much of it, ruins America's drive. Reality television promotes watching instead of taking part in; following rather than leading; sit down, not stand up. Quantity of reality TV is bad, yes.

For a while there I was a little concerned from all the shows and how much America paid attention. We had Real World. Road Rules. We had At home with Flava Flav. "Come on," I was thinking. I was like, man, if we do not use self-restraint this will break our backs.

We could be out *doing* what we see on TV, getting exercise, instead of *being at home*, watching it. But action takes moves. We have got to move to be a country worthy of the title, "Land of the free." United States can only be the land of the brave so long as we stand up from our seats and take a long hard look, and walk into the outside world.

Healthy living is living. Aligning the human spirit with the Spirit of our creator should be of the highest importance.

If we have little motion of enjoyment, we are but carcasses, idly sitting shotgun in the Volkswagen of life. Quality of life should be paramount.

"Why not walk?" a woman should say instead of driving.

"Why not run?" instead of walking, a man should wonder.

In doing so each of us maintains the self-control; we then hold accountable our own bodies to move freely, quite less inhibited by disease or other discomforts that could form within us.

Overcoming our national weight problem is the way to reach heights we have been capable of, but have never ascended to. Fast food plays a large part of the problem, though chains like McDonald's are making positive changes.

Fast Food industry received national scrutiny due to Morgan Spurlock's film Super Size Me for which he won Best Director in the documentary competition at the Sundance Film Festival. The movie chronicled Spurlock as he ate three McDonald's meals a day for a month trying everything on the menu. He gained 25 pounds.

"My body just basically falls apart over the course of this diet," Spurlock told Newsweek magazine. "I start to get tired; I start to get headaches; my liver basically starts to fill up with fat because there's so much fat and sugar in this food."

No matter where a person is from, she has the choice to build up the body or tear it down. So when people come under convulsions when stepping away from alcohol after a binge that person better understands the gift of life's intricate fragility.

Challenges keep things fresh. A life without challenges is a life without room to grow. People need change in life to reach a point of strength. When men get comfortable, they become dependent on other men to lead them.

The human body can take punishment. But that punishment can only be endured through discipline. A person must be willing to sacrifice to get to discipline. Without sacrifice no man may obtain discipline.

I saw men walk through the free weight room doors at 7 p.m. on Friday nights. They were in it 100 percent.

Discipline can give a person the ability to do many things. If we believe we can move mountains. One song goes,

They say that I can move the mountains
and send them crashing to the sea
They say that I can walk on water.
If I would follow and believe—
With faith like a child.

Discipline comes from yearning to be childlike. You wanna shed the nasty cloak of the world and be free. The Rec Center was a place I could be a child. I felt like, you go in there, and you are building up your temple. Only those who accept the Kingdom of Heaven as a child will enter therein. People accept you inside those walls. You work hard. And people respect that. I could go blow off steam like a seven year-old plays in the sand. It was all gravy. And it was where I let it loose.

A small part of this freedom can come through the weight room where a man has the capacity to completely transform his body.

The Student Recreation Center is where I found rest at SIU. The Rec became my sanctuary.

It was one of the best in the country. The Rec had a huge lit up swimming pool, a weight room 50' long by 25' wide, and six full-length basketball courts. In rough times and so many periods of adjustment during that first year the weight room was where I went to find my place, to see where I was going in life, to relax, to find myself.

The first semester I spent some more than 100 hours in The Rec Center. I divvied evenings between the weight room, basketball court and upper track, and lower track. I also played a little racquetball with friends. It was one of the few friendliest places on campus.

Bodybuilding was an aesthetic sport, and once again it was building something up, into something special. It felt like, you were building a house. You work on the very foundation first. In construction it is pouring the concrete for the basement, what the home will rest upon. In weightlifting this foundation is the gluteus maximus and quadriceps right in the upper legs. This is where power comes from. This is a highly important section in the vast majority of sports, and where most of the work is accomplished in, say, football, or track.

Then you add support to your house with the long boards that span the home, giving added support. These boards are akin to your abdominals, which help you keep balance.

Then come your adornments, such as a ceiling fan that would be similar to the trapezius, the muscles in between the shoulders, and right behind your neck.

The best bodybuilders treated their bodies as temples rather than amusement parks. The sport received my appreciation around sophomore year at SIU. These men put in hours of toil in the weight room, living with the weights, breathing with the weights.

I was lifting a considerable amount of weight in the free weight area, being around that iron 10-20 hours a week. Lifting was my burning desire. Grades crept up at school, like in a bad dream, haunting me back to my lack of preparation in high school. There was this terrible sense of urgency, an excitement. Weights were exciting because when I was in there I felt I could do no wrong. I worked out hard, building up my body into something special.

Stepping into the weight room was like the point that sticks out on the tire gauge, the side that releases the pressure. Weight room de-pressurized my body. I sensed this exhilaration in there. All these guys I worked out with for years. Since I arrived at school, many of the same guys were right along side me, using the same machines, sweating, just like me.

Vince Rhomberg was a fellow with a chiseled 5 foot, 6 inch frame. Vince was scraggly looking on those heavy metal nights, with a pointed nose, furry face, and round cheeks, the crown of his pumped figure. He carried himself diligently in the weight room, with a swagger of experience, a knowledge in there of everything iron. Vince was utterly talented at expressing his body, and transmuting his mind into raw, packed muscle. He knew of the best ways to perform exercises. There was no getting around it—Vince was cool, an anomaly in that he often carried a red apple in his sports bag, with that zipper undone, materials revealed.

Vince showed me weight lifting from doing—explaining technique was not nearly as effective as performing the reps and creating a style. He rose on the lat pull-up bar, and, muscles flexed, came up in a gracefully controlled motion all the way, no stutters, no jerks, just as effortless as the swan flapping wings on ascension from a sparkling lake. His grace was downright beautiful. It was obvious he had worked on this with deep concentration, keeping focus, even with the random slamming of 200 pounds on a cleans bar on one side of the weight room, and a man yelling under a squat rack on the other. Rhomberg was like a veteran halfback of sorts, answering various questions from the physically younger guys leading up to the Mr. SIU bodybuilding competition.

Vince encouraged speaking of lifting sometimes pointing out what were my best attributes. He would come to me with theatre affirmation as well. He studied graduate level theatre at SIU, and every time he wore one of those button up dress shirts, his chest expanded his ensemble, and hairs burst forth just below his chin. During the last two to three semesters at SIU, when I watched plays, Vince walked out just below the stage, introduced the program, and asked people to turn off their cell phones. Vince had this commanding presence that stuck with you. I appreciate him teaching me for all those weight room sessions. I don't think he saw it then, but the man was taking me to school.

Vince displayed dogged determination. He possessed a drive around the weights that is an indicator of a fundamental truth since the beginning of man's existence: physical strength does not make the man.

I see far too many brothers looking up to models of physical strength as prototypes of perfection. My mother said the other day, when a person has the physical, the spiritual balanced there is a glow about them. I say, "Wow!" to myself upon seeing somebody who has that glow. He has it going on.

I try not to notice the flesh of women. Sometimes difficulty hounds me. When looking around the world every day, for a man to recognize a woman is a delicate creation worthy of great honor, even that of a queen, that man should stop the looking at her ankles.

He who exalts himself will be humbled but he who humbles himself will be exalted. In the trials we face each of us will be brought low at some point. The object lesson is, however, whether we will suffer humiliation or humble ourselves.

I saw familiar faces at the Rec often—people from my dorm or Thompson Point in general.

DRUGS AND FOOTBALL

Making friends there was easy, too, because people congregated in the wide open basketball courts space while waiting for games.

All it took was asking who had next.

"Do you care if I run?" I said, mimicking others I had heard. If the person who had next did not have five players, he usually picked me up.

People commonly say nobody is happy with the way they look. I believe that is false. People go on camera all the time on the movie set. They look impressive. Bodybuilders show their bodies off in front of hundreds, sometimes thousands.

Discipline my coach taught us in high school enabled me to be fine with the way I was becoming. I used to be black. I saw myself that way. I wanted to be white. That didn't matter now. I was who I was. I was special. I was becoming unique. I began to understand, with all these folks from Chicago down here and all these people from across Asia...

"They're beautiful," I thought. I can be beautiful, too. "Wait...I am becoming beautiful..."

I wanted to be in a black group. I wished to be identified with black people. I sought to be...blacker. More and more walking through the University halls I wanted to understand blackness more completely. I wanted to understand *being* black. I sought to grasp the black experience.

I enrolled in a black history course with Dr. Pamela Smoot. I purposely sought out black friends initially based on the color of their skin. I had no, who you could accurately call black friends in Staunton. Met some in East St. Louis and that's about it.

I knew some here. I wanted to understand my blackness. I heard the National Association of Black Journalists was planning a trip. They were trying to attend a Howard University job fair Washington D.C. so I hopped on it.

We met to plan for the journey in a standard Communications classroom, about 18' wide, by 25' deep. Modest 15-year old chairs made the room look similar to a high school. We had good lighting, and a postings board for anyone who wanted to advertise for free. We spoke about just regular things everyone speaks about, but in a different way. People spoke with different inflections. They left off the ends of words. I learned from them, and wanted to be like them.

Howard University showed me first-hand the diversity we are capable of as a collective people.

Educated black men and some white men graced the Howard University inner city campus. Howard set at least a small trend in fashion for the East Coast. Hey, Phylicia Rashad went there. And so did P. Diddy. Fellow members of NABJ and I walked down the streets of America's capital and saw a large black man prophesying. He stood on a box elevated above passers by. A man stood next to him. I looked at him in wonder as thousands of people bustled through the city.

The lot of us also went to the subway. A man came up to us at the top of an escalator. He asked if we wanted to purchase some perfume. Some smooth talker from the city, I figured. He stood about 6' 4" and was a convincing speaker, calm and self-assured. The man said he stayed in a halfway house across the street and had been homeless before. He used heroin in the past. Junk screwed up his life royally. But there was something about this man magnetic and mesmerizing. He had been through so much. I listened to his whole life story, crude language and all. Other NABJ folks stood and reclined at the top of the escalator resting from our walks.

But this gentleman had me. He was humble, unassuming. I looked at him, and understood he had the ability to influence people with story. I saw how all people can influence with story.

He said he was clean and I was happy for him. He had somewhere to go in life, not wanting to stay where he was, but tell others about his previous road—the one not to go down. The perfume smelled cheap but he had a purpose to him.

Donovan, a husky, baldheaded jokester from East St. Louis, was one of my closest friends. He made me feel good inside even when things were looking hopeless around campus.

He stood 5' 10", had a black mustache, laughed like Krusty the Clown, and was black as a blacktop. One of our mutual friends, J.D., said after Donovan is in a dark room, even after turning on the light, someone asked, "Where's Donovan?" J.D. said, Donovan was so black, when standing in plain daylight you would have to ask Donovan to blink to see him.

I am so thankful for the absence of difficulty in friendships with people of all ethnicities. Refining fire I had gone through at an early age prepared me for this. J.D. stood 6' 1", lanky, but firm. He taught me all about myself, much how guys from my hometown taught me. J.D. worked hard day in and day out. He was concerned about integrity, and it was seemingly effortless for the man.

J.D. made the most out of his college, shining a light to me he probably did not recognize he was flickering. He was unpretentious.

He spoke casually, glancing over with his lazy eyes in a gaze that became his trademark and accentuated an exceptionally inviting demeanor. We went to Vineyard together in my third year at SIU, some of my last drinking days on earth. I just tried to imitate J.D. sometimes, as his calm personality was easy to mimic. And he was the antithesis of abrasive, displaying a sense of humor, and allowing a good friend to poke fun at his style. In halfway sentences, J.D. would say things.

J.D. said things to me in halfway sentences like, "I was watching the Cincinnati game the other day, and, um, with under five seconds to go…" He interjected with, "ums," and occasional, "likes." He just was giving the person a chance to catch up in his friendly monotone.

Only time when it was significantly hard for me to be black at SIU was at the bar scene. Black folks shimmied up onto the mid area at Carboz Night Club as artificial lights pierced the crowd, bending through dark bodies with precision. I felt alone, like the only person lost in the jungle. Black folks could contort their bodies and just hang. It seemed when I went out onto the floor, my body just became lame. Or maybe I was just inebriated.

Sure, not everyone is happy with the way they look. But I became increasingly comfortable with my appearance *in the light*, away from the dance floor lights. I went to the clubs less and found something beneficial in this. I was black and white and began to understand how to transition from immaturity into embracing the cornucopia of culture I was.

I was blessed to have the resources to deal with self-consciousness effectively. So many good teachers taught us discipline through the game of football. Choice was ours whether to use it.

The way we can change our physical selves and own awareness is through self-restraint. Through that self-control no matter what I looked like it was fine. Transforming the human body takes discipline. Just to live every day to its max people have to discipline their bodies.

Some people are funny about their bodies because they are not sure how to utilize their equipment. Physical fitness was such a complete release then.

Self-control is beneficial into every aspect of the day. Very first moments of the day, however, are crucial. A person should get out of bed as soon as she becomes conscious. Wheels start turning. Blood is pumping.

A reverse scenario is unfortunate. He becomes drowsy soon if he chooses to lie in bed, slugging along before the day starts. Men should plan walking outside into their days. Going to a weight room weekly would help also.

Picture your eyesight as a tunnel if you run. You can see through that tunnel because there is light. A light shines all the way down through your vision and light through that path is bright. At the end of the tunnel, however, there is great light; a luminescence brighter than a lake's reflection in a summer's noonday sun, a light brighter than anyone has ever seen.

This light allows you to see things to sides in addition to things which were already at the vision's forefront. When a person uses this ability to see, she should use all effort to stay focused. Distractions are off to the sides, on the periphery. It is imperative not to break concentration, lest the runner's vision falter. When the vision begins to sway, the runner becomes irritated, by the rocking of the boat, his body.

This vessel contains the heart, lungs, head, eyes, ears. These provide senses people utilize every day. So when people go to run they need to remember to keep vision clear. Focus is essential in this time of stress relief. This is relaxation time.

When I run I feel free. Running is the single most exhilarating exercise discipline, a training most men can do daily, and with relative ease. Feeling is euphoric, but in a natural way, and gets a person high the way our creator intended. Run is simply an extension of the walk and people have been doing that since man began his journey.

Regular exercises simply prepare the body for everyday action, making motion automatic. The human body needs to be cared for as a tool, a tool to praise one another.

When I lift weight, I tend to picture my body as a machine, working to get the most efficient workout possible. After the workout, people can relax completely. One shouldn't lean on the body to keep going. Humans should beat the body and make the body a slave, as the apostle Paul spoke about in the New Testament so eloquently.

Weightlifting makes me feel sexy. I suppose it's also called being comfortable in your own skin. I don't need to wear tank tops. When a man considers himself, he should consider himself as a vessel for service.

I had a good self-perception by halfway through that first year. But I faced other challenges. I faced challenges left and right. I put myself up to some also.

Southern Illinois University at Carbondale was unique. Thompson Woods blossomed in the heart of campus. Squirrels scurried by the cracked walkways. I walked to class, wondering what new philosophy I would soon discover. The scene was breathtaking in the fall: red leaves, green leaves, brown leaves tenderly floating to the downward throughout the town.

People from other nations such as India must be among the elite in their schools to attend *any* American colleges. Our schools are our most valuable resources.

I pondered all that could possibly be on the campus of 20,000 people. Any university in America is a great institution. They operate so others may learn knowledge. But this school had my fascination. It was not unique to other colleges, in all their innate grandeur. It was just…this was *my* university.

I was going to make it work.

I would make it.

I needed a challenge. I long thought writing would be a strong point because my brother excelled at it. My mother was a Spanish/English teacher.

So I said in my bosom, "Yeah, I am going to apply at *The Daily Egyptian*."

The Daily Egyptian was our school newspaper. It was an excellent student newspaper evidenced by the fact we won the General Excellence award of all the collegiate daily newspapers in Illinois.

I did not realize how much current event knowledge being a journalist required.

Faculty Managing Editor Lance Speere gave me a test to match up names of prominent public officials, and others who appeared in the news with regularity. Lance stood about 5'8" with a black mustache and goatee. He leaned slightly forward due to a spinal cord condition. I tried to show him I wanted to report. I wanted his admiration and to journal for such a fine publication.

There were about 20 questions. But it was tough. It was something fierce. I did not get the job.

I figured, "I'll try next semester. I'm new at this, whereas most of these people have been at this for at least a year."

Luke Schuette was an exceedingly athletically gifted, 6'1" friend with black hair and an ironic laugh. He spoke with me about doing something I was *already* good at.

We were friends in high school and played on the same undefeated football team 1997. We met up down at Southern and became better friends immediately.

"You should come play rugby with our team," he said. "We're looking for guys to play." So I said I would play rugby. There, we were sealed. We already shared some team success.

"This rugby would just draw us closer," I thought. Then he asked me to church. And that drew us even closer. We walked through the glass doors into the lobby of Vineyard Community Church one Sunday morning, and the whole place was lit up. This light was a special, supernatural light that hung above the door. It was this profound, remarkable glow. This presence just sort of dwelled there, above the entrance to the auditorium. This was the fullest, most visual feeling, I had ever experienced.

But other than the lobby glow, underneath, in the midst of it, people stood in the space, 50' wide, and 18' deep, talking with one another. People chatted as though they thoroughly enjoyed being with one another.

DRUGS AND FOOTBALL

The whole encompassing atmosphere, however, felt like this connectedness, this unity among them. I *sort of* felt this on the football squad. But not like this. These people looked good. They acted like they loved being there. I was floored. I wanted to know more.

Donuts lay on a shiny wooden countertop on the right side of the room. An assortment of designer coffee was also available just past the donuts, through double doors leading to a cafe. Folks went inside to hang out, pray together, get more coffee etc. Thick, cheap couches lent the room an easy, congenial feel.

Cafe was approximately 35' long and 28' wide with at least two good-sized windows, providing a healthy splash of light. The whole place brought me closer to Jesus, as well as the people I would meet.

But the design was completely breathtaking. Back out the cafe and into the lobby, just catty-corner to the right was one side set of double doors leading directly into the auditorium. The large expanse that made up the auditorium measured approximately 32 yards wide and 26 yards from back to front. Green chairs abounded. More important by far were the people.

Sandor (pronounced SHAWN-Dor) Paull was a minister with a cheery disposition, strong, taut muscles, and hoping to easily please. He was hip. He used to drive a motorcycle until he wrecked it, putting him out of commission for a while. Sandor made these kind faces. He said things such as, "Hey buddy" and "Rats!"

There was this yearning to get closer, to be closer to these people I started to consider family in a warm, peculiar way. These people differed from most I had associated with.

They were unique, and incredibly special, a people who listened to you, in a city where a sometimes intense learning environment too often hardened the hearts of a student body and faculty. The general campus population at times lost perspective on the most important aspects of this life.

But Vineyard folks were extraordinary. Come Sunday morning, hundreds of worshipers filled the auditorium, lifting up hands in praise. Some closed their eyes and shouted. But, then, in the midst of the assembly, the crowd was moved by The Spirit, and the congregation became as one body.

>
> Father of Lights
> You never change
> You have no turning
> Father of Lights
> You never change
> You have no turning
> Every good and perfect gift comes from you
> Every good and perfect gift comes from you
> Father of Lights

We were drunk in the Holy Ghost, as one of my preacher friends called it. We moved sang, and came together, moving in unison as the entire mass of water particles that makes up the sea crashes to the shore, waves enveloping. And we were in love.

We sometimes became frustrated and puzzled at circumstances in our daily lives, but when we came together, and shared our sorrows in the lobby or at friends' homes we were okay.

We sang that music, lifted up our songs as one voice, and perspective entered in our minds.

The Holy Spirit is when a man 90 years of age gets up of a Sunday morn, just to put his hands in the air, ceiling light shining on his silver hair. Not that we had many 90 year olds in our assembly, if any.

But the Holy Spirit is the Spirit of the Messiah—Jesus Christ—being poured out into a congregation. The Holy Spirit is good, like nothing else in the world. We can certainly feel its presence when we drink water, and abstain from food, devoting ourselves to the scriptures, with the sole purpose of gaining closer proximity to God's Spirit.

Holy Spirit goes from one person and if another person is willing to accept, that person receives the Holy Spirit also. Holy Spirit is without limit. Whenever the Holy Spirit moves, there is no containing it, because the Holy Spirit lives in all creation of the universe. Stars that give light in far off galaxies get their power from the Holy Spirit. There He may be called something different, in another language completely, however, wherever there is life, there the Holy Spirit dwells. An effervescent glow hung above the auditorium of sinners.

Cares washed away like the room was electric. The band played, as if in the same Spirit and in the continuation of the psalms Jesus sang with disciples at the Last Supper, stretching over centuries of days and nights, with one resonant cord. We sang in unity the triumphant words:

We cast our cares on you, Jesus
We cast our cares on you, Jesus
We cast our cares on you, Jesus Cause you're the only one.
The only one
The only one
So faithful
So righteous
You're so essential
Jesus bread of life

It felt like we could put worries aside and be happy together, if just for those 60 minutes during worship and the sermon. And then we experienced the ineffable joy in fellowship, moments we did not have to be with one another. We delighted in a common faith. We delighted in one another.

David Roberts taught at John A. Logan College in Carterville, just up the road from Carbondale. A picture painted could not do Roberts justice. He had a full black, wiry beard, stood 5' 8", with a soothing voice, perfect for a Community College professor. He was scraggly, with a comforting disposition, and calm enough to accept criticism and reason an argument with candor. Hair in his upper lip rose when he spoke, disclosing a distinct space between two of his front teeth.

David led a group and one of the topics was getting closer to God through prayer. My brother was going through a tough period in his life, as he was staying with me. I came to Roberts for advice.

"Be Jesus to your brother," David said. Amazing. Roberts was a sensitive man, and contemplative. He gave me three people to look up to—human beings who were willing to die for their beliefs: Gandhi, Martin Luther King, and Jesus.

I wanted to be sensitive and dynamic, just as the principles all these people really strove for. I wanted to be like that.

Jharmel *was* going through some things. I did not really understand it. Jharmel had been like a father. He was like a big brother-father. We were back at grandma's house in Staunton.

Jharmel lay in bed at 6 p.m. His room was dark and I wondered what the matter was. I peeked in the medium, 15'X 10' space, only seeing 1/3 of it clearly.

"Jharmel," I said. "Why don't you get up and do something." He had been like this for a few days now. He kept on. He kept lying in bed, night after night. I was thinking, "How is this man going to get *anywhere* like this?"

Mom and grandma spoke about his condition. It was crazy. Jharmel was not working. He did not…do anything. Mom told him he needed to go to the doctor. He would not comply.

Finally grandma and mother started talking about hospitalization. They spoke of getting him some serious mental health attention.

I went into his space. I looked into the hollowness. He was in there. "I have to find him," I thought. I thought I've got to go for him. I've got to go for him even if I never come out.

"Mom and grandma are going to take you to the hospital, Jharmel, if you don't get up and do something."

This comment seemed to ruffle him out of his dingy slumber. Out of the cavernous walls of his mind he rose. But it was not better. In fact, it was on some level worse than what I had expected.

Jharmel walked around, hands over his eyes, speaking to me as though the bright shining light of his capability was too much. He told me some things. He said its all about control. He said people, they only want to control you. I looked at him, and he wasn't doing a thing about it. In my mind, he was cooperating with whatever limitations anyone put on him.

But eventually he made his way to grandma's small, meager bathroom. Door hung open to the inside.

Jharmel stood there. He stood upright, looking at himself in the mirror until I thought he would drown himself in the image.

"What are you doing?" I asked him. I wanted an answer. I sought some sort of response. He reminded me of Narcissus, the Greek god who gazed at himself for so long his own image turned him to stone.

He looked as though, Jharmel appeared as though...he would turn to stone. I mildly panicked, walking back and forth through the living room, and past the bathroom. Jharmel stood there, looking at himself, frozen in an inanimate glare for ten minutes. He just kept looking, and I could not find my brother anywhere in there.

He came out into the open again.

I said, *"Jharmel, mom and grandma are going to take you to the hospital if you do not leave."* Grandma and mother instructed me from the other room not to let him go anywhere. I went to the front door. My shorter and lighter brother stood there.

"What are you doing," he said faintly. He said it in such a way he could have let me make the decision for him and been better off.

Jharmel was a grown man. Sickness or not, he was my big brother. I was not my brother's keeper. He would go where he saw fit.

"You need to go," I said. "Or else mom and grandma are going to take you to the hospital."

Jharmel went outside, shaken. He entered his small brown Ford Ranger. He left. I slept abnormally, for five hours.

Jharmel came back over to grandma's house the next day.

Mom said Jharmel, her and I had to "go down below," or, south of Staunton to the St. Louis Metro-East.

Jharmel got into mom's white 1994 Chevy Cavalier and so did I. We made it 27 miles to Collinsville. Mom bought us some fast food. We pulled over to a gas station. Mom took care of the gas pumping. Jharmel lay in the back seat. I looked back to him.

"Jharmel, you need to get up and go... Jharmel, you need to wake up. Jharmel you need to get up."

Mom returned and had an unusually determined look on her face. She was set.

We took off. We drove about 14 miles to Gateway Regional Medical

Center in Granite City. We parked in the cold lot. We told Jharmel we had to go up now. We had to get going now. We said we had to get a move on. I stood outside the car, not knowing exactly how this whole thing would work, you know. Mom asked for my assistance.

I told Jharmel we had to get going upstairs now. I took Jharmel by the arm. He sort of held on to me. I basically carried him, with mother. We made it to the front entrance. We signed in. Mother told the attendant our situation. She advised us to go upstairs, and someone would be waiting. We three got to a hard metal door in a short, well-lit hallway.

We were standing in front of the Behavioral Health Center. We spoke on the little speaker, telling them who we were. We entered. We heard some moans. We heard speaking. Some outsiders sat in a quaint room visiting with residents. We went to the desk, and they kindly told us to proceed to a waiting room straight ahead. Jharmel's head was reeling. He did not understand, really why he was in there, I don't think. I put my head down, drained of energy. It was night now. I felt release. But then again I felt culpable, as though I could help Jharmel from going to a psychiatric ward. A woman entered the waiting room.

"How do you feel, Jharmel?" she said. She peered deep into him, past her glasses and, with a serious disposition, asked the question again.

"How are you doing?"

It's all in the same I guess. You are looking for a response.

"When was your last bowel movement?" she said. And I didn't even want her to go there. It made me feel uneasy. Jharmel was unresponsive. She looked at him seriously and said she wanted to give him something that would lessen the edge. She said it would calm him down.

She brought a needle in. I felt as though I was in a bad movie.

"Should I take it," Jharmel said. He grabbed onto my shirt. It felt like I was his last chance, his only lifeline, a phone-a-friend, who was right in the room with him—right in front of his face.

"Should I take it?" Jharmel asked, bewildered, and clutching me, like I was his last gasp of breath.

"Yes," I said. "Yes you should take it," I blurted out. I got it out of my system. I removed from my system an answer that in any other circumstances would be anathema to my entire way of doing things, my

DRUGS AND FOOTBALL

whole belief system. At that point I did not believe in drugs. Drugs only controlled you, I thought. You need control over anything you put into your body.

I said yes, in a moment of weakness. I felt sleep deprived, on the edge of hallucination, as though I should be in there with him. I seriously thought of it. I thought, "I should go in here, too. Jharmel and I are never going to be the same if I leave him in here." I was responding to questions I wished I'd never been asked. I guess I felt like Senator John McCain did in the POW camp overseas. He gets asked a question, then he doesn't know what to say. He is in a different country. These people are speaking Greek to him, and he only knows the language of hamburgers and apple pie.

What he was saying was all gibberish. I expected Jharmel to always be there. Completely, I expected Jharmel to always be there mentally. I wanted him always there. But now I was stuck again, stuck in a strange place, and this time it was bad. Where we were was horrible, because you forfeited so many rights.

I felt as though I was in some horrible, cheap movie. This was the cheapness—that Jharmel had to be like this. I wanted to say, "**Wake up!!**" but felt like that would not do any good.

Jharmel took the shot in his arm. Shortly thereafter mother and I got up to leave. I leaned over to Jharmel. I hugged his slender, slim frame. I kissed him on the cheek. I looked at him desperately. I longed for him to come back. And then walked toward the door, slowly and lifeless with mom. Nothing else mattered. No other people were in the room. No, it was Jharmel and me. Jharmel and me. Jharmel and I looked at one another. Mom and I were to the door now. Our door opened. I kept looking at Jharmel. I looked at him, like, this is wrong. There's got to be some other, better way to do all of this. But this was the only way. I saw no other way...

I came back and saw him about four days after that. I sat with him. I don't know exactly what happened then. We did not speak anything. 'S surreal. 'cause when you see someone no matter their condition in a place such as this it gives you more hope. I guess it is all the old motion pictures that depict mental health facilities as drab and uncaring. But I did not feel that way after getting in there. I met a nurse, and she seemed loving, as though this was the right occupation for her. Patients played cards. They sometimes made crafts. They joked around with each other. It was kind of like camp, I guess.

I just sat with him as a sort of booster. I hoped to lift his spirits. We sat... I listened to residents ask for things. Jharmel breathing. Television. I looked at Jharmel. His eyes were innocent. His soul had gone through the flames. He was my brother. And he was still my hero.

Some details in my life are not clear when I live through them, but later the purpose becomes evident. Problems arise, and I was reading in the "Purpose-Driven Life" about how God uses problems in our lives to make us more like Jesus. Behind every trouble we face, we are being refined. God is using it for good, even though the enemy meant it for bad. God uses bad circumstances to build character.

While being away from school I guess I felt as though I needed to be father to others, or in charge some way. But I needed a father. I was in acute need of someone to look up to. I looked up to another David in my life... I looked up to David Cheri.

Now David went to the Vineyard also. He was a strapping lad, about 6' 2" tall, 190 pounds and strong. Cheri came to SIU on a track and field scholarship. He could dunk a basketball with two hands. He had a regular brow, normal in size, framing his round face discreetly. David led a Bible Study. He played the djembe, a single drum approximately 9" in diameter, to a sweet worshipful melody. Lights were dim, and the few of us sang. We then waited in joyful expectation for David to begin the study. He was so fluid with his teaching he took the Bible and threw it upon a chair to begin.

"It's just a book," David said. From then on, I still had a reverence for the words, but the pages and the book was just another thing. Stories inside were the important part.

I looked so much up to David, though he was a year younger than me. He was more faithful, and I learned a great deal from his constant demeanor. I learned a lot, because whenever we hung out, I watched him. I took notice of the steadiness of his hand. I observed the words delicately pouring from his lips. David was a sharp person. He was on the right road. I wanted to be on the straight and narrow. I wanted to learn more from him.

Jane Huh, our mutual friend, David and I sat at a kitchen table at my apartment a short distance from campus. We snacked.

"There's no *(%$#*&way I'm going to eat that," I said. David looked me right in the eyes, on impulse and unflinchingly.

"Brett, that language might have been okay before, but you know better than that now."

He cut to the heart. It was like, "Whoa." I didn't really know what to say. I didn't know the proper response. I was humbled. David brought me low. And I had no desire to cuss thenceforth.

Cheri was a guy you could count on. He led the group, sang occasionally in the worship band, studied for classes at the University, and had a steady girlfriend.

Cheri and I walked to McDonald's in the Student Center one day. We regularly did these little get-togethers. We had been close friends for several months.

"I feel like you're my baby," David said. "I feel like I've got to let you go on your own now." He meant in the faith, as he nibbled on a fish sandwich with tartar sauce.

"Keep in what I've been teaching you, because now that you are following the Lord, the enemy is going to try and take you out." I listened in rapt attention, as Cheri tilted the bun up, to lick the tartar sauce off his hand. We spoke of new steps in life, remaining ever-vigilant.

"Let's go," he said. We walked down out the long Student Center. A bright sun warmed us, as we were cool and full of new, righteous expectation. We stood under Faner Hall, and as we walked along the extremely long structure, I paused for a moment. This was where I was to go up winding steps to class.

"Here's my stop," I said, looking somehow for David to direct me. He was to point in which way to go now. I clung to him emotionally in a deeply meaningful way. It was interesting. He was a year younger than me, but I looked up to the man like an older brother.

"Let's pray before you go into class," David said. As hundreds of students passed by on the busy summer day, David put his hand on my shoulder.

"God, please walk with Brett in wherever he goes in life. Be with him every step of the way. When the enemy comes near him, please give him the armor of you, Father, and, just give him all the strength he needs…Amen."

After that day David said I needed to join another Bible Study group, because his group was to multiply. I was hurt. This guy, who walked with me, who looked out for my well-being on so many different levels all this while, was leaving me. He was leaving me…and was insisting I leave him. I cried inside. I felt unwanted.

I felt a little abandoned, though Vineyard Community Church had dozens of other capable male role models behind the sanctuary doors. In hindsight I guess I was a little too expectant, as a naive mother expects her child to come out all nice and cute. She anticipates him being obedient to every word she tells him, straight out of the womb. But that mother has unfair suppositions.

It was just idealistic looking back. If you consider it, David was doing me a huge favor in the first place, because he was letting me go to the bible study. He taught me how to serve in a more substantial way. I had not known that level of steadiness actually, up to that juncture. David was great. Everything he did mattered. We now know one another on a deep level of affection. We know each other on a cosmic level, in an everlasting memory of friendship.

A whole atmosphere that lived inside Christians at the Vineyard was cool, and yearning. Though we sought after inward purity, people in church succeeded in adapting with new fads. Jeans hung down, saying, "JNCO" in large, obnoxious print. A friend's shirt said simply, "Love," with hand displayed as men and women's bathroom signs inside retail stores. But the hand had a hole in it.

Cheri regularly wore a discreet bracelet.

"WWJD," was printed on it, meaning, "What Would Jesus Do?" People *believed*. People sought. They reached out, and grabbed for a fire that burned inside. Like they wanted to share their faith with everyone on Earth.

DRUGS AND FOOTBALL

When stepping inside the Vineyard church down at college, there were so many beautiful people. Physical symmetry abounded. People all over were good looking, and there were others who were fun with which to speak.

Paul the apostle, one of the great missionaries for the Christian faith, said, in a letter to the Philippians in the New Testament, "Your attitude should be the same as that of Christ Jesus: Who, being in very nature (or, in the form of) God, did not consider equality with God something to be grasped, but made himself nothing, taking the very nature (or the form) of a servant, being made in human likeness."

People want to be noticed in America. But, taking the role of a servant, disregarding status, by, listening to people, even in a lull in the conversation, that's fine. Now this is exceedingly difficult. And at first takes intense training. If, however, we can actually forget ourselves, humble ourselves for the periods when we are up, then there is no reason God will not automatically pass on that joy to others, through your humility. Just standing and listening is where it's at, refusing to talk unless the topic has quite direct relation to you or unless somebody asks you a question. Perhaps someone has something they want so bad to share with you, whether guilt, shame, uncertainty, doubt, or maybe even joy, a report of praise in their life, or great mark they just received on a test, or lovely compliment for you but they think their many words will give them the opportunity to put it off 'til another day. Possibly through your self-restraint you will open up something hidden in them for the past 16 months! Silence is the patient faith sharer.

I repented and was baptized in Jesus' name. I could now speak to Him without compunction. I had access to Him at all hours of the day—when frustrated, or stuck on a test question, lonely or lost. I would speak. He listened and responded in wonderful and mysterious ways. He counseled on levels beyond human comprehension—through visions (This was one of my primary spiritual gifts), as I wrote in a journal, prompting me to do something which turned out to be profoundly helpful to another's condition or mine, and in that still small voice.

I came to know Jesus' teachings most authentically through living the moments. A group of us once drove out to Giant City.

Giant City State Park was a vast forest with open areas scattered throughout. Natural, wide walkways abounded, allowing a view to massive boulders, cliffs making people feel as though they were in one big city.

Jon Farn, medium in height, round in face and athletically built, smiled incessantly. His smile, like everything about his facial appearance was rotund. Farn had a deep voice and even more resonant laugh which made him very approachable. He worshipped in the band. He sang, and hoped to connect to the living God with every strum of his acoustic guitar.

He and several others ran out on the wide expanse of a field more than one score of acreage deep. Sun shone brilliantly, but never overly so. We played random catch with a regulation-size football. We also threw around the Frisbee beneath the tranquil and breath-taking afternoon sky. This was our moment, when homework, boyfriends and girlfriends did not matter. We shared the field as brothers and sisters.

And the physically stronger threw as many passes to the physically weaker participants as to the buff guys. We were equal on all levels. We felt as though we were in a different dimension, in an alternate universe. There was nothing above or below that could separate us. Many moments played out in my days attending the Vineyard similar to this one, such as 7 a.m. pick-up games at the courts behind the Student Recreation Center. We worshipped while shooting hoop too. One of the guys got hurt while playing ball, and Gary Darling, a new pastor for the Vineyard congregation, laid hands on him and prayed. This physical interaction was necessary, and common among us, as, at any one moment, any one of us could lay hands on another for any injury, disease, sickness or hurt in life, and pray. Most of the instances we laid hands on one another and prayed, there was simply a sharing of faith, a reassurance that somebody was indeed presently looking out. There was no need to fear, because somebody had your back.

But with regularity the supernatural would occur and people actually described a regeneration. Anybody could be a part of this community, but opening ourselves up to the community, as the apostles did, and persistently seeking members was wrought with difficulty. Opening ourselves up, being wholly vulnerable to the Carbondale multitudes, at the mall, or at SIU football games, was tough.

Football was a sport that could commonly be violent if a player had not a control on his physical abilities at all times when on the field—one of reaction, instinct. Football was a game where the purpose was to bring people closer together through camaraderie, not at all a brutish endeavor, but one bonding of the players to become one pulse. Church was the same way.

When I needed to get something done in church, I had to work from the same instinct. In football, instinct was guttural. It had to come from the very base of my physical self. In church, however, the expression came from my very soul. Church was not something I could simply wish for. In football there was a preparation. Working up to the season, the team went through two practices a day, and agility drills therein. Richard Barber, three years my junior, hopped through the ropes drill in the heat of the summer. Ropes was one of the more demanding of the seven drills we endured throughout two-a-day practices. Barber possessed a large, imposing build at only 14, with curly blonde hair and strong body odor come midway through practice. He had a soft face, one with features like a baby, in a body, on a football field, bent on big muscle.

But there he was sorely out of shape in those first of his two-a-days. His legs chugged up and down, up and down, as he cried out, "Oh!"

Barber said he could not get through the drill. "It's too tough!" he said as I stood on the side. I assured him he could do it, and he kept going. Barber wanted to play. He reminded me of a rough necked kid who played for us and was a senior the season our team went 10-1. Cory Buse was his name, and he looked similar to Barber, same build, blond hair, but Buse practiced all season with us even though he was ineligible to play. Such was the level of commitment he had for the game he sweated, the game he bled for. Barber was just like that. He worked diligently for all he got, he didn't quit that sunny day, and he became a better man for it. Religion is like Barber's stance that day. You feel like giving up, like packing up and going home some days, such as when the heat index is 110 degrees, and the dust sticks to your face like particles of earth slapped on a piece of bologna…like every particle of stale dust sticking to your face as soon as it comes into contact. On some occasions the fear would tempt you like a hideous monster, not to show up to practice, or not to endure the grueling process of sprints and twisting the body in positions alien to the considerable majority of human beings, but there was always the fact, the knowledge by God's grace, that other people were doing this same exercise with you, and it was fun after getting into it. There is joy when all us folks toiled out there together, sweating profusely, but with purpose, bending our wills to go even further, with fervor. Same thing was the case with church. Church was a battle. Getting up in the morning on Sundays, on many occasions I did not want to go. There was little else I could hear Steve Morgan preach about, I thought. Morgan, a large man, 6 feet five inches, approximately 240 pounds with a baby face, in his forties, walked with a purpose—he wanted to win souls for Jesus. Virtually every syllable he uttered was clear as crystal, as he had earned a doctorate degree in speech communication. Morgan was towering from a distance, but after he began speaking, it was easy to tell he was a man of purpose. He had a direct goal in being a minister. He wanted to enunciate every one of those words, because his message was too important for somebody who was contemplating suicide to miss. There was utter responsibility in the man, an inner grace that shone on the crowd of Vineyard, which gave him authority to preach what he knew best. He did it quite well. But as kind as the man was, through his powerful presence, there was still little reason to show up on Sunday morning it felt like some days. I was just spent.

    Men like Kurt made me want to get to church Sunday mornings. He was another man who made a significant impact on my life. Especially Kurt made an impact because he showed everyone he could be a holy man, and filled with emotion, while being a large physical presence. He was tall and gentle, more than middle aged, and with a flowing grey/blond head of hair. He wore glasses and talked with an extraordinary voice, in tone and clarity. Kurt's voice also contained a slight lisp, which was fine. I respected Kurt, as one would respect a general, yet he had this disarming quality, which put you at ease whenever you were around him. He was masculine *and* cool.

    In Kurt was a dichotomy of sorts, in he was an exceptional athlete. Kurt played volleyball, a sport where some of the best hits were called kills, and a person would be looked at as a skilled player if he batted a ball the size of a man's head so forcefully it would ricochet off the opponent. Kurt played at UCLA more than 20 years back. He has this athletic build, with a firm grip and unwavering grasp on things. Kurt's hand shook when we were in service at the Vineyard. He prayed for me, and, for anyone he would pray for, his hand would tremble. This was a sign a person had the Holy Spirit living inside.

Kurt would not let the fire quench. He was awesome. Kurt had a slow, sure voice, and when he would pray for you, there was a feeling you were in God's arms, like the Lord's loving care would wrap you up and hug you reassuringly not letting a thing harm you. Kurt was just that kind of man. There was no getting around it.

He, like scores of folks at the Vineyard, cared.

I learned great things there. We all studied together. We prayed together. We sang with each other. But what was most amazing was the root this faith was taking in me. Like a firm tree planted next to a river, the torrential downpour came. Water came, however, it would not take me away. I would not be moved. I would not be shaken. I began to embrace faith. I would not be denied. No, not if I went after it. I would be okay. I so sought to impact my world on a level that I had reached yet. Some talent lay hidden in my breast. I was compelled to draw it out.

I had this feeling about my fingers that just made me miss these keys. Something about that, I can't quite put my fingers on it, but, wait a moment, here it is. My fingers are home. I have found a soothing quality behind this computer, which is such blessing to own. I can express myself through the use of this machine. I have known what I know only through grace, not by anything earned on my own. I have done some evil acts before, but, somewhere, God was looking out for me.

I had continued to apply at *The Daily Egyptian* semester after semester, still ignorant of names currently in the news, and no job. But after my fourth try they hired me.

"We figured if you are going to keep applying you must really want the job," Lance Speere said. I became *Daily Egyptian* news clerk in the summer of 2002 as one of the first two correspondents in the publication's history.

Challenges indeed make people stronger. I wanted to prove myself early on. I stayed late hours and loved it. Sometimes a group of us huddled around the television at night during a breaking story of national significance, considering how fortunate we were to cover news as students and get paid for it.

We were to write two stories a week, which takes usually only ten to twelve hours. But I behaved like a voluntary slave for paper, in there day and night enjoying simple tasks such as putting newspapers on racks and cleaning.

I was challenged, indeed, through temptation. I gave in one time when editor in chief Marleen Trout sent me deep into southern Illinois to do a story on Camp Ondessonk.

I didn't know totally what to do there in the first place. I figured…describe some things. Then ask people questions and get their answers. I was ga ga over this counselor. And I became a little too fond of her deeply radiant countenance. She looked as though she were an angel who fell from heaven. I told her she was pretty and this was not smooth for any cub reporter.

Marleen said the comments disturbed her. I apologized to the woman and learned a lesson.

Another one of my first stories was on the local farmer's market. One of my sources insisted to give me a container of honey. He would not accept a no. So I took the container of superior pure honey home.

I later asked an experienced reporter and also my professor at Southern, whether I should give the bottle back or give it to the tummy. He said it probably would not hurt to accept the thing on this occasion if I insisted to pay for the next gift if the honey man and I met again.

I consider now the impact journalism can have upon the masses. A good journalist reports the truth as he discovers it. He does not embellish, and refuses to operate off subjectivity. When he writes down what the interviewee says, he responds not by word of his mouth, but with a patient and cautious hand, taking down information. The words from the notebook then go into the computer just as he has written. Thus, truth has to come out.

During wartime it is of utmost importance to report on both sides.

Iraqis are human beings. Average, politically and militarily neutral Iraqi citizens are just as, if not *more* in need of news exposure than our own troops are, because the Iraqis are the *other* guys. American soldiers work on getting what is necessary accomplished to be able to exit the country. Iraqis, on the other hand, are responsible for building the remains of the former regime into a stable society.

Our Bush Administration supported barring news outlets from publishing photographs of slain soldiers at funerals. However we go about this issue we need to proceed with utmost respect to the families of those killed servicemen. Though not every citizen believes what they are doing is a service to our country, *they* do. Soldiers believed in it so much they were willing to put their lives on the line for the freedoms we enjoy. Though violence is a weak way to increase strength, these men and women put themselves on front street to protect us from foreign threat, that one day we may be in a world where violent action has been mitigated to such a degree we do not even consider it anymore something to be feared, but a sick condition to be treated with a mother's gentle love individually, strategically truthful in the masses and nonviolent in scope.

An amendment to the U.S. Constitution directly prohibits the abridgment of the freedom of the press. But we must behave tactfully when we exercise this freedom. Just because something is permissible does not make it beneficial.

As I have studied the teachings of Jesus Christ, Mohandas Gandhi and Martin Luther King, I have found there is Truth in society, that is, absolute truth. Exposing evil, or something morally wrong, is the only way to mend the wrong and bring good from without. I have, therefore, a job which is awfully relevant, to the day's issues—to report the solution or the problem, the victory or loss, each by gaining fact from people. Wherever the lining of truth lies is up to the discernment of reader. I chose journalism to write about issues that affected my community.

If your mother says she loves you, check it out. Journalism was based on fact. If somebody says something, check it out. It clears the air. Truth is liberating. No other job can be said to be more pure than journalism by its very nature. Journalism at its very core gives us a chance to understand what a person we do not know says—and such is the business of reporting. I don't know what exactly to put into these pages sometime. But sometime that's the lot of the journalist—to provide *something* in these pages to comfort the reader. In doing so we may share community. I give a little to the reader. She writes back a letter to the editor, or column or responds to a poll/survey and so on. With news, that is daily communication from an outside source. I wanted to be, and still seek to, be that voice on the page, the reader can connect with on a regular basis.

A fellow resident assistant, Emily, said she used to deliver mail in Winnebago, Illinois, and elderly folks just waited for you to deliver their mail. They waited all day to receive something new and fresh, and all theirs. This was the highlight of the day.

I learned some great things at college. I learned extraordinary doctrines in journalism school.

Best things, however, I learned from people. And none more so than Li Nan, my roommate at Lewis Park apartments. Our relationship was a peculiar treasure. It was as a woman finding a pearl of great value in a field, and then going, and selling everything she had, to buy that field.

Li stood 5'9", slim, and wore glasses. Nan was from Xianjiang in China. He was so full of laughter, and gentle. He chuckled easily and upwardly. Nan laughed in a high pitch from his stomach. Sometimes he took in the air instead of releasing it.

He was distinct. Li walked with grace and integrity. When he tried to remember something he needed but could not recall exactly he snapped his fingers.

He was just heading out the door one day. Then, "click, click, click."

Nan bought his food from the international grocery store on route 13. He cooked on a wok in the 8'x 5' kitchen area. He made pork stink like I'd never smelled it, cooking some vegetables alien to my taste buds.

Visiting with one another was a shining hallmark of his culture. Li listened to other peoples' positions on anything. He was polite and often let others speak first. He deferred out of habit. Li held a cup of tea in hand, his eyes beaming in wonder relaxing in the wooden chair, taking it all in.

I appreciated Li. I guess it is because he is different—different culture,

DRUGS AND FOOTBALL

different accent, different intonation. He has built his body differently. But it made me think of how we are all different.

Made me think how nobody is exactly the same. I was beginning to see how much I was like other people. This whole blend of faces, ethnicities and cultures. I was no longer the odd man out, and, more importantly, I never was. We always had these different bodies. We had these different minds with differing interests. Our religions often varied.

I saw this myriad of color through the media before. But now we lived together and we blossomed for that very reason. We complemented each other, our various experiences adding flavor to the melting pot. We are America. Only in America. Only in America do we save money in an old shoe. Li Nan was curious. Yes, I saved loose change in a worn running shoe.

"Brett," he said. "When are your shoes gonna make money?" He became acclimatized with our culture and enjoyed it. As I saw more and more people I wished to be like them and learn from them. I met more people every week who possessed qualities I aspired to gain.

Greg Padesky was a stand-up type individual. Greg was Habitat for Humanity leader. He was also awarded distinction of Eagle Scout, the very highest honor in Boy Scouts of America.

But he showed me how to live. In fact, he made everything seem right. He was the kind of leader who could not be shaken, no matter what storms arose. Greg was an odd fellow in a comforting way.

He was the kind of guy you wanted to go everywhere with you—from the football game for entertainment, to Wal-Mart SuperCenter for groceries. He was *the man*.

He stood 6', weighed 180 pounds. But the most telling part of Greg was his hair. Greg's curly, black hair flopped this way and that. It was as though his collective strands had a mind of their own.

He carried a pursed lips-look when he prepared to respond to a question. His laugh was contagious, and erupted from flared nostrils. He laughed in a most ironic laugh.

In everything he did, he did with class, and I thought he did it better than the rest. His nose was short and punchy, carrying thick-rimmed black glasses. He bought his attire from second-hand stores mostly.

He rode his bike to all sorts of places on campus. I seldom saw him drive his car. I didn't even think he owned a car for the first year I knew him. I reported to him various aspects of the Habitat for Humanity work.

"Fair enough," he said, with a reassuring look as to say, "you did well," or "keep up the good work."

When each person comes through with a their piece of the pie, sticking as a cohesive unit, the whole operation runs like a well-oiled machine.

Each person should seek to recognize others for specific efforts. We mustn't let people just slide by in doing their jobs, assuming jobs are simply people's duties. Work is more than just duty alone, for a job *just* to pay the bills would be mere drudgery. People need encouragement to see how they fit into the whole operation with those unique talents. Compliments are divine. A person perks up when he has been vocally rewarded in the presence of colleagues. Congratulations at work for a job well done is what drives a man to get out of bed of a morning. Men thrive when people let their good works be known.

Hope we will be congratulated should not be a single force behind why we work, but as human nature, it is. We all want to be praised. Every person wants attention. Encouragement is the single most gratifying gesture a man can receive, and essential, more important than gold. When a man is congratulated at work, he is uplifted. A specific instance mentioned as to why what he did was stellar galvanizes that man in his drive to succeed. When a man has been complimented in the presence of others on a specific piece of work, he actually uses that to improve his own work. Job then translates to service. From service comes fulfillment and from fulfillment people are completely in and the team is complete. They want to win it. And at that point a man is not lying down on the job, he is ready to go, bolt cutters in hand, pen pumped and ready to scribble, gloves on, tie fastened because when a man has received congratulations in the presence of his colleagues. He is uplifted.

Inclusion is a big part of uplifting. And there was none better at it than Greg Padesky. Greg was a man of the people, and did not feel uncomfortable speaking with anyone. Other men who look like him nowadays look trendy, because Greg set the trend with his unabashed nerdy/goofball manner. He looked like the typical stylish guy. He set the mark and never missed. You could always count on him for anything.

He was always prepared to smile, but never in a naïve, placating fashion. He exercised an enduring, even stately, self-control. We spoke of ways to improve the community through our beautiful organization, Habitat for Humanity.

We sat in Father Chris Piasta's Newman Catholic Student Center office at night, as Greg perused through various pictures he took for Habitat for Humanity—workers, his girlfriend Jackie Donavan, Father Chris, and so on. We sat together.

Greg blinked at the screen. He chose some images to keep. Some he discarded. I looked to him, trying to absorb the warmth of this young man. Everything, actually, seemed good coming from him. He was a ray of light, shining the way in an often-dark university world.

'S crazy he was living with me. We were together—one body, as the Christian doctrine goes. We lived to serve others. We all are, and were, one body.

Some have this gift…possibly it is photo-taking. Others have this talent…possibly building things, bridges for instance. Whatever talent the person possesses is by grace and by no goodness that person inherently has.

Greg knew his gift. Greg knew his talent. I sought after mine, like great spoil. I sought after mine. After you seek so long, you *will* receive. When you persist, you *will* come out, all the way on top.

We wanted to serve other people in the most selfless of ways. We sought to give unto others. And we got to share all that together.

Greg's **self-control** was *the* most appealing part. It separated him from the rest of the crowd. He leaned over in this methodical way, sipping a light beverage, his heart beating at few rates per minute.

Not only did we sit in Father Chris's office. Greg was *always* at the Newman Center, it seemed. Either he was speaking with the Newman Center Director, or creating brownies in the kitchen, or taking part in Lite Supper.

Greg was the very best Catholic of similar age I knew. He is one of a handful of the best Christians I've ever known. Just speaking about him sends chills down my spine.

He was excellent in all he did. You could tell he tried his hardest at everything. He had some good raisin'. You could tell.

He was somewhat of a father figure. He was, yet again, a year younger than me. But he seemed like someone to model behavior after. Though we were peers, on equal ground, he had something I wanted. I looked for those qualities in him that were unique. I wanted to be like him.

Obviously, idolatry is destructive—duh. Just consider, however. Consider Greg was like a father.

I hung on his every word, as though he was Mel Gibson as William Wallace leading soldiers in Braveheart.

I wanted some of that. He was *just* what I wanted to be like. I wanted to be assertive, decisive, yet not take myself so seriously where people think you're uptight.

He *was* Habitat for Humanity to me. Habitat was an organization where you look up to others. Some of the best learning happens after school, working in the community and getting the hands dirty.

People feed off the best of each other's character, gleaning commendable attributes. You've got this universal, renewing spirit constantly at hand.

In the November 2004 issue of Men's Health magazine, one of the responses to who have been great leaders in history was Jesus.

"No greater following, no greater message. Made the ultimate sacrifice, accomplished the mission, and went home." Jesus and the message he brought was a no-brainer. People have known this for around 2,000 years. Responsibility lies in our hands to achieve what he wanted for all of us.

One response was simply, "Oprah." Winfrey was a great response because she is in the now. Oprah takes some of the challenging topics of our generation and makes them known. She deals with emotional subject matter in a society wanting nothing to do with genuine emotion. Oprah is right on cue because she is completely willing to show her feelings, and on national television. This takes a good dose of intestinal fortitude. She represents caring, compassion, dedication, follow-through. She is an excellent candidate for President of the United States according to Michael Moore, famous documentarian and author. Moore first brought up this point when trying to think of people we should send to the White House. I figured, well, Oprah has all the important qualities of a leader, and she's got it goin' on.

Winfrey is special also because she has the wherewithal to manage a gazillion dollar television production company. She also runs a large monthly magazine. Whoever should lead among us should be like the youngest.

One person replied to the leadership question, Bill Parcells. Parcells coached NFL teams such as the Buffalo Bills and New York Jets. He always takes underachievers and soon has them believing in themselves and winning. Parcells comes to struggling programs and teaches them how to win, and usually rather quickly. Figures, he accepted the job of General Manager for the lowly Miami Dolphins, and they are now winning again. I see in Parcells the same as watching Michael Jordan play in the 1990s.

Jordan had this itching passion to achieve. He brought teammates together. He was highly disciplined. Jordan elevated the play of whoever was on the floor wearing a Bulls jersey. When he touched that ball, he was like a kid in a candy store; like a toddler in daycare with a ball in his hands going for the mini-hoop, while the other little guys were busy running in circles, getting *dizzy* in the playroom.

Accomplishments, for them to mean anything, must be coupled with humility, and love, to be worth their salt. Whoever is great among you will be your servant, and whoever is chief will be servant of all.

A person *must* recognize a way to serve others selflessly in whatever profession she chooses. First way we can serve others is consistency. C.S. Lewis wrote in his book *Mere Christianity* thrills come at the beginning and do not last.

The thrill you feel on first seeing some delightful place dies away when you really go to live there, he wrote.

People buy things; they go places because it makes them excited. When looking for a mate, or when looking for a job, look for something which is consistent because that flame of love at first sight burns out like dead wood the morning after a bonfire.

Lewis wrote,...If you go through with it, the dying away of the first thrill will be compensated by a quieter and more lasting kind of interest. So, even though a woman looks attractive or a particular job appeals to you, look into how able you would be to serve after the first couple months. People admire those who are in it for the long haul.

Another way to effectively serve others in their occupation is through self-control. Men *must* be loving and considerate. Men judge women too quickly. First impression, immediate impression of a woman is her outer appearance and this is not reflective of the substance in the woman's character.

Thinking about pursuing women for their physical attributes is tiring in itself. Picture walking down the street then seeing a five-foot eleven inch, 125-pound blond female with an athletic build approaching a Toyota Camry 20 feet in front of you. If a man gawks at her buttocks and breasts he intentionally does work which will automatically make him think lustful thoughts. What is the good in this?

Fish are all over the sea. If one swims in your direction, best to make her feel comfortable and this comes through controlling the thoughts. You can only concentrate on a woman's words during conversation when the mind has been trained to avoid the flesh. How do you train the flesh? Through the palate.

Men must give all diligence as to what they ingest. Eating is responsible for how the body naturally works throughout the day. We eat to live, we do not live to eat. When we live to eat we give into sensuality. Every other part of the human body is then more difficult to restrain. It is like a lake's spillway. The apparatus holds in the waters. We go about, trying to do well unto others. When the waters of life rise, we have given into the flesh; our floodgates have nearly been opened. Then when we disregard self-discipline completely, waters of sensuality pour over the natural boundaries, into unnatural behaviors.

A man of utter self-control, on the other hand, possesses peace in all he does. He cannot be shaken. The storms beat against his house; he will not be moved. No, he will not be moved, because he has set himself upon the rock of self-control. When he gives up that subsequent, unnecessary pastry, we'll say, or some other delicacy, upon hearing that still, small voice, he forbears. Just then he gets under his body and makes it his slave, that after working for the good of others, he will not himself be denied the prize.

Someone said, Life is 10 percent what happens to you and 90 percent how you react to it. Standing firm deals with relationships and relationships are built through work. Men should always work to train their minds to view women as sisters, not as prizes.

In training the eyes to see a woman's face rather than her fruitful parts a man opens himself up to a woman's intellect; he views her as equal; he recognizes what sparks her inward motivation; he sees her true desires.

Job said through the scriptures in the thirty-first chapter, I made a covenant with my eyes not to look lustfully upon a girl. Most people just want to be listened to. They want someone there who will validate what they are feeling. This is the very best of what we can give to one another. We can be there for one another. Most people, they just want people to listen to them speak. Best thing we can do for each other is to learn the art of listening.

In America especially we have a loneliness about us. This loneliness is poverty. It is poverty on a tragic level, because we have everything we want here. We've got so much, we are often glutted as a people because of the superabundance. And then this excess tends to make us preoccupied with ourselves. But we must diligently strive to consider others. He is a perfect creature who is selfless, and relates every situation to the thoughts, feelings and emotions of the other person. He is perfect who puts himself into the "shoes" of the other person, to walk in that other person's situation for a while. Most people just want to be listened to. And to an amazing degree this is a profound way of showing them we love them. They see we listen, and our agenda is secondary to their condition. We do the best when we give another person our attention, as though he or she were the only person in the world.

Sex should be the utmost expression of a man's love to his wife, and in my estimation only for the means of having children. I am finding this more and more to be preferable. When a man and woman sleep with one another they do strengthen bonds. They become closer, in the flesh.

What is better, however, than a man serving his wife, the partner he has chosen to reveal his soul to in all aspects of life, from deep devotion, and the woman to the man? Is there any greater accomplishment? I think not.

From the outside it seems as though when a man and his wife look at each other with sensuality day after day, over and over, they look at one another in a carnal, worldly sense. But, when a man and his wife look at each other as brother and sister, a team who has chosen one another for the means of service to humanity, they have something special.

When a man sleeps with a woman out of wedlock, he will be left emotionally hollow from the physical relationship. A man can say, She has a nice body or whatever. Point is the woman's flesh is only a shell. Seeking women for pleasure will only lead to pain. I won't tell you not to chase women. I can only share my former grief. When a man meets in the bed with a woman, and they do the nasty, because out of wedlock, that is what it is, nasty, the man can only get so much pleasure, no matter how remarkable pleasure seems at the time. The day after, the man can think about what he did and say to himself, "Self, what was I doing?" Or he can shut himself off emotionally. Most men who were not in a drunken stupor do the latter, I think. When men someday somehow can control their carnal desire, then men will be great. Men who can save their virginity until marriage are the strongest men alive.

College was tough. But I figured to definitely go to church still, and I wanted to attend Catholic services as well. The Catholic tradition had been such a part of me. Those beautiful cathedrals were home to my own faith foundation. Whenever I was at a loss I always felt safe in church.

Newman Catholic Student Center was excellent. I wanted to be around Vineyard also. I was spending time at both churches.

At Newman you could sense caring as when a parishioner entered. She could see a large board on the left hand side of the foyer. Stacks and piles of leaflets hung on. They set, and were overlapped by more mini-booklets of information. There was no lack of service to find about. There were activities. People actually made an effort to **be** Christian and Catholic.

My feelings of loneliness were similar to the rest of the nation of college freshmen. There was this persecution, this underlying notion I was different. But difference was okay. Because if everybody were the same this world would cease to be interesting.

We were made unique to make a new mold.

I met Mary Mertzlufft, a woman with a gentle spirit and kind disposition. She was one of the first folks I met during the traditional ice cream get-together following Sunday morning services. Mary was large—very tall for a woman and with a solid frame. She had short red hair and was built like a lady defensive end. She emanated warmness. She gave hugs to where they simply flowed from her. Mary was like those Catholics you think of when Sainthood comes to mind.

She never married, had a heart for the oppressed, and was a staunch opponent of the death penalty.

All Americans are schizophrenic. We have the tendencies to lock our doors, legally kill people who have killed people, etc. By connecting with the mentally ill, we give them strength, and in essence, strength to the whole planet. It is difficult to take the extra effort to listen to those mentally afflicted souls, castaways of this, allegedly greatest of all nations. We, however, build others by lending them our ears.

The Christian part buried in Catholicism on the whole was brought to the forefront at Newman. Sunday services at 11 a.m. were made up of mostly City of Carbondale folks. And then during the 9 p.m. mass, the crowd was almost all SIU students.

Openness We must lay down pride and go for letting ourselves be seen. People, especially church folk, need to be transparent. One thing which troubles me about the beautiful Catholic Church is the tendency of church-goers to keep hearts well below the surface. Maybe I'm wrong here, but I don't think I am. People see each other in different ways. Maybe I am wrong on this one, but I don't think I am. People get bottled up. Getting bottled up creates pressure. If a Coca-Cola bottle has the cap on tight, the container holds a good amount of pressure. Release of that cap and the twisting of it, makes the bottle say fizz. Ah, what a sound. Same with people. When we get something bottled up inside of us, and we keep it pressure builds. Pressure can help us excel in serving one another. Pressure should not be put on by the self, though. As a people, we must realize our limitations.

Overcoming fear must be done with help from others.

My awakening to Jesus Christ came during the Newman services. People had this reverence for deep, prayerful reflection. Candles burned on each side of the altar, where Brother Chris Piasta taught his sermon and performed the ritual. On most Sundays a beautifully detailed wooden cross with Christ hung serenely, portraying the suffering a man underwent to maintain his religion in the face of persecution. Piasta, a chubby Franciscan Friar, who was priest at Newman, had short brown hair, with distinct features on his round face. He wore an intense passion along with skinny glasses. He learned street smarts from the avenues and boulevards of Manhattan as a graduate student at New York University. Piasta was German. He was fond of soccer and moved well for a Catholic clergyman. He laughed easily and was warm with people. When Chris first came to Newman, about the same year I arrived in Carbondale, he was shy, and stressed, with just cause—he was a leader in a considerable-size congregation, and young. Piasta I knew, but it was only because Julie, my friend from a stagecraft-scenery class, introduced me to him on one of the frequent nights we students randomly hung out in the Newman Center, sharing each other's company. We spoke with one another at our first meeting in passing, and would not exchange conversation again for another two years. We worked on Habitat for Humanity and Lite Supper. We would just be as one team, like a living, breathing organism unified in the spirit of service. My goal is to combine the two—faith and work—that I may be so very consumed with my faith whatever work I do will be an extension of my devotion to the One who created me. No one can take those memories away.

A pen my mom bought has the words written on it, "**Teamwork** is the fuel that allows common people to produce uncommon results."

Habitat was awesome. We had *ownership* of that.

We created memories and left it all we had on the build site.

We traveled to Battle Creek, Michigan for a Spring Break Build. We took off in vans. I rode in back as Greg sat shotgun in the same vehicle. It was a beautiful ride.

Others sat to my right and left asleep. It was midday. Greg's girlfriend Jackie drove.

DRUGS AND FOOTBALL

I was hunched over, a little sleepy like. I looked up. Greg slowly reached back. He had these gentle eyes that were paradoxically on fire in the same instant. He looked up at me. He just looked, in a steady gaze. It had to have been at least six seconds. Greg was glad we embarked on this trip. He was glad we were going for the trip of our lifetimes.

We arrived at a nun's dormitory in Battle Creek. A sanctuary was on the bottom floor of the two-story building.

We played games on the bottom floor, in the commons area. There were about 13 of us. We played Catch Phrase. That game is so much fun. We played some more. We played board games. Mm. Mm. We had some good times. After games were over everybody else was in the kitchen or in bedrooms, or wandering the building.

John Scarano, Newman's Director and Habitat's adviser, spoke with me in the downstairs. It was just us. We sat near one another at the spacious table. I had something on my mind. But it was great us two there, having a conversation. Those are actually the best memories in life and all eternity—when you sit there and speak and things come from you.

"John," I said. "I need help with my brother. I try to be there for him. You know, I try to be around and all."

He listened intently. He nodded in everything I said.

"He's got schizophrenia," I said. John shuttered. He immediately, instinctively drew back. His eyes got big, but we kept talking. This is not your run-of-the mill adviser to advisee conversation. No, John was being laden with a burden heavy to be borne. He pretty well listened. He only said a handful of words. John was a gifted listener.

I felt so out of sorts. Jharmel was on my mind every day. Most days he was what I thought about most.

I called him from my room in the convent. He was in a hospital. I said it was good to hear him. We sat hundreds of miles apart. But just hearing his voice was all I needed. I just needed to be there with him. I had to know he was all right.

Battle Creek was straight other than that.

We made meals together. Making meals was one of the very best parts of the whole trip. Greg, and Jackie organized it to where some cooked the meal and others cleaned the dishes afterward. We lived a divine existence. We thrived as a community. We worked shoulder-to-shoulder, way we are supposed to live.

We labored during the days. We worked on one house in particular called a rehab. A rehab has a good foundation, but the top is in need of repair. We tear down the top just to build it up again.

Organizing the people was what seemed to be a daunting task for a tall, mustached Michiganite named Dirk. He was our build supervisor. Dirk spoke with a slow, soothing, reassuring tone which let us all know he was in charge.

We got gussied up at night. We went out to eat. This was different than what I had done in the past. In high school I went out and drank with the buds.

But on this trip we went to the nunnery from work. We got into our respective showers and got to smelling good. Guys wanted to look good for the ladies and vice versa. It was clean. I was finally part of something *clean*. Yes!

We worked during the day. We learned. My brain works at a scattered rate in some instances, but this housing work made me come alive. I could see absolutely no fault in it.

John marked on a piece of wood (He gave me responsibility of a power tool) at one of the three or four build sites we undertook.

He said make this cut. I made it. I felt flawless. I engaged my whole being with Habitat for Humanity in Michigan. Building houses was now my hobby, my pastime, my work, my muse. I felt impeccable, because together we were perfect. Nothing could stop us. We did everything right. It was like football all over again. But no glory and all guts.

We gave of ourselves because we believed it to be the right course of action. We felt this was the way you create a euphoria, or as the religious scriptures have it, the Kingdom of Heaven.

We arrived back in Carbondale after a week's work. I was more engaged than ever.

I sat in class day-dreaming about what we would build next. It is nuts how the project worked. We had an incredible response. I arrived 7:50

a.m. at the Student Center, entered the doors, and saw 30 students standing around, or sitting on the palatial steps. At one point we had to turn volunteers down. Scene was jaw-dropping. These 18, 19, 20-somethings could be at home recovering from a hangover but they want to build houses for poor people.

We drove to our build site behind the University mall.

I stood on a ladder and screwed drywall up to the ceiling. People gathered around to watch.

They gave undivided attention. We were all on the same page; they learned from me and I from the job. Women and men took an *active* interest in building our community and there was the difference.

Serving became a **tangible excellent** for us all. **Us** was the operative word. We were pudding in the pie.

Another day about ten of us worked on an Oak street house laying the surface on the outside deck. Five of us stood inside the body of the deck with hammers. We punched nails into 12' boards. Workers from outside the zone handed the boards, sliding them our way ever so carefully, but at a continual pace, as we developed a distinct rhythm.

As we popped nails through boards and into the beams those handing picked up and prepared new boards to slide in the constantly-filling deck. Space became less and less. Some of us hopped out as the space abated.

We finished the day with a deck. The lot of us worked together in unity to make the community stronger through action. I asked God if He would make me cool in a composed and collected sort of way if I would follow His lead. This was a long time ago.

When we assist others in creative ways we are doing something constructive. And when you are doing so with a *group* of others. Man. You are doing something special.

We achieved concrete—literally—concrete results when we assembled in unison.

I felt useful with Habitat. God began to develop within me a talent of menial service.

Everybody's got a story to tell, is what my mentor at college told me more than once. This digging, this searching—it's worth it.

Mike Lawrence inspired me to run. He was my mentor in college. I went to Mike's office, and we talked about running. Mike said he ran several miles a day. It was amazing, talking to a person who ran so much. I sat there—three feet from him—a runner.

I used to associate with pot-smoking football buddies. It took power. Football required some endurance. Running at the level Mike ran, though, took a *serious* mindset. And that's where I came face to face with a model of consistency.

He ran every morning. Mike was did not waver, see. That's something I appreciated about the man. Constancy is something I admire in all male role models, but especially Mike.

I went into his office and I know he could see through me. He would know if something was up. Mike could sense it. I admired the self-discipline he exercised. He got much of this through an ardent dedication to physical fitness.

Mike was an avid runner. Every day he went out there and ran. And you can tell. For anybody out there who exercises regularly, you can tell when you miss. You can see in attitude, if you are insightful or perceptive, when you miss when you know you should have run. It affects sleep as well.

Mike looked at me across the empty space between us. He gazed past his discreet glasses. The air was heavy and he would be able to tell if anything was going wrong. Mike was a sound judge of character.

"How are you?" he said. Seconds rolled by. He would not breathe. His eyes peered into mine giving me his undivided attention. I always admired that straightforwardness.

"Fine," I said.

"Really?"

He always got me with the question. He taught me on a deep level with that question, because when somebody asks, "How are you?" The asker needs to listen. You should be giving him your undivided attention. Other person needs to take a personal inventory right quick. He needs to give something accurate.

It was about the time Mike gave me the question, "Really" I began to think a little deeper. I began to understand better the depth of this man.

Then I started to seek out a way to utilize my very best talents. I made a serious quest to become serious about what it was I was doing.

Franklin Roosevelt said once, "There is nothing to fear but fear itself." What's more, we decrease anxiety when we *prepare* for a presentation, a test or a basketball game. Fear of death or dying is an irrational fear. We will all perish from this human form. We needn't worry about what is going to happen with the safety of this nation. We as a people should be concerned with making things better at home. All of us can find ways to improve the life we have been given. Only through mercy have we been given these cards, no matter how unfair they may seem. Through faith of a brighter day we can lay them down on the table. Any one of us could be hit while in a car tomorrow on the way to work. Not to be morbid, that's a fact.

Carpe Diem means seize the day. The maxim is from a Latin poem by Horace. Now the saying has some weight to it.

"Get as much education as you can because they can never take that away from you," my grandpa said once. When we learn we can grasp; in wondering we understand the possibilities of an effervescent tomorrow filled with a myriad of technicolor opportunity.

Fortunately education was all around me growing up. Family skillfully taught me. Mom was a teacher. Grandmother taught classmates and me at St. Michael's preschool. My cousin Louise taught and still does so in the Southwestern School District. Education was in my genes as well, as Bobbye taught art at Rock grade school in East St. Louis.

A university allows you to go after what you want. In literally pursuing dreams in education, a person develops into what he always desired to be. She can work the profession she dreamed of as a child, making the dream right there, and tangible.

Learning in America is absolutely fantastic at the University level.

For an intelligent opinion to adhere to truth it has to be well-researched with **at least three resources**, Jack Young, my professor colleague (he was not much older than I), said. Dealing with my own conviction, I had to weigh ideals and come up with the most honest one, and best one. Mine was not always the correct conclusion. And it shocked me at times these people would tell you so.

School is a place where intelligence thrives and ignorance dives.

Successful people came to speak about all sorts of topics when I was at school. Some people had been on TV, others were icons in their own right, one guy wrote a book on the works of acclaimed author T.S. Eliot. All these people traveled on a quest for knowledge. Their desire definitely influenced my own.

Our human race has come so far in history. I walked along the rows of Dell desktop computers on the rustic first floor of the great, noble and majestic seven-story Morris Library on campus. Some friends would be working on last-minute research projects, while others looked for Internet gaming amusement at Internet sites

I regularly went to the library when simply bored, if nothing else, during my senior year. I didn't need to hang out at Lewis Park and watch reality shows. Friends showed their faces—Yusuke, Hiroki and Hideki, from Japan—in the long aisles and filled me with joy.

Pursuit of truth is a daunting task, especially when so many half-truths abound in the world today. Libraries provide us with an outlet to smash half-truths where they stand feebly, aiming to debilitate the public consciousness.

One of the most enduring sayings grandpa ever gave me was, "get as much education as you can, because they can never take that away from you."

One night I sat outside the Interfaith Center along Highway 51 in Carbondale during a candle light vigil with one of my war protest buds. Cars passed by and passengers regularly yelled evil at us.

Seth, my buddy, was a vegetarian. I asked how he found out about vegetarianism. He had thick blond hair down to his shoulders. He was scrubby just like all protesters were, as though they had not missed a beat since the Nixon administration. Well, I was a hippy-wannabe, and I sat out there, through some wind, through some slurs, through some vegetarian discussion.

Seth hunched a little, grasping for protein in his low calorie diet, and looked up to me with his unique model gaze.

"I just started reading up on it." Seth's reading made me think: "If he can read about being a vegetable eater, I can read up about what I feel is important in this world."

So I told him, "Man, that's what I want to do. I've always wanted to find out about Martin Luther King Jr. with all the change he helped create…"

"Go for it," he said. And there, with a verbal, commitment, I was a man on a mission.

My journey to thoroughly understand nonviolence has been exciting in these past few years. Not since football have I found something so stimulating, though this time the stimulation is mental rather than physical.

King taught us to use our thought process coupled with love as a means to eradicate injustice. Dr. King said, Not until I entered theological seminary, however, did I begin a serious intellectual quest for a method to eliminate social evil.

I *did* go to Morris Library soon thereafter and picked up the book of Martin Luther King Jr.'s writings and speeches. I began to understand blackness.

Very soon in the book, after reading the foreword by King's wife Coretta Scott, I got the sense this was a deep man, full of wisdom, like one of those Old Testament prophets. Turned out King was new and exciting, provocative of the very thoughts and prejudices of his day. He was a man beyond myth, sprinkled with the tranquility in words he uttered, in search of truth. King looked for a set of law that could not be shaken either here or in the heavens.

I sat in the back of Ben my friend's small, fancy car on the way to Staunton. My friend was Ben Brimer, a black-haired Jewish brother with pudgy cheeks and a stocky frame. Things were funny to him as he laughed casually. His poetry in our English class was of an intense nature, direct and to the point. He was a fan of Henry Rollins. He looked into the rearview mirror.

"What you reading?" he said. Well, seems when folks are reading, people ask what they are reading, God bless 'em.

"Martin Luther King," I said, engrossed. As I looked back down to the pages, my eyes were fixed. Day was a bright, gleaming day, one of those shiny afternoons that nearly seems too good to be true when you are there, breathing it, and then wishing for it come mid-February. Grass was so very moist and tender it was almost palatable.

Dr. King's writing basically stuck to my face. Martin Luther King, Jr. said in essence every person can be great because every person can serve. A man does not have to have a doctor's degree to serve. A woman does not need to know Einstein's theory of relativity to serve. Every man can be great, because every man can serve, which will lead to what King referred to as *The Beloved Community*.

It was vivid. It was intense. He spoke directly, as to say, "This is truth. Please believe it. Because these principles have no turning. They are immovable, set as the hand that changes time."

He gave detailed descriptive accounts, backup. I was reading the writings of a man, who *knew* truth. He presented information in an extremely difficult way by making it confrontational and caring in the same vein.

I thought these guys were only in novels and old Bible stories. "These men were not tangible these days," I figured. "How can this be?" But then I wanted to *be* the words. I wished to reach out and grab the words and put the words in the precious treasure chest of my mind and seal them tenderly in my heart.

There was no reason for me to believe prior to picking up this book, this was the same Mr. King whose birthday we celebrated each year. Some of his writings were succinct. Some were compact.

Yet he could also expand an idea into an eloquent essay on social justice. King's best language usage was flowery, attractive in the sheer poise, and with enough content to draw the reader to verbs, as a bear paws honey.

There was a cosmic connection as my eyes gazed at the words, dumbfounded, in total captivity by the words of a prophet, a man who changed my life, not through some physical dexterity as a football player, but by a mind used to better the human condition.

My eyes, as they felt wide as tangerines, analyzing the writing from this man who acted as a conduit for the living God. I read sentences, words and paragraphs literally twice in succession, astonished at the clarity of expression; the technicality and lucidity of these adjectives. Metaphors jumped off the page.

DRUGS AND FOOTBALL

Jeremiah the prophet was hounded by people every day because he spoke out against how hypocritical they were. Some even wanted to stone him. Jeremiah, even though he did not ask to be a prophet, became one because he was *led* by his faith.

God spoke through Jeremiah when he said, if you can find but one person who deals honestly and seeks the truth, I will forgive this city. Jeremiah replied that they made their faces harder than stone and refused to repent. He was in a difficult position. But God was with him the whole way.

A man becomes uplifted when he knows he is part of a team.

A sign in the Daily Egyptian newsroom at Southern Illinois University said a team is a group of common people who come together to get uncommon results. People come together, work and when they achieve, the end result is spectacular. Secrecy, however, separates us from God. Organizations that leave people out, or have an exclusive attitude, make others feel out of the mix, and this ends up hurting people's feelings. Openness needs to be at the forefront of any organization, or government, to avoid corruption.

One sign that hung over the campus desk in the newsroom was, "If your mother says she loves you, check it out."

I failed to heed the tip on a story about how drinking equals popularity in college. I put a woman's quote in my story who I did not actually interview, but who was quoted in my news story. I got the information off the Internet and somebody else did the interview. I wrote it down without attributing the information procedurally correct and that was wrong. Learning was a regular occurrence inside the newsroom.

I remember one instance in which the enemy was trying to get at me hardcore. It was getting on toward the end of my Senior year. I figured, this question has been on my mind, and I must ask it before I leave, and get a straight answer.

A trusted advisor, Lance Speere, was my faculty managing editor at the Daily Egyptian, and possessed keen newspaper wisdom. We sat in his office and I asked him why people report murder as news. I did not understand why homicides were simply stated in newspapers without regular follow-ups. I wished to know more of the use of journalism as a tool for the common good of the community.

I saw no use in reporting about the crime if people were not going to at least make an attempt into finding out why a person would do such a thing.

He said, "There must have been some reason you came in here." I was terrified. All I wanted was a starting point from which to begin discussion, because with more in-depth reporting, I felt, we could contribute and, hopefully reduce murders across this great nation.

Speere said with self-control, when an event happens, when life is lost, the incident needs to be reported about. Lance told me reporting on such stuff showed the judicial system is working.

When asking a serious question, I could expect a serious tone.

I asked the same question in the middle of Bill Recktenwald's Investigative Journalism class. Recktenwald was fit, with glasses on a 6' frame. He had blondish gray hair with a rugged look. Recktenwald had been an editor at a large daily newspaper. He cussed casually with a Chicago accent, but taught a brand of journalism that was highly practical, and hands-on. He prepared us for life after school in a strong manner.

"Should murder be reported in the news?" I asked. He looked down, then spoke about something about which I cannot remember. He right away took it as a non-serious matter. I was quite serious. Less than a couple weeks later, Bill brought in a video to our computer lab. He told us about when he worked for the Chicago Tribune the reporting staff took it upon themselves to do a story on every child who was murdered in Chicago for one year. This was exactly what I was looking for.

A major television network did a story of their own on the Tribune's coverage. Newspaper articles from the broadcast presentation had pictures of children who had been slain.

Upon asking the same question of why we report murder in newspapers if we do not follow up on the story to another of my professors, Gerald Stone, a doctorate degree holder, he said to me that was just what he had always been told to do.

Redemptive value is where news shines for a community. Where we can get to the very best use of our occupations are where we will take our world to the next level.

On some occasions I get filled with vision. Like I get confirmation in what I am doing in a certain situation. When I submit to the Creator. I see myself with wide eyes, the way the Lord sees me. Even now I feel like what singer-songwriter Michael W. Smith referred to as a conduit, or, a circular band of wires, because this is what I was made to do. Smith said when he gets out onstage he sings and it is like this current.

School frazzled my wires, though, at the end of senior year. School means testing ones' self in order to be better than before. I kept on testing. I kept pushing myself.

Stress comes with school, so, one must be prepared to know when that stress is coming.

It was the week before finals senior year. My brother stayed with me then, sleeping on the floor in my 8' x 8' room at Lewis Park, so home was not a place of relaxation for me.

I had no food of substance in the refrigerator. I was taking five classes, working 10 hours at *The Daily Egyptian*, building with Habitat for Humanity Saturday mornings, attending weekly National Association of Black Journalists meetings, and going to church Sunday mornings. And I was feeling it.

I had been getting 6 hours and three hours of sleep in two consecutive nights in the middle of the week. night when I could not reach slumber, my resolve said to take a blanket and pillow, and go camp outside of the church, one mile up the road, where I had safety from fears.

I bowed down to the wooden cross with a purple sash draped thereon outside of the Newman Catholic Student Center. I released all the unconfessed sins imaginable. This was around midnight on the edge of campus. I was 25 feet from the sidewalk. Students could have passed by. They could have thought me a fool. Everything was dark.

I received a vision of Christ walking up to me in the midst of my terrible darkness. He approached. He looked at me as I turned over and said with a fixed, flaming gaze, "Get up and testify."

I rose. I set my blanket down in front of the Newman Student Center doors and lied—**laid** down. An artificial light shone above the entrance. I still could not grasp sleep. I just wanted..........sleep. Minutes passed. I heard weird noises inside the church. I entered to see what was the matter.

Greg Padesky and Jackie Donavan were hanging out inside. Greg's lower back tightened up giving terrible spasms as he sat in a wheelchair.

"Aahhhhhhhhhhyyh!" he said.

Jackie and I tried to move him or he tried to scoot himself, however—

"AAHhhhhhYyyuh!"

His back became even more sensitive. He continued wailing.

This continued for half an hour. We resolved to take him to the hospital. Getting him toward the van was an arduous chore. So we wheeled him at a turtle's pace. We prayed for him right there. Greg finally got in with much effort so Jackie could drive him to Carbondale hospital.

I went home and slept.

Nathan, one of my roommates, drove me to the Health center on Greek Row. Yasoda Modali, my psychiatrist, met with me and all that was on my mind was **need sleep**. I didn't care what she was telling me. My head tried to keep focus on her countenance. I was reeling.

I explained my lack of sleep and she told me to go about my day, to go to classes and work. But I was completely spent and said I just couldn't do it.

After further prodding from Modali, my pride would not let me give in and she gave me a prescription for sleeping medicine. I went to Vineyard Community Church, laid on a couch in the children's crying room.

So peaceful and quiet, serene and light. Auuhhhhhh.

I missed all my classes, calling off work, and overcame a major battle. Triumph gave me indescribable strength. Overcoming gave me understanding. Life meant more to me after that as grace had just showered down upon me. I felt a new appreciation for circumstances which were before insignificant.

Next week John Scarano called up. You could tell vocally he was deeply concerned about me, and my condition.

"Brett? This is John Scarano at the Newman Center. How are you?"

"Oh, I'm fine," I said.

"Listen, Brett, if you need a place to stay, you are welcome to sleep inside the Newman Center."

He cared when so many other activities were going on. He completely comforted me.

Whatever my hands scribbled down on the final exams seemed incoherent as exhaustion took its toll. I wasn't as bad off as the end of the previous week, but spent nonetheless. Church was my sanctuary through daily, incessant prayer. I read my Bible. I sought out friends. And sport became a profoundly important outlet for me. I began to put the pieces back.

Sports as Uplift

I began revving up my motor at the Student Recreation Center. I started a flexible routine of running a couple miles, going to play a pick up basketball game or five, and there was stress control for the day.

I practiced in that side basketball court in the summer, completely alone for long periods at a time, shooting the basketball, battling all the voices in my head saying I would not finish, my brother was no good, I wasn't good enough to be a reporter…and the ball kept flowing from my fingertips, somehow.

Just kept on shooting. I ran on the Rec Center upper track that summer, and felt a breaking off of chains. Mike, who was about 60, said he ran four or five miles six days out of the week. Something happened up there on the track, leaving slavery behind.

Other people passed by. I stayed in step with some. I passed others. A certain wind, it felt like, was lifting me through five-ten-fifteen minutes—something unexplainable. My whole being just wanted to run. I considered all the while, "How high should I bring my legs up? How far back should my kick go? How much should I cut back on weightlifting?"

Running was my muse, a new hobby, a sport my mind dwelled upon, even when not trying to purposely think on it. Running provided a freedom I had never experienced before. God guided me along this beautiful journey marked by sweat and inward emotion. I breathed the experience, and it permeated everything around me.

I looked out to the inner track. People played basketball... "Gotta stay on task here," I thought. My whole body came alive. My legs kept kicking. "Pat Pat Pat Pat Pat," I brought 'em up, put 'em down, "Pat Pat Pat Pat." Pain and suffering temporarily away. It felt like I was on a different hemisphere or another planet completely. All that was happening, all the troubles and challenges I faced the semester before were easing off me.

I felt the pressures sliding off my back, a shedding of old skin. God was doing a *new* work in me. The only other times I had experienced this was at church those past couple of years—this wholeness and togetherness—a complete unity. But now the unity was inside myself. I felt as though I had not been treating myself with respect. I had disrespected the very vessel God had given me for service. He did so much for me. And by weighing myself down with unnecessary obligation I was disappointing the only real Father I ever had, one who was there with me in the most difficult times...when my bed was wet...when Mom and Dwayne kissed and it was so strange... He was with me all through all the pain and suffering before, in football, when feeling as though I had terribly and irreparably disappointed the team through poor decisions...He was there...He was right by my side, even through serious periods of feeling a disenfranchised state of emotion. When I felt *so* different. He was right there telling me—you *are* special. You *are* wanted. "*Brett, I love you,*" he said in a fatherly way. I gave to him my fears, and he was lifting up my head. I now knew **nothing** could hold me back. No, not now. I had come too far. My mental health had been pushed to the very limits. I had been gone. I had seen sleep-deprived hallucinations. And now I knew how to handle all that. I now knew how to beat my body and make it my slave. Yes, my Father had disciplined me. He who does not chastise his son hates him. This discipline was borne out of a profoundly exhilarating love; an ineffable joy. For His joy, was my strength. When I had strayed He showed me the very depths of human existence. He allowed me to stray so very far from what He wanted for me, to show me my own image, as in a mirror.

I had damaged my own self-esteem. I high jacked my sanity. All because I wanted to feel accepted. I wanted to feel important. I pushed myself. Now my ultimate Father let me see what He wanted was for me to run like a little child. He wanted me to run, as on an effervescent summer day, with Him. No worries. No strain.

But I regularly started to feel this worship in day-to-day life. My life became wrapped up in His existence. Monday through Sunday matured into a living, breathing faith.

Then I prayed for God to show me *His* truth. I asked Jesus to show me the way.

I dreamed at night of being in a school in some town, a small town just like Staunton, only a new school. I was behind a set of lockers and I heard the principal speak over the intercom.

"Students, listen up," Hustling and bustling youths shuffled to a delayed halt.

"The President has just passed legislation scaling money from the Department of Defense to the Department of Education." And the crowd went wild. Students jumped with upward excitement, jubilantly dancing, only for a brief moment.

Then back to the studies with a focus and appreciation for learning. It seems when bearing weight under the most intense pressure I have faced, there was a light to point me toward better days, an inspiration to continue on. No matter how dark the road got, no matter what storms raged within my breast, there was a way some how.

I have been praying the Prayer of Jabez lately found in I Chronicles 4:9-10. Bruce Wilkinson wrote a book, titled, "The Prayer of Jabez," a work that guides people through the short Prayer of Jabez found in the Bible. The prayer says, "Enlarge my coast." When someone is active and asks God to enlarge their coasts, or territory, He will put them to work. This is all right when coming to rejection. Jabez's prayer is powerful in that his mother bore him with sorrow. Jabez means, to bear with sorrow. Wilkinson said the mother was probably in a rough part of life. The baby's father may have abandoned the family before he was born. The father may have died. In any case, Jabez's mother bore him with pain.

He overcame the odd name. He rose above his environment. He was as the Phoenix, ascending from the ashes.

Jabez rose up from his unfortunate place in the earliest stages of life. He lifted himself up by the bootstraps, as it were.

God will use people when they want to be used. This means He will send people to houses if people yearn to do something with their talents—to wash dishes, to rake leaves, yes, to scrub toilets—for people they barely know or have never even met. This is all for the benefit of service. Jabez was more honorable than his brethren. He sought the reward. A great reward is there if people are willing to work.

Humans need the will for there to be a way. Without a desire, there is no road to travel. It is merely an idea of the journey.

Voices creep into the equation sometimes.

"Aughh, you're not worth getting in shape," people say to themselves. "You've been fat for so long."

This is straight nonsense. All people have intrinsic worth, a basic and essential value. Each person is equipped with a gift of service to the human race.

People find out their worth by going after what they are good at; in essence, what they have fun doing. Folks commonly look up and feel trapped in jobs they *do not* enjoy. Taking focus off what motivates a person directly inhibits the individual's ability to serve.

The next school semester I found something fulfilling. Our university chose me as a resident assistant.

A keyword as an RA was **team**. But training was **fun**. Man was it. Training was fantastic. The eh, 48 of us went to the Rec and the resident directors from our three campus residence areas split us into teams. We had the whole place to ourselves. The entire vast, huge facility, was ours for a week of training. Some RAs wore red shirts, some green, and others yellow. I got to wear blue, my favorite color!! Yes.

We played different games with each other to build teamwork. It was awesome, all of us running around in there. Afterward Tina Horvath, my resident director, gave us leave to go play whatever sports we wanted to.

I met many cool people there. We became acquainted with each other. We met new friends, and we all thrived knowing we had each others' backs.

We went down into the basement of Grinnell dining hall further in the training week. These several speakers came and spoke with us.

Our diversity director walked in painted blue. He had a thick mustache. He looked so funny, and talked sensitively in front of all us.

Then another man came in. He seemed like an official type, but from outside the university. He spoke frankly about some things. We had gone to war in Iraq less than a year before.

"If you see someone doing anything suspicious, we want to know about it," he said. He went on to say that if we saw anyone of an Arab background acting suspiciously they wanted to know of it.

Then Love, a 6'7", 302 pound black man, rose his hand.

"I got friends who are Muslim," he said. Jason, an RA in the same category with Eddie, in healthfulness and skillful speech, sat near me, and said, "Ooooh…"

The crowd became visibly relaxed by Love's comment. We were thinking along similar lines. How could we make a preference to someone who groomed his beard a certain way, or had a certain hue of skin? Then the man said something.

Love said he would not tell the man of Arabians on campus and, "Somehow you sleep at night."

Another day in training we all got into a circle and Ben, a spunky veteran RA, led us in an exercise. We each had to say our names with an action, such as a wave, or peace symbol. We went around the room in rumbling laughter, at the funny motions our peers came up with.

The week was strenuous, not for the physical exertion, but for the sheer time it took from us. We were spending about 12 hours a day together, preparing for a variety of situations, and new students who would be utterly unfamiliar with this campus setting. It was not as though we *had* anything better to do. We were training there weeks before school even began.

A resident assistant's duties included advising residents on where to go to on campus to find what they were looking for, instructing them in case of any emergency and so on. Counseling students was also a high honor.

Rachel Benjamin, my friend and Mike Lawrence's secretary, often informally counseled me. She said something that stuck. She said I could be a positive person for others to go to when they need somebody to talk to and listen to them. This was uplifting to me because my mentor had been a journalist for 40 years already, and she told me *I* could be a person for peers to lean on.

Listening to and advising students was highly satisfying—as satisfying as any job I had done. I was being a father to these students. They came to me, away from home, in need of direction. I tried to give them some accurate advice. I was now in a position to give them some of what I had learned. All the while I learned so many things myself.

Jose Manzano let me stay with him and mom at his Collinsville apartment over the Christmas break.

He was always a role model for me. He was my favorite of mom's significant others in her life.

Jose stood 5'5", weighed 180 pounds, and was a health nut. He enjoyed working out at the Fairview Heights Bally Vic Tanny's gym.

Jose moved from Puerto Rico and began working at the Wentzville, Mo. GM plant when he was 18 years old. He had already spent over 45 years at the plant as a maintenance man.

"When I come here," he said through a stutter he tried to get a hold of even then, in his early 70s. "I was at the bottom of the pole. But then I work. I work more and more."

He took his paycheck stub out to show me.

"No, no," I said. "Jose I don't want to see."

"Look," he said intently, standing up to me, less than a foot from my chest. I glanced down and saw he was making more in one week than anyone I had ever known for sure what they made. He *wanted* to show me, too. His earnings were to him something to show people, a badge of honor.

"After I keep working," he said, "I made it to the top."

He told me things. He said you should make sure to eat fruits. He told me to be sure to eat grapefruit. He took different natural juices and pills. He was healthy indeed. Jose had a breakfast regimen including bread, fruit, and either some oats or eggs. He ate all this in his 9' x 5 ½' kitchen. He displayed in the 14' x 12' living room a little statue of the virgin Mary with a serpent under her feet alongside a picture of her mother on the same small table. He slept in a 9' x 9' bedroom and used a bathroom slightly larger than that of an airplane. But Jose had it. He had it all. He was determined. Jose was the man.

"Heat 'em up," Jose said about the eggs. "You scramble 'em up. The—n you put 'em in the microwave for a little while. They taste good."

Humbling Experience

Belleville (Ill.) *News-Democrat* gave me a chance on an internship that same break, December 2003, right after I graduated from SIU. My mother let me use her 1994 Chevy Cavalier for the three-week period. Tension at the News-Democrat was thick and heavy.

News-Democrat Editors Brad Weisenstein and Gary Dotson handed me stories every day the first week. Pressure mounted, swirling like a tornado. Stress came from home as tension built at work. I arrived at work by 8 a.m. and this gave me an opportunity to read through the paper by 8:30 a.m. and then walk in the door.

Brad usually had something for me to report upon by 10 a.m. Getting off work at 4 p.m. was usually out of the question. Working for a professional newspaper was a special opportunity, a cherished learning process. My work needed help practically every night and Mike Koziatek, the night editor, frequently would be hung up with something else, making my wait longer.

I spent my night reading the day's paper or browsing the Internet.

I, of course, did not just come home and plop down in front of the TV. Edwardsville YMCA was only a short drive.

I fantasized of the dozens of fitness center isolation machines. These different engineering marvels filled my head while at work giving me an excitement to get to the gym every night. I sought to work my musculature hardcore night after night.

I rolled home around mid-evening and mother was gracious for the first while.

This plan worked for about a week.

She told me one day she needed to use the car one day.

"Mom," I said. "I'm only going to be at this internship for three weeks."

She looked at me with a baby look stern and unabashed.

"Let me tell you in your language," she said. "You taking the car and being inconsiderate of my transportation needs is not Christian."

Her statement cut to my heart, silencing me.

When she broke me down, I really could not think of a comeback.

My throat tightened, my eyes were literally opened wide to where I could not physically open them any farther. I was essentially judged for my evil and am now far better for it.

She revealed to my eyes the selfishness I displayed.

Going along living my life, trying to make a concerted effort at an internship, while my mother showered me with grace made me consider the relationship I neglected. She brought me down to the very essence of the teachings of Jesus Christ—Do unto others as you would have them do unto you.

Friendship with my mother was and is stronger than any columns of a newspaper. I used a car which was not mine and stayed at an apartment without rent. People fed me and I usually did not pay for it. I somehow did not consider my mother's feelings about using the car. Lo, and behold, she taught me. She woke me up to the fact teachers need to learn also.

I jogged at a steady pace on a brisk, cold night down Collinsville Main Street. I approached a bar.

"Brett!" someone said.

I wondered who could have known me. I knew two people in Collinsville—Jose and a relative who was a Public Library administrator.

I looked over and saw a friend and resident from college, Talia Gilmore who lived near Collinsville.

She told me Ayesha Judkins, her best friend, got into a car wreck and did not survive.

Judkins was my friend and a resident at SIU. I just wanted to be there for Talia, so I stood there in the artificially lit street, not responding with more than five words as she spoke sternly. Somehow I naturally, instinctively was able to block out pain, the first thunderous crash my heart felt. I felt like, when you hear tragedy you go on instinct then. 'S all you can do—consider your training and listen to what's inside. I listened. I tried to be a rock. We each departed in a healthy manner.

I went on about the run.

It was in the chill of winter.

I was saddened and stunned. But something came to me: life goes on. Her smile was so beautiful and warm to behold. I'd never see you again Ayesha. I'd never behold your tender smile. Never again would I understand you here. You receive and let go. Things are given. Things are taken away. That which is dearest is taken away in the twinkling of an eye—and on to eternity.

A group of Black Catholic men gave me a better understanding of that eternity during a Christian retreat to New Orleans. Actually, these men made me feel as though Heaven had come to Earth for those few days. We walked together just beyond the shallow waves bumping into large rocks along Lake Pontchartrain. It was so warm there. We ate shrimp etouffe together, we read scripture together, we sang hymns together. We sang a song together

Walk by faith
And not by sight
Trust in God, it will be all right
The door is open,
It's waiting for you
God is going to see you through

Step out, just a little bit further…This was a dynamic time because with all the older men in the room and some younger guys in there—all sixty some of us, we just let our spirits meld in worship. We moved in coordination with one another worshipping the Ancient of Days. Uplifting is when you have all these men together with you, and you each have an abounding faith also in one another. The experience changed me. Uplifting each other is important for many more than two reasons. I'll name two, though: 1—You are a child of God. 2—We are social beings.

No. 1, you are a child of God, you are God's creation. You didn't just magically appear some day. Your spirit was created, all that, by a force greater than you. That is what makes you awesome. No. 2 We are social beings. We eventually need to turn to somebody, even when we get down and depressed. A song goes,

Lean on me,
When you're not strong
I'll be your friend
I'll help you carry on
For, it won't be long
'til I'm gonna need, somebody to lean on.

A team benefits from ideas of each member. A man can contribute and uplift his team in a myriad of ways.

Brother Ferd Cheri and Brother Joseph Brown were completely encouraging to me, and the whole group. They led us through worship, showed us how it was in the days gone by. Just the two gave the rest of us such strength through their courage to relay stories that were hard to tell about the persecution of black folks.

Makes me think of an amazing story of a Christian man William Wilberforce. He had a particular zeal for public service as he came before parliament in Great Britain pushing for the abolishment of slavery. Wilberforce used his mind, body and soul to accomplish his goal even having his tailor make extra pockets so he could carry more books.

Abolishment of slavery was constantly on his mind, as he presented to Britain's governing body every year for about 45 years, despite heavy opposition including an attempt on his life. While in his mid-70s, however, Wilberforce lay on his deathbed when Parliament passed legislation making slavery illegal. Even though Wilberforce got the news from a messenger and died within two days, throughout his struggle he had a faith to move mountains. He did something just as important as taking a mountain and placing it in the sea. The man married faith with knowledge. Wilberforce took what he knew, worked with the conviction slaves should and **would** be free, and got things done. Even though he could not see what was going to happen, he trusted his God, even through the fire.

Lance Pitluck, a Pastor at the Anaheim Vineyard showed up at our Vineyard for a weekend conference. He had lost a young son. Right in the middle of his grieving, he praised God for his child. There was no bitter shaking the fist in the air. He knew what the Lord had done for him. There was no denying the gift that was placed in his arms. The child was of indescribable importance to him. But the child was here and then gone. His boy meant a great deal to him, but God actually **made** him. Pitluck felt a deep longing, but in the midst, he gave God some praise.

"If there is one thing I wanted you to take out of this whole conference it would be, half the battle is just showing up."

That was his great wisdom. When you do not feel like going anywhere. When you have anxiety about how to go about something, or starting a project, showing up is what is most important. So pat yourself on the back. You have already overcome the challenge of getting out of bed this morning. You wanted to throw the alarm, didn't you?

Life is like a mountain and the only way a person can get to the top is recognizing the strength gained through terrible disappointment and failures past, in seeing scrapes already endured from rocks, spread trees dodged, and loose gravel trudged through.

Pitluck stood up there in front of the hundreds of people.

He stood at 5' 9" 190 pounds in the wide space in front of the drums and backdrop and told us about the Kingdom of Heaven.

He spoke with a surfer accent. He was part of the Jesus movement of the 1970s. He had to have provided for the family in the most important aspect, the spiritual, because, when he was faced with adversity in about the worst given situation, he took what was broken and made it whole by standing like a rock for the rest of his clan. That's all a person's got to do is believe for his family. Such faith is contagious like a wildfire.

Simply using the discipline in getting out of covers is a large part of success. When you get to where you need to be during the day you can respond to things as they come, but you have to be counted "present" first. If things go wrong, ah, so what—you gave it a shot.

I made the cast of a musical called Parade that spring semester.

I ate some Wiseguys pizza one night before practice. Pizza was tasty, but during the night after eating it, I went to the bathroom because of sickness. I proceeded to throw up in a trash can I brought in from inside the lounge next to my room. After hurting and trying to go to sleep I got nauseous and went to the bathroom again, though I barely had the strength to hold myself on the trash can, which was holding my whole body from tipping over.

During practice the next morning at McLeod Theater, just moving was a chore. My role in the production was mostly technical. My responsibility was with the stage crew mainly making sure set props were in their proper places.

As the cast sang the line, "Georgia home of the strong and sure," I hung over the stage properties, unsure of whether my presence was doing any good. All I did while offstage was hold onto furniture like I was completely out of it. I asked the director if he would allow me to go home and he said no, a little miffed. (He must have thought I had drunk a good deal of wine the night before!) But without asking I would not have known.

Possibly I should have carried the trash-can to rehearsal that morning. Maybe the incident taught me what to eat and what not to eat. Possibly it was food poisoning.

At the present I eat little dairy. My experience with limiting dairy intake has been beneficial. Please consider, in 1991 and 1996 no state in America had more than 25 percent of residents who were obese, according to the Centers for Disease Control and Prevention Website. As of 2004, at least nine states had that number. Something about dairy makes it worth limiting. Anything that spoils easily and we should be wondering what integrity the substance has and what purpose that serves in our physical members.

Plant foods last outside of refrigeration for days, and they are also the best for the human body. A vegan (plant foods only; no animal products) diet has no cholesterol. It has very little to no saturated fat, and many plant foods (i.e peanut butter, guacamole, olives, canola oil) are high in monounsaturated fats, which actually benefit the cardiovascular system.

I failed because something was bad with the Wiseguys pizza, which had to have been a handling issue within the company or their affiliates. But then again, I can control what to eat, and that food can be such that does not spoil easily, as cheese does.

To control the body, one must first bridle his eating habits. The food guide pyramid is a nice guide as to the portions of what food types to eat. If a man eats vegetables primarily, and pastas, as his main foods, he should have little problem keeping himself focused when a woman walks by, or when talking with a woman. Fruits Nuts, rice, beans, salsa are all good at keeping the animal at bay.

We **must** follow the lead of others who have gone before us and faced trials. Through trials we persevere and shine the resilience we possess as a people. I recommend people to look into the lives of Jesus Christ, who made the ultimate sacrifice, and Martin Luther King, Jr., Mohandas Gandhi etc. because these men were people just like us, yet they lived their lives with an intensity.

We must look to the prophets so we may learn from their trials and suffering.

People may think I'm crazy, but I know Jesus loves me no matter how much I make on my pay check, or how much I've lied. He has always been constant, even when I have been erratic, changing with the wind. I need to tell people, uneducated folks the story of Jesus Christ, my hero. Jesus was born in a manger in a small town of Bethlehem to a Virgin according to the Bible. He grew up to be twelve years of age and when His mother and His earthly father Joseph walked back from the temple, they wondered where the boy Jesus was. Mary became concerned and troubled she could not find her baby boy. So eventually she found Him in the temple where they had left from. Mary told her son how she had been worried sick over his absence. He said to his mother, Momma, I'm just doing the will of my Father. And Jesus did many other weird things such as this growing up; to make people sure he was out of this world. Jesus and his momma went to a wedding in Cana when he was much more advanced in years, about 30. Mary said, Son, they have no wine. The groom and bride had run out of wine to drink. Jesus said, Mother, don't concern me in trivial matters. It's not my time yet. Mary insisted. Jesus got ready to work through the grace of the Heavenly Father. Mary told the attendants at the feast to do everything Jesus told them. So, Jesus took the barrels of water and made them into wine. All the people at the banquet were amazed at His character and grace, and people were pleased with Him. Jesus went on. During the same period, he fasted forty days and forty nights. He was led up to a mountain by the Holy Spirit toward the beginning of his abstaining period as he was tempted by the devil. The enemy told Jesus, if you are Son of the Most High God, turn this rock into bread. Jesus replied, but man does not live on bread alone. Then the devil wanted Jesus. to look over a cliff. The enemy said to Jesus, if you are the Christ, jump off this here ledge and you will be saved. As it is written, Angels will come concerning you. Lest you dash your foot against a stone. Jesus replied, it is also written, Do not put the Lord your God to the test. So Jesus outwitted the slimy devil like he would end up doing for the remainder of his tenure as God in earthly form. Jesus loved being with people. He would go from house to house healing people from their sicknesses, curing folks with infirmities. Jesus chose twelve people to follow him closely, to watch what He did so they might be able to copy what He was doing some day. He chose people, Andrew, Peter (called Simon), Judas Iscariot, another Judas, Matthew, John, James, Timothy, Thomas and some others. Jesus taught these men how to pray.

> Our Father who art in heaven
> Hallowed be thy name
> Thy kingdom come, thy will be done,
> On earth as it is in heaven
> Give us this day our daily bread
> And forgive us our trespasses
> As we forgive those who trespass against us,
> And lead us not into temptation,
> But deliver us from evil.

Jesus taught the disciples self-control. He was a disciplinarian, but not in a cold sense. Jesus was a loving, compassionate guy who cared about the opinions and inquiries of his friends. The disciples followed Jesus, largely because He was unafraid to tell them how to do things. He said to his twelve, when you fast, do not fast as the hypocrites do. The Pharisees like to keep phylacteries on their heads and walk in flowing robes. But it is not to be this way with you. Don't be somber and falsely mournful. Wash your face and put oil on your head, so people do not know you are fasting. And don't tell people you are fasting. Let your abstaining be a secret between you and your heavenly Father. What you have done in secret between you and Him will be rewarded in the open. Jesus did many more things to show his disciples He loved them by the discipline He gave. Jesus was awesome because He showed the disciples how to be tough, and rock steady. If a man strikes you on the cheek, turn him the other one also, He said. Jesus also stated, if a man makes you to walk one mile with him, go with him an extra mile. Jesus was awesome in his wonder. On one occasion Jesus, filled with the Holy Spirit, looked out on the lake, where his disciples were. The disciples were in a boat, as the storm raged. Jesus walked on the lake, moving toward the disciples. Peter and the rest were freaked out, as they thought the man was a ghost. Jesus said to Peter to come to him. Peter said if it was the Lord, he would come. Peter took a step out onto the lake, walking, but when he looked down to his feet to see how he was walking, his faith was shaken, and he began to drown. Jesus then grabbed Peter and saved him. On another occasion the disciples and Jesus were out on the boat together. Jesus was sleeping. A storm began to brew and the disciples began to get scared. Lord, get up, they said. Jesus told the waves to be quiet, calming the storm and the men were amazed. Jesus told them if they would just believe they could do more than this.

He told his men, disciples who were as spiritual soldiers, Wars and rumors of wars must come. But do not be disturbed, for these are merely birth pains. When wars come this is not the end but the end is still to come. Just as a woman who gives birth has pain in herself before the baby comes, so it is with this age. After the baby comes, the family rejoices because a baby has come into the world. After this point Jesus said many wonderful things and preached repentance to people, because, if they were not sorry for all the wrong things they had done to people, folks would live in unforgiveness, hurting themselves and others. The Kingdom of Heaven could not be reached by simply being nice to people, but by repentance, that is, rejecting all the sinful ways of one's life. He said, Woe to you Pharisees, hypocrites, for you put loads on men's shoulders you are not willing to help them carry.

Eventually Jesus began to get closer and closer to Jerusalem, the place where prophets had been rejected and persecuted in the past. Jesus said to his disciples, Guys, I am going to be handed over to the non-Jews, whipped and beaten and then crucified. And on the third day I will rise. His disciples did not understand what He was saying so they kept on listening to Him. As they were coming into Jerusalem, he sent two disciples ahead of Him, telling them to go to a certain house complete with a furnished upstairs and to take a colt which would be tied outside and bring it to Him. If people asked what they were doing, Jesus said to tell them the colt was for the Lord. As they went on, the scenario happened just as Jesus had explained. As the rest of His disciples came into Jerusalem with Him, they all supped at the inn. Jesus told them all about how he would be offered up to the Gentiles. He would be scourged, beaten, and crucified, and on the third day He would rise again. They did not understand what He was saying and they were all too afraid to ask Him. As He broke bread on this, the day of Passover, He gave thanks and shared among His disciples, saying: Take this, the bread of my body. It will be given up for you. Then He gave them the cup, saying, this is the cup of my blood, a new and everlasting covenant. It will be shed for you and for all so that sins may be forgiven. Jesus said one person among His friends would betray Him that night and they all looked around wondering who it would be. Jesus said he who dips with me in the cup is he. At the same moment, Judas Iscariot dipped bread in the cup with Jesus, and Judas said, surely not me? Jesus told him, What you are going to do, do quickly. At that moment Judas left, and headed toward the Pharisees to tell them where Jesus was. Jesus and His disciples went out to the garden of Gethsemane and He prayed, "Father, if thou art willing, take this cup from me, but not my will, but Your will be done." He came back and saw His disciples sleeping, and said, "Could you not watch with me for one hour?" and He was sore distressed. He went a stone's throw out again to pray, kneeling down, and was greatly troubled, so much that His sweat was as drops of blood. He got up again, to find the disciples sleeping again. The spirit is strong, but the flesh is weak, He told them. Again He went out to pray, and prayed, that maybe the hour would pass before Him.

He walked back to His disciples, and saw Judas Iscariot. Behold, the Son of Man is betrayed into the hands of sinners, He said. Now the chief priests, and the elders and servants came out with clubs and swords. Jesus asked them, "Why do you come to me with clubs and swords when I taught at the temple courts day after day, not harming anyone?" At once, one of His disciples cut off the right ear of one of the chief priest's servants. Immediately Jesus touched the man's ear and it was restored. Jesus said to his disciple, He who lives by the sword, will die by the sword. The elders then led Him off to Pontius Pilate, as Jesus' followers fled.

Pontius was head official in the region at the time. People all over a crowd below Pilate's palace had conflicting stories about Jesus, some saying Jesus said He would destroy the temple and rebuild it in three days, others that he said He was greater than Caesar. Pilate questioned Jesus, saying, "Are You the Christ, the Holy One of God?" "It is as you say," Jesus replied. Pilate then asked Jesus whether or not the accusations the people were making were true. Jesus said nothing and Pilate was amazed. Pilate said, "Don't you realize I have the power to save You or have You crucified?"

Jesus said, "You would have no power if it were not given to you from above." Then Pilate's wife came unto him, saying, "Have nothing to do with this man, for I have been tormented by a terrible dream because of Him." It was now day and Pilate went out to the people, saying, I find no fault in this man. The crowd said, "Crucify Him!" And Pilate was stuck. "Why, what has He done?" he said, and all the louder the crowd cried out, "Crucify Him!" As the custom in Jerusalem was, during the Passover, one prisoner would be freed, and Pilate said, "Shall I release to you Barabbas (Barabbas committed murder as he took part in an insurrection) or Jesus, who is called Christ?" The crowd said, "Barabbas!" Pilate took a bowl of water and wet his hands before the crowd, saying, "I wash my hands of this man's blood," and gave up Jesus to be crucified.

Roman soldiers put on Jesus a crown of thorns, a purple robe, and paid homage to Him, mocking Him. They then took the robe off Him and spit upon Him and whipped Him, with leather straps having metal similar to barbed wire at the ends. Soldiers and the chief priests then made Him to carry a wooden cross, all the while they spit upon Him, and punching Him in the face. Eventually He was led up to a hill named Golgotha, or the place of the skull, the same place where Abraham offered Isaac as a sacrifice more than 1,000 years before. Soldiers drove nails in Jesus' hands on each side of the cross, along with nails into His feet. They hoisted Him upward to where he hung by his own weight. People continued to yell insults upon Him, saying, "if He is the Christ, the Son of God, Let Him come down from that Cross." Another said, "He is going to save the world, and He can't even save Himself." All the while Jesus said "Forgive them, for they know not what they do." About the ninth hour, darkness spread over the land, and people dipped a sponge into wine vinegar, and lifted it up for Jesus to drink. After the sponge came to His mouth He said, "Eloi, Eloi, lamasabachthani?" which means, "My God, my God, Why have You forsaken me?" At that moment he gave up His ghost, and the veil inside the temple was immediately split in two.

One of the Roman soldiers took a spear and pierced Jesus' side, to fulfill what was said about Him in the ancient scriptures, "And they will look upon the one they have pierced." After Jesus died and was taken down off the cross, Joseph asked for the body, laid it in his own tomb, and three days later (exactly) the women went to the tomb and found it empty. Later on Jesus appeared to His disciples while they were walking along. Jesus simply walked next to them, asking why everyone was so sad. One man said, Are you not from around here and don't you know of the things which have just taken place? Our Lord has just been crucified, and we know not what to do, for, He was everything to us. Jesus then began to tell them about how the prophets spoke of the Christ and how His crucifixion had to come to pass so prophecy would be fulfilled. They then came to a place and Jesus was radiant in all His glory. The disciples were terrified and overjoyed at the same time.

Even though some of the eleven remaining were with Him, Thomas was a ways off, and, when the other disciples told him about Jesus' resurrection, Thomas did not believe, saying, Unless I see the nail marks in His hands and the pierce mark in His side, I will not believe. Jesus then appeared, showing Thomas the scars in His Hands and the piercing in His side. He asked Thomas, Do you now believe? Thomas said, my Lord and my God. Jesus then told them if they would call on His name, they would be able to pick up serpents and not be harmed, and drink poison and not die. He instructed them to wait until they were given power from on high, and He would be with them always, even to the end of the age.

Jesus is the summit of perfection. He is my pinnacle. Jesus Christ said, if a man makes you walk one mile with him, walk with him another mile. Jesus made sure people understood relationships were important. Come to think of it, He was like a father to me, when I was at my lowest point. I had somebody to talk to familiar with loneliness, familiar with being different.

His renewing Spirit now lives in billions of people. When the human body is filled with good, a person responds consistently well in all facets of life.

Jesus had second thoughts, about going to the cross the night before he was to die. He prayed in the garden alone and his emotional pain was so intense his sweat was like drops of blood. So let us learn from him, if for no other reason, because he is a great man and because we can take something from his experience.

Rev. Martin Luther King Jr. laid down his life for civil rights and nonviolence, knowing he would be in danger but going ahead with the plan. We may derive so much courage from these teachers who speak to us still. We can each teach each other something in this life.

I felt this same acceptance with Habitat for Humanity. The organization was full of warmth and acceptance. By and large, folks were kind and understanding. If people hurt each other, it was unintentionally.

Men should feel all right in a team atmosphere with other men or play boxing at the Wal-Mart or even wrestling at the family get-together. Men can find all sorts of ways to rascal around legally. It is fun, too, because it is fulfilling. When men engage in sport there is a primal yearning that calls back through the beginnings of man, when we had hair all over us and testosterone coming out of our ears.

Point is—even if men are poor in sports they can take part in a unit. If men try diligently, they can watch ones who are talented and learn.

Playing on an undefeated football team feels great. But when it comes down to it building a house for Habitat for Humanity *is* greater. I think the latter trumps the former, though both are beneficial. A group of individuals come together to create something transcending the person. Self is lost in the equation. People put this effort forth to put the puzzle together. They yearn to contribute without recognition.

You work together erecting this house. You take part in this almost supernatural feeling; you work towards a common cause to help others with tangible results. But the whole project is above feelings because you can sense it with *all* your senses; the experience is above emotion.

SIU Habitat for Humanity went for a build at Myrtle Beach, South Carolina with SIU Habitat for Humanity. A group of us hit the volleyball around in a circle on the beach. I continued to hit line drives when the ball came to me. I felt a bit uneasy because the balls sailed wide or I would hit it too hard so the person across from me could not catch up. Students from Washington College on the East Coast were there to build houses with us, too, staying at the same facilities as us. The volleyball team's coach gave me some pointers.

She told me to lock my hands when I hit the ball. The woman also said to use the shoulders in punching the ball upward. So that was my lesson and I got it from a woman who knew more about the technique than I did. My shot improved as we continued behind the waning sun of the Atlantic.

Fellowship is knowing you have people you can count on, that you have friends—that helps in any situation. Friends are essential in life. As my mom put it, the best people in public office have others around them who will be frank. Best public servicemen and women will keep people around who will let them know when the ship is sinking.

Teachers with the most significant influence on their pupils have the ability to, first of all, listen attentively. Teachers who influence their students can make an impact by being involved in the students' lives in sharing with students' embarrassing, enlightening, humorous, but altogether personal, stories. Teachers who have the ability to connect with students in the classroom have the opportunity to impact lives. This can be oh, so difficult. To do so, you become attached to those you are trying to teach. This is why to teach you must prepare the body for service. You must ask yourself, what is the furthest length I am willing to go for the very best education of the least of my pupils? If it is all the way you are doing a *great* service to your students. I think you should be willing to lay down everything you have for even the most unpopular of your pupils. There is where you allow yourself to learn from them, and it is a reciprocal relationship. You can still be the one authority. You are both human beings and the other person must respect that. He yearns for that discipline like the summer longs for the rain. Give a little and students do ask questions. Questions from students provide a teacher herself with insight. I studied English at the graduate level for a semester after receiving my bachelor's degree. My best professors were those who, when asked a question, let it soak in. The best instructors gained insight from students' responses.

Teachers should get paid more as they have the duty of raising tomorrow's leaders. Teachers could stand salaries twice as much as today's standard salary.

I learned from the many outstanding teachers that educating folks is at its best when people are willing to step out of their comfort zones and be different—this is the good news. Family can teach you some things. Family teaches you the essence of life. You are with these beautiful souls the most and they teach you the essentials. It all begins with family.

Family

When the family comes together memories come alive and people can reminisce. Families make all the difference because when the world tells a person she cannot go to Hollywood to become an actress, family reminds her how to take care of herself while she finds the way. Family units care about one another in the sense that even if they do not like each other, they can still look out for one another and show where the bed is to get some rest on.

My mother and her siblings, my grandmother and my grandpa grew up poor in rural Bunker Hill, nestled in southwestern Illinois. Even now my grandmother has far too many items she can do without but still holds onto because of memories when needs were met, but wants were put off.

Grandma continues to shop at the chain thrift stores regularly, such as Salvation Army. His Service Station, a thrift store run by a group of Christian Staunton women is where grandma went to before relatives laid pressure on for her to discard her household clutter. She still goes here and there.

Amy's Clean-Up Project

Since I was back from college, my grandmother, brother, and I lived on a 12-acre plot of land in the summer of 2004. My cousin Amy and Uncle Louis lived 40 feet away in a trailer on connected land. This time was of an educational nature.

Amy put my brother and me up to cleaning projects.

Amy was the eldest of the three of us, one year my brother's senior. She was a Marine Corps Drill Instructor at Paris Island, South Carolina. Amy taught organization and work ethic at home solidifying and strengthening us new recruits. Near every afternoon Amy had some plan going on about what to do next with the miscellaneous farm clutter.

All three of us revamped a 25' x 30' area behind my grandmother's wash-house out back. Amy and I broke down a wooden outhouse that had been on the farm since I have been alive. The tin-roofed structure had been sagging in a dramatic sway like the leaning tower of Pisa for the past couple years. Amy let me separate boards from one another. This was especially fun as I got to whack away with a hammer. We exhausted ourselves attempting to destruct an obstinate camper shell window, swinging a heavy hammer, laying into it over and over.

We raked piles of leaves, vines and sticks but shortly thereafter we could see the dirt clearly. We loaded some heaping masses of remains into the back of Uncle Louis' black Ford Ranger. We then drove them to the burn pile way out back inside the long fenced-in horse area near the train tracks. Sticks and tree limbs poured over the back, caught by the ground, scratching earth all the way out a quarter mile to the weathered pile of ash.

Making light of all the work had been eventful. Amy made her uncanny impressions of Uncle Louis's horse Fireball, sounding like a chipper character from Saturday Night Live named Pat mixed in with a talking horse from an old television show, Mr. Ed.

Jharmel's strength increased since he started working heavy duty with us. He grew physically stronger more than he had been at any juncture in his life. He was also challenged by the noon wake-up time he had to follow. (We had to arrive outside and start work before Amy yelled at him [and me])

I had been blessed as we cleaned up around there just in the physical strength to perform strenuous labor.

We had to dig fence posts, four inches in diameter out of the ground. We hauled bicycles to Mullins Salvage, a junkyard 14 miles north of Staunton. We drove over to Mullins, probably eight times since we had begun work. They accepted seemingly any kind of metal!

Mullins Salvage, located on Route 66 between Staunton and Litchfield, is on a sort of island, with a field stretching the eyesight toward Interstate 55. A road leading into the quaint community of Mt. Olive is located on the other side of the junkyard.

Heaps of scrap metal as tall as a two-story house line imperfect rows up and down the Mullins junkway.

Mullins men wear grimy dirt on their faces such as a fellar who stood approximately 5' 9" with a red mustache and slightly balding head, stout, about 180 pounds.

A certain friendly man, roughly 75 years of age who looked like he has been doing the job since he was 17 called out on the loudspeaker when it was okay to pull forward off the scale after first weighing our vehicle.

Cars need to be taken care of and people need to be cautious. Any broken windows or busted tires are not ownership's responsibility—as posted. I had to follow Amy to Mullins with Jharmel's 1973 Dodge Dart Swinger and drove past my cousin who was parked on the scale. I rested the Dart just in front of a car, unbeknownst to me, ready to be demolished.

I hopped out and stood at a distance, waiting for my cousin to finish our business. "You'd better move your car before it's junk," said a scrappy-looking gentleman in sunglasses.

He startled me for a moment and then I hopped up out of my shell and moved the car. Amy and I proceeded to work with a rhythm to empty a load of miscellaneous metal off the Ford Ranger.

Amy borrowed her dad's Rangers. One is of middle age, blue and sturdy. Black Ranger, the other one, is worn out but not played out. About a 1989 model, it has rust dotted around it, but still does the trick. Trucks around here keep going, just like my family. Being together while cleaning up has made us strong. Makes me think of how grandpa worked hard to keep us all together.

Team

I would like people to take good things from my life and use them; learn from them so they can overcome, too.

Best part about teaching people is what you can *give* to them.

When it comes, it comes just like a friendship. When the reporter asks questions, he is asking the source to share a piece of himself with others, to teach others. This interviewing process has to be reciprocal. Just like teaching has to be reciprocal. Teacher instructs and yet the student does so much of the teaching in the relationship.

I was looking over my news clips five years ago after considering what job to look for in and/or around Staunton. After looking for awhile, my attention was drawn to an article I had written for *the Belleville News-Democrat*. Its headline included the phrase Purloined Pooch.

The story was good, but what was remarkable was compassion and building community. I sat there interviewing this woman Lori Womack and she showed significant concern for a dog which was not hers that, she assumed for a period, ran away. The purloined pup did not run away, though. Womack said she walked out to the highway about 400 yards down the street from the animal shelter in fresh snow and no doggie tracks. An anonymous reader gave information leading to the dog's safe rescue and the world seemed right again.

The story was enjoyable to read over again, because this woman shared with me how the furry chow mix with scarcoptic mange was once lost but found again.

DRUGS AND FOOTBALL

Just sitting there, something welled up inside me because of the teamwork the piece took to assemble. The word, Purloined, in the headline, *was* in the dictionary, but none of my doing, as the adjective was not even in my vocabulary before I saw the published copy. One of our photographers took the photo of Lori holding the pooch, and there it was—the finished product. We created community by each throwing in our unique talents.

Even then, I looked. I searched around. I met up with people who I had known in my former life. I was new now. I looked for people who were new also.

My old friend A.J. Underwood's mom saw me one day and asked if I wanted to go to her church. I figured it would be good. So I went.

Pastor Anglin asked if I would like to coach the boys' basketball team. I accepted.

I felt good about it. I wanted to coach. I told him I accept. There is some special, you could go so far as to say, mysterious, quality, when men come together doing what they enjoy for good. Finding what it takes first requires a person to find out what that, "it", is. Courage, stamina, humility—(possibly the most important). A mixture of all these is the special recipe. Whatever that recipe is, people have to play to their strengths. Through all the sorrow and the pain, I am still breathing. Standing in the midst of adversity takes a certain fortitude anyone is capable of. I have to believe this. I choose to be a Christian, though I am unfit and not worthy of the title. Christians believe. That is the gig of any faithful Christian—believe the unbelievable. So when Jesus said his followers can move mountains, and when he was disappointed because His disciples could not heal because of their lack of faith, He yearned for them, His closest friends, to believe. Belief is what makes the best in people. Believing we can ourselves be born again is amazing. I was now able to give to these 6th grade boys what my coach had cared enough to instill in me: discipline.

My grandpa was my role model. I had a man not exceptional in intelligence and physical prowess but a steady model of behavior. I came to him. When a child approaches any man for advice, that man is the most fortunate of all men, because the child is asking that man to lead him into this next generation. This man is given an open invitation to be part of and even contribute to the best generation known yet.

We are only effective insofar as we can help other human beings. I will be judged on how I have helped others. Cars, homes, love interests, etc. I have had will be of no interest to the Big Man up there. He is concerned with results. I know this. I spoke with Him last night and He told me we are too anxious about things that *can* go wrong with us. He said, we need not worry, because He made us, and He does not worry. He is too busy providing for us to worry about a thing.

Furthermore, we see what is in front of us because we are still concerned with ourselves. Yes, we must take showers, brush our teeth and eat. Yet, when we see ourselves as superior to any act, whether it be washing the dishes, or cleaning up vomit another worker chucked up, this reflects poorly on us to the Man upstairs. See, the Man upstairs is concerned with what we can do for others. In doing for others, to do for others effectively, we must cultivate such a proper love for ourselves, we merely forget about ourselves. That's right, to gain big treasure we must disregard our very selves, where we have possessed self-denial. Should we work on this denying earnestly, we would gain treasures no man or woman can possibly store in his storehouse. Indeed, the storehouse would topple over into his neighbor's yard many times over. For, giving out of obligation, or, to feel better is a tarnished cheer. T.S. Eliot said the only thing worse than doing something wrong for the wrong reasons is doing something right for the wrong reasons. Let us deny ourselves for the sake of others. Deny thy self is a maxim worth living by.

We assembled at Zion Lutheran School for practice. We shot hoops in the back-court, a standard blacktop with goals at far ends, with a fence keeping the area from the road and sidewalk. My players listened intently.

We got into two lines. One line would go for a lay-up. Another line would get the rebound and throw it to the next person in the lay-up line. It was fun.

"One, two, three," I said, listening to the rhythm. Christian went up. Then Seth, then Sam, and Sam, and David, and Russell, and William.

"One, two, three."

DRUGS AND FOOTBALL

They are supposed to release on the "three."

Pastor Anglin played the boys at the end of practice. We were much larger than them. Our beefy, muscular arms were so much bigger than theirs. We were quicker. We had the agility. We played on the same team, passing the ball to one another, over the heads of these pint-sized defenders. It was almost too easy.

"This is great," I thought. "I am teaching these boys. This is great. Yes. I get to teach these boys something enjoyable.

"I absolutely love playing this game," I said inwardly. "I thoroughly enjoy playing sport. This is fantastic. Now is *my* turn to share. I am a father to these young guys, concerned with their needs, learning, and skills growth.

I am concerned about what they are watching on television. I want to know who they are hanging out with. I even want to know when they will be home at night."

I was so in to their overall development. I wanted to be there for these guys like my dad was not for me. I wanted to be the guys who displayed the intestinal fortitude. I wanted to be the guy I wanted to be when I started looking out into life. I wanted to be like I wanted to be when forming a life long vision over at Shirleys' after seeing Dwight big and strong. I wanted to bounce these guys up on the bed, or push them around the basketball court; I was taller than them now; I had the edge, and so many things to teach. We were in it to win it.

At last I figure mine was and always has been a story of redemption. It's been a recollection of triumph.

Yes, here in America we live in a dream, but this is a dream not only those described as Americans should embrace. By world, I mean a new and beautiful place where people try fervently not to sin, going after the Kingdom of Heaven in our own bowels by force.

Because immoral behavior perverts the behavior and character of fellow men and not just those engaging it. A land where men can be free is a picture of beauty, not tangled by societal or national boundaries. In order for man to rise above and crush the bonds of iniquity, he must accept all men are created equal—in Iraq, in Philadelphia, in East St. Louis, in Bangladesh, in Japan, in India, in Great Britain—wherever men go, they must remember they are of one mold. My American brothers must recall they go to the bathroom the same as folks in Vietnam, and kick soccer balls with the same bone structure as those in Senegal. Wherever men lie in life, they must recall they are on the same equator of equity in personal dignity as rice farmers in Xianjiang and own the same integrity as female seamstresses in Calcutta. Not only for us to make of this world a new world do men have to recognize they are on the very level of worth in God's eyes with beggars standing outside Busch Stadium at St. Louis Cardinals games, but they are of the same importance of the Pope in all his flowery apparel. Only way anybody, though, can see significant change in his neighborhood is to see the alteration in himself. M.K. Gandhi said, You must become the change you want to see in the world. What we do here only matters insofar as we impact and contribute to the lives of people around us. The book has to come out of me, mom said. I want to bring this book to people, so they can read and be encouraged. The book has to possess a redeeming value. I want people to bring their hurts, their fears with them in the receiving of this, my story, because everybody has a story to tell. I'm not saying everybody has hurt as little as I have. We are, however, tied in a network of mutuality, wrapped up in a single garment of destiny. We are bound by each other. I cannot be all I can be until the oppressed at any part of the world are all they can be. And we fight on with this struggle. I want to be as good of a person I can be for those out there. I want to be a hero. I think everybody wants to be a hero, standing up for what they believe in. Lifting others is what life is about. I lifted people up in football. And then in college so many lifted me. Jack Young, Pamela Smoot, Joseph Brown—all lifted me. Youth at Mercy Christian Fellowship look up to me, and I guess it would be not very different if it were some other little guys, and adults even with their wide eyes, hopeful for the future, a desire to impact souls. Just like my Pastor said, We should have walls but no ceilings.

 This book has touched some people hopefully. People need to see their passions. Gandhi said love or truth is more real than is a tree, or dinner table. I use the Christian doctrine the Apostle Paul used as inspired by the Holy Spirit. We look not to what is seen, for what is seen is temporary. But what is unseen is eternal (2 Corinthians 4:18). Football was a major thrust of my education on this earth. Football was so much more than a game to me. Football was and still is a way of life. Coach Tonsor molded so many of my ideals. I wish I could repay the man for all he did. Hopefully those boys can look up to me. They have a teacher in me. Possibly this is *the only* way to pay it forward—To give others that intangible gift you possess and become a teacher to disseminate it to your students…to draw out of your pupils that which you before had not seen in yourself, but someone cared enough to draw out of you. Those boys, hopefully, they can see they have an even better friend in Jesus. If he were in the flesh, he would tell them how very important they are, of that I am sure. Oh, in a world without words, we would be living more simply. Somehow if we did not even speak, we would be far more equipped to tame our desires. In the future, truth has to be the ship's rudder, the rock's sturdy base. This is what I want to get at with my Drugs and Football. This has to be a book that comes from me. It has to be based upon Truth in my life. Only this is my walk. I have seen a great light. But possibly your path is beaming with lights of a different color, maybe brighter than my own. My hope was to inspire. Hopefully my job has been done. I hope to write in the future. But my work is done now. I wanted to provide hope. This is all I have now.

Through it all I was persevering. It was from God, it was from all my family helping me along, but mostly from my only Creator. I appreciated it. Bobbye was *not* there. I needn't be bitter, however, because millions of black men and white men went through the same agony of not knowing why they were unwanted little children wading through a hole of frustration. But overall, in the final analysis, I made it through.

By the way, Bobbye has been calling and coming by to see me more in the past three months than in any five-year span in my life. He is making a concerted effort to know me. And because of this, I have to give the man some proper respect. We had a three-hour conversation one night about two months ago, just about his likes, public policy, comedy. I am glad to understand his sense of humor.

Hope. I wanted to bring it, through grace. Where people do not have hope, I want to be able to give them some through grace given to me.

With hope we can build a world where darkness cannot enter. Bringing forth a bright future is where hope comes from. By seeing what we are accomplishing and then saying, we can do so much more because we've done this much, now that's hope.

I suppose I was like President Barack Obama some. His story was that of uplift. We both made it. We both didn't have daddies right there, ones who said they'd be there for us from our conception to their natural deaths.

Then again we also had some straight up men. They set apart time away from their own families or schedules to be with us. We were each black and white children who grew to maturity in white communities with racial undertones. We knew we were not fully accepted in our world. So each of us worked to make this world our own.

Even though we human beings know conflict—everyone knew—they were different. They were fat, or short, or too tall, or too black, or too pasty. Maybe we did not all come to the same conclusion about how we processed this difference. I was fortunate. I was fortunate enough to know where I came from. I was fortunate enough—men showed me how—to understand a trailer park is a family. A private school is a distinguished upbringing. You take the good with the bad. You hope to come out ahead. You *always* remember where you came from. You must. This is a rule no one should forget. It has to be written in stone on some far away field, distances from untainted shores we can only imagine. We must remember. Because where we are from, this is what made us. We are not who we were. We are who we are right now at this very moment. Hopefully we may each embrace this.